REPORTING THE RETREAT

PHILIP WOODS

Reporting the Retreat

War Correspondents in Burma, 1942

HURST & COMPANY, LONDON

First published in the United Kingdom in 2016 by
C. Hurst & Co. (Publishers) Ltd.,
41 Great Russell Street, London, WC1B 3PL
© Philip Woods, 2017
All rights reserved.

Printed in India

The right of Philip Woods to be identified as the author of
this publication is asserted by him in accordance with the
Copyright, Designs and Patents Act, 1988.

A Cataloguing-in-Publication data record for this book
is available from the British Library.

This book is printed using paper from registered sustainable
and managed sources.

ISBN: 9781849047173 *cloth*

www.hurstpublishers.com

For Len and Isobel Clark

CONTENTS

ACKNOWLEDGEMENTS

The lives and work of war correspondents from the Second World War can be difficult to research at a point in time when there are few survivors from the 1942 campaign. However, one of the pleasures of researching this book has been to make contact with some of the relatives of the correspondents, all of whom gave generously of their time and help. I am very grateful to Mrs Jinx Rodger for allowing me to look at the archive of her late husband George Rodger which she and her family have lovingly maintained at Smarden in Kent. I also thank Mrs Anna Patterson for providing photographs of her late father, Alec Tozer; Mr Anthony Foucar for letting me see photos and other material relating to his late father, Emile Foucar; Professor Christopher Wallace-Crabbe for the photo of his father Kenneth Wallace-Crabbe; and Sarah de Graaff-Hunter for memories and a photo of her late father, Richard de Graaff-Hunter. I received very helpful comments from Dr Stephen Inwood of NYU in London and Dr Eleanor Bavidge of Kingston University, London. Dr Michael Leigh generously allowed me to adapt maps from his own book on Burma evacuees. Thanks also to Luke McKernan (British Library), Linda Kaye (BUFVC), Richard Morse and the late Terry Gallacher for their advice on the issue of 'faking/reconstructing' scenes of battle in wartime newsreels. Needless to say, the conclusions I have drawn in this book are my own. Professor Steven Casey (LSE) kindly let me see a draft of his forthcoming book on 'The American Media and Military at War against Nazi Germany, 1941–45', which sets the standard for future research and writing on war correspondents.

ACKNOWLEDGEMENTS

I am grateful to Professor James Chapman, editor of the *Historical Journal of Film, Radio and Television*, for permission to use material on the newsreel cameramen which was originally published in that journal. I am grateful too for the wonderfully efficient archives and libraries which are available to researchers in this country: thanks especially to staff at the British Library, the National Archives, Kew, and the Imperial War Museum. An archive that I was unable to visit was that of Kenneth Wallace-Crabbe at the University of Melbourne, Australia, but I had excellent research assistance from Abigail Belfrage of the History Department company. I also had very efficient help from Lee Grady and her colleagues at the Wisconsin Historical Society, Madison, who provided me with copies of Leland Stowe's notebooks.

I have been very fortunate with my publisher, Hurst & Co, who are everything an independent publisher should be. Thanks to Michael Dwyer, Jon de Peyer and colleagues for supporting this book throughout.

Last, but very much not least, I thank my wife Judith for putting up with my obsession with this subject for the last few years, providing valuable comments and encouragement, and for helping me to improve drafts considerably.

LIST OF MAPS AND IMAGES

MAPS

IMAGES

LIST OF MAPS AND IMAGES

ABBREVIATIONS

AA	Anti-aircraft
ADC	Aide-de-Camp
AFS	Auxiliary Fire Service
AP	Associated Press [agency]
ARP	Air Raid Precautions
AVG	American Volunteer Group
BFI	British Film Institute
BIA	Burmese Independence Army
BMN	British Movietone News
BPN	British Paramount News
CBI	China-Burma-India theatre
CBS	Columbia Broadcasting System
CDN	Chicago Daily News
CIGS	Chief of Imperial General Staff
DPR	Director of Public Relations
GHQ	General Headquarters [Army]
GOC	General Officer Commanding
IWM	Imperial War Museum
MOI	Ministry of Information
OIOC	Oriental and Indian Office Collection, British Library
PRO	Public Relations Officer
RAF	Royal Air Force
SEAC	South East Asia Command
SPRO	Service Public Relations Organisation
TNA	The National Archives, Kew, London

ABBREVIATIONS

UP   United Press [agency]
WO   War Office
WHS   Wisconsin Historical Society

NOTE ON PLACE NAMES

Main Place Names as Changed Since 1942

Place names in 1942	Today
Akyab	Sittwe
Arakan	Rakhine
Chungking	Chongqing (China)
Magwe	Magway
Maymyo	Pyin Oo Lwin
Moulmein	Mawlamyine
Pegu	Bago
Prome	Pyay
Rangoon	Yangon
Tavoy	Dawei

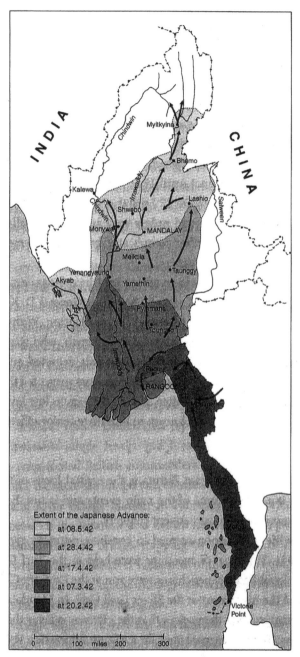

Map 1: Japanese Advance Through Burma

PREFACE

'THE FIRST DRAFT OF HISTORY'?

It has always been my contention that a journalist who writes truthfully what he sees and knows on a given day is writing for posterity. The scepticism and criticisms that I met in some quarters during the Spanish conflict made me feel at times that I was working more for the historical record than for the daily reader.

Herbert L. Matthews, *A World in Revolution: A Newspaperman's Memoir*, 1971

Journalists, especially war correspondents, are here to write the first draft of history as best they can.

Wilfred Burchett in conversation with Phillip Knightley, *Memoirs of a Rebel Journalist: The Autobiography of Wilfred Burchett*, 2005

The aphorism 'journalism as the first draft of history' dates back in its most widely used form to the 1940s but has its origins much further back in time.[1] It has become something of a cliché which is widely used to describe what journalists do. It is useful to unpick the various uses of the phrase and to consider its usefulness, particularly in regard to the study of war journalism. Most obviously, it seems to reflect on the role of journalists as eye-witnesses to historical events. In the case of war correspondents, they are often early on the scene of conflicts and need to make sense quickly of what are very often confused situations. Burchett's deprecatory comment that war correspondents are 'here to write the first draft of history as best they can' suggests that journalists are aware of the limitations of what they write in these situations, but that first-hand reporting offers special qualities which may be used later in writing more considered accounts.

One needs to consider also the reception of the journalists' work. Historians still turn to newspaper archives as a source for studying the past, although they will be aware of the limitations under which correspondents' dispatches are written and eventually published. They will be conscious that journalists have to turn out regular dispatches or articles, usually to an editor's order, to deadlines and within strict word limits. They have to pay regard not only to their editor's requirements, and sometimes those of the newspaper proprietor, but also to those of their reading public. War correspondents face very particular problems because they are flown into conflict zones, often with little background knowledge of the area, and then must try to make sense out of the confusion of war. They may not know the local language and are forced to rely on the armed forces for their information and for any opportunities to report the fighting at first hand. They face dilemmas about their patriotic duty in wartime, particularly whether reporting truthfully about the progress of the war or its conduct will undermine their nation's war effort and perhaps help the enemy in some way. Journalists become close to the soldiers they accompany, and one of their key imperatives is not to let these soldiers down by their reporting. Even if they do find a true and honest account of what they are witnessing, there are still major hurdles to overcome in reporting it. The most important obstacle is wartime censorship, which will rule out much of what they would like to write. They must transmit their reports quickly, for otherwise the news will be stale and no-one will be interested in reading it. This may mean they have to take short-cuts in reporting and that they do not have time for quiet reflection and deep analysis. They are in a very competitive business, and their ambition is to 'scoop' their rivals by writing 'exclusives', stories that their fellow journalists have not managed to report or transmit as quickly. Stories are required to be first-hand, 'eye-witness' accounts ideally, and should be exciting tales of direct involvement in conflict. The temptation to fabricate stories to meet these exacting requirements is ever-present. Even if not a question of fabrication, it is easy to blur the lines between reporting second-hand accounts and the reporter's own involvement in a story.

The idea of journalism as the first draft of history may sometimes fail some of the basic tests of truthfulness, authenticity and reliability. The distinguished BBC foreign correspondent John Simpson summarises this view:

> They [the war correspondents] are simply doing their best to puzzle out what on earth is going on, then trying to fit their interpretation of it all into an unrealistically small number of words, before spending a disproportionate amount of time working out the technicalities of getting their material transmitted back home. As everyone who has ever done the job can testify, reporting, especially from abroad, isn't so much a first draft of history as a form of escapology.[2]

Michael Nicholson, another distinguished veteran BBC war reporter, argues that 'there is a popular myth about journalism that it is all about getting it either right or wrong'. He then cites a quote from Max Hastings in the *Evening Standard* at the time of the Falklands War: 'You know very well in fact that what you are trying to do is have a sort of stab at the truth, in which case if you are getting it right about half the time, you are doing pretty well, in war that drops to about thirty per cent.'[3]

The limitations of war correspondents' dispatches and later memoirs as outlined above do not mean that historians should ignore them, as there is a tendency to do, but rather treat them with caution as they would with any other sources. They need to understand them within their historical and journalistic context, to be aware of the potential propaganda and myth-making role that correspondents may play in wartime. In the era before television news, newspapers, magazines, newsreels and radio were the means by which the public received its information and interpretation of events in wartime, and a close study of the press and how it works is crucial for this.

The two radical journalists, Herbert Matthews and Wilfred Burchett, who are quoted above, may intend different meanings to this idea of a first draft of history, and they are ones that relate particularly to the role of the war correspondent. Both journalists saw themselves as writing against the grain of the establishment version of events: Matthews was reporting on the Spanish Civil War from the Republican side and Burchett reporting on the Cold War, often from a stance that was sympathetic to the communist side. Therefore, there is a sense in which what they are writing will be better appreciated by posterity than by contemporary editors and readers. In addition, there is the distinction they make as war correspondents between the restricted information that they can report in their dispatches at the time and the greater freedom they have after the event to write more fully in their books. It is these books that will provide the better evidence for historians—evidence that is still based largely on eye-witness accounts.

This book will use the case study of the war reporters' writings on the first Burma campaign in 1942 to test the value of their work to historians. Each of the different texts, whether it be newspaper or magazine articles, photographs or newsreel, it is argued, will provide valuable material for historians, provided that they are understood in the context of the circumstances in which they were produced.

INTRODUCTION

WAR CORRESPONDENTS

The historian will find very little that is useful [in the news reports of the Second World War].

Henry L. Mencken, writer and journalist, cited in Robert W. Desmond, *Tides of War: World News Reporting 1940–1945*, 1984

This book is about war correspondents, men and women, who reported the six-month, one thousand-mile retreat of the British and Chinese armies from Burma in the first half of 1942. There have been many excellent military histories of this disastrous campaign, the longest retreat in British military history.[1] This is not a military history, but rather a study of how the war was represented to the public back home in Britain, the United States and Australia, partly in contemporary newspaper reports and partly through books published by war correspondents shortly after the campaign was over. It focuses on the role of named war correspondents rather than analysing the complete media coverage of the war. Published newspaper reports were often composites made up of correspondents' dispatches, news agency reports and military communiqués provided from various locations: Burma, India, China and London, for instance. Some newspapers tended to restrict the use of named correspondent reports, bylines as they are known. Limiting this study to the published work of named correspondents allows for the role of individual journalists to be tracked, and for comparisons to be made between their newspaper dispatches and their later

1

published memoirs. Although some correspondents have achieved fame and heroic status, most have vanished into obscurity. It is important to recognise the contributions of the war correspondents and to be aware of the strengths and limitations of their work for the historian.

More recent studies of the first Burma campaign have taken it beyond the military narrative and placed it in the wider context of the challenges to colonial rule posed by the remarkably rapid Japanese victories in Southeast Asia and the growth of indigenous nationalist movements.[2] There has also been a greater emphasis on the experience of the civilian populations, which has led to studies of the previously rather neglected experience of the large number of civilians who fled Burma during the Japanese advance.[3] Hundreds of thousands of men, women and children, predominantly Indian, but also British, Anglo-Indian and Anglo-Burmese, fled, and tens of thousands died in this retreat, and their experiences have now been properly recorded.

One group whose experiences have not been analysed is that of the war correspondents who came into Burma at various stages of the retreat. Indeed, historians have tended to avoid using their testimony, either because journalists are considered to be too close to the event and to lack perspective or because their memoirs of the campaign are thought to be too self-serving. The journalists' dispatches to the newspapers may be thought to be too subject to military censorship and too dependent on army communiqués to be relied upon. Altogether, they are suspected of being unreliable witnesses—too keen to 'scoop' their rivals and too ready to alter the truth in order to make a good story. Their published accounts of the campaign are more likely to have been used by historians to provide contemporary colour, to add a sense of 'being there' to the more arid military accounts.[4]

There have been very few studies of the way that war correspondents actually worked during the Second World War. Scholarly studies, influenced by more recent approaches to media and cultural history, have focused more readily on post-1945 wars, especially the role of war correspondents in the Vietnam War and after.[5] The studies of wars before 1945 tend to focus on the 'heroic', often romanticised, role of individual reporters or groups of reporters.[6] The antidote to these books is Phillip Knightley's classic study, *The First Casualty: The War Correspondent as Hero, Propagandist and Myth-Maker*, which has been issued in multiple editions since it was first published in 1975.[7] Knightley takes a very different view in which his heroes are the minority of correspondents who, in his opinion, had the courage to tell the truth about campaigns, even if it reflected badly on the patriotic cause, and who often fell foul of the authorities for doing so. Of those reporters who failed this test, most did so, he concluded, from a mistaken sense of patriotism, from conceding to the censors, or from over-reliance on official communiqués. Hence, he argues, the public were misled into believing that campaigns were going well and were shocked and demoralised to find the British run out of Malaya and Burma, for instance. Knightley's arguments have been criticised by Max Hastings, war correspondent and military historian, who insists that for correspondents in the confused situation of war, it is not a matter of 'choosing between retailing truth and falsehood, but between reporting a fragment of the reality or nothing at all. All journalists must compete with official deceit, in war and peace. In war, not only do commanders tell reporters lies, often they themselves do not know the truth.'[8] This study of the first Burma campaign gives some support to the arguments of both Knightley and Hastings. The contemporary media reports were too sanguine for too long about the Allied chances of holding Rangoon and Burma. This is particularly true of the newsreels which operated under their own particular pressures to present audiences with a sanitised view of the war. However, print journalists did usually try to tell the story accurately and fairly, within the constraints of tight censorship requirements. The problem was that they suffered from the 'fog of war' and could rarely piece together the various parts of a fast moving campaign. Although they never criticised the soldiers or their commanders, at the end of the campaign they analysed where it had gone wrong and tried to use that information to recommend ways of avoiding repetitions of the same mistakes.

The Burma campaigns are often described in a clichéd way as 'The Forgotten War', but this is certainly not an accurate description if one considers the amount of attention given in the British media to events in Southeast Asia in the period from December 1941 to May 1942. The defence of Malaya, and especially Singapore, was certainly given much more attention on the front pages of the newspapers, but the Burma campaign figured prominently and was often given lead billing, especially after the fall of Singapore on 15 February 1942. There were approximately twenty-six war correspondents in Burma at some time during the retreat (see Appendix 1).[9] They included two newsreel cameramen and one photojournalist and the rest were reporters working for newspapers or news agencies. The correspondents were a pretty international bunch: thirteen were British, six Americans, five Australians, one South African and one French. English language local reporters, for example for the *Rangoon Gazette*, did not apply for accreditation, which would have allowed them to report from the front, which was surprising as some had acted as stringers (local reporters) for international papers.[10]

Of the twenty-six international reporters, nearly half of them published books or sections of books which included their Burma experiences. The books were published usually within a year or two of the retreat but all while the war with Japan was still being fought. It was considered almost a perk of the job that journalists could earn additional money from writing their memoirs, but the motives were not entirely pecuniary. Most of the books were based on copious notes and diaries taken during the campaign, but the majority of the material could not be used at that time, either because it did not meet editorial requirements (for instance it was too long or too expensive to cable in full) or most likely because the material would have been cut by the censors. It does seem, therefore, that as soon as the retreat was over the correspondents wanted to put on record their experiences and the lessons they thought should be learnt from the defeat. They were, perhaps, conscious that they were writing 'the first draft of history'. Their books, although mixed in quality, are a valuable and under-used source for historians. They have inevitable drawbacks in that the correspondents are often too close to the battlefronts to understand the larger picture of the campaign, which is sometimes filled in by military correspondents writing from the head offices of their newspapers. Their books were still subject to censorship, although far less restrictive than that applied during the campaign itself. There is a tendency for self-aggrandisement in such memoirs, and the journalists, when complaining of the way that editors cut, changed or added to their dispatches, tended not to make allowances for the reasons behind these decisions. However, despite all their limitations, the correspondents often provide first-class eye-witness reports of the fighting and to a lesser extent of the civilian experience of war. Because they are not in Burma very long they rarely manage to set a good historical, political and social context to the country. This leads them to overestimate the powers of the colonial government and to be unable to judge accurately the attitudes of the Burmese people to the war. Even so, their writing usually shows a good understanding of the military, tactical and strategic situation and is often not out of line in its judgments with more recent military histories. Some of this analysis appeared in their contemporary dispatches, not just in the books written when they had further time to reflect on the campaign. Indeed, a minority of the correspondents were able in their memoirs to reflect quite philosophically on the process of war reporting and their roles as well. A number of them had been through military retreats before—from Spain, France, Thailand, Malaya—and they were keen to have the lessons from the Burma retreat understood and acted upon.

It is not just historians who have been wary of relying on the war reporters for accurate information and interpretation. After the retreat, various members of the civil administration of Burma took issue with the books that some of the journalists rushed to publish. Indeed, this public repudiation of the journalists' accounts of the colonial government's role in wartime is remarkable and perhaps unprecedented. These criticisms are dealt with in detail in Chapter Nine but, in essence, some of the correspondents were accused of sensationalism at the cost of veracity. The journalists were seen as making a 'fly-by-night' contribution, without appreciating the problems that the civil and military leaders faced during the Japanese invasion. Some of these criticisms were valid but they owed not a little to a failure of the Government of Burma and the armed services to take the correspondents into their confidence sufficiently, and to understand the difficulties that they faced in reporting this campaign.

It is important to realise the multiplicity of constraints on the correspondents publishing 'the truth' about the war as they saw it. The most important restraint they experienced was the tight wartime censorship imposed by the government which is discussed in Chapter Two. Although reasons of military security were the main purpose of the censorship regulations, they could be, and were, interpreted widely to include any reports that might give succour to the enemy or undermine confidence in the Allied war effort. These restrictions undoubtedly tied the hands of the correspondents pretty tightly but some correspondents managed at times to find ways around them. Self-censorship also marked another important restraint on the correspondents. For a variety of reasons, they did not report on aspects of war which they regarded as likely to undermine the war effort, either in Burma or at home.[11] They did not try to report, for instance, criticisms by ordinary soldiers of their commanders: no 'lions led by donkeys' stories, even if they could have passed the censor, which they would not. There were no stories of 'atrocities', such as the killing of prisoners carried out by British troops, though these undoubtedly would have taken place, if only in revenge for outrages committed by the Japanese on their comrades. There were no stories of cowardice or mental breakdown under fire, only of the bravery of the soldiers. This is understandable in that correspondents saw themselves as part of the war effort. They were, in modern parlance, 'embedded' with the troops, they wore military uniforms and were treated as officers. They ate, slept, drank and sometimes even fought alongside the troops. Although by regulations they were not allowed to carry weapons or be anything other than non-combatants, most did so for self-protection, and some did, inevitably, become participants in the warfare.[12]

There were also practical constraints on reporting the fighting or other events at first hand. These will be discussed in more detail in Chapter Four. However, they go some way to explaining why dispatches often gave an impression of first-hand reporting, when journalists had to rely on second-hand reports from retreating soldiers and civilians. The Evelyn Waugh scenario from his novel *Scoop*, set in the Abyssinian War, of the journalist sitting comfortably in the hotel bar many miles from the front, and sending reports based on Army Headquarters communiqués, marked 'From Our Special Correspondent at the Front', has some basis in truth, but is a gross caricature of most war correspondents who constantly risked their health and lives to report as directly as they could.

Another constraint, but one that was very important, came from pressures within the newspaper, magazine or cinema industries themselves. These were all competitive businesses which needed to turn a profit, or were heavily subsidised by wealthy owners, usually with some political agenda. In wartime, the media industries were compelled to compromise on some of their normal competitive practices, for example by pooling arrangements in the newsreel industry to cut down on the number of cameramen reporting events, or by restrictions on supplies of newsprint or war film. Editors held the whip hand over the war correspondents, urging them to out-scoop their rivals by speedy coverage of the fighting and by gaining exclusive stories. At the end of the day it was editors, or sometimes proprietors in the case of Henry Luce of *Time-Life*, who would decide whether the correspondents' dispatches would be used and how they would be used. The correspondents had to keep this, and their reading public, in mind.

Finally, there is the problem of how much correspondents actually knew of what was going on in the war. There certainly was a major problem in reporting a fast-retreating army across hundreds of miles. In the early days, the reporters were pretty much confined to the capital Rangoon while arrangements were being made for transportation, conducting officers and permissions. This meant having to report the battle in the skies and conditions in Rangoon, particularly in the docks where the movement of Lend-Lease materials was a major concern. The correspondents had to rely on Army Headquarters for information about what was going on in the south of the country. Things improved from the middle of February 1942 when the Services Public Relations Organisation (SPRO) was set up and the correspondents managed to acquire jeeps to give them greater mobility. There was another information hiatus, however, when non-essential civilians were ordered out of Rangoon on 21 February and the correspondents had to move to a new headquarters over four hundred miles away in Maymyo, the government's summer retreat. In this situation, correspondents were not able to report properly on or understand the most important episode of the retreat, the battle for the Sittang river crossing, the loss of which opened up the way to Rangoon for the Japanese. The loss of Rangoon almost inevitably meant the loss of Burma but, of course, the correspondents did not report this in their dispatches. The battles that they were able to report most fully and dramatically were not necessarily the most important ones, but rather those where they were able to be present. Sometimes, their presence was in itself part of the army's propaganda. For instance, the battle at Shwegyin on the Sittang river in March 1942, which George Rodger and Wilfred Burchett reported, was really only a temporary diversion to provide some relief for the British forces leaving Rangoon, but was presented as the first successful offensive against the Japanese. The battle at Pegu around the same time, which was presented so heroically by correspondents Bill Munday and Thomas Healy, was in reality part of another retreat. Did the correspondents know the broader picture, that they were reporting an inevitable and humiliating British defeat and withdrawal into India, or did they maintain the army's propaganda line depicting a phased withdrawal into northern Burma where forces could regroup and reverse the enemy's progress?[13]

It is interesting in this context to contrast the contemporary dispatches of one very perceptive female correspondent Eve Curie with her later book *Journey Among Warriors* published in 1943. Curie paid a short visit to Rangoon and to the fighting front at Thaton in mid-February 1942. Her reports, published in the *Daily Sketch*, give a positive gloss on the military situation. She quotes the general that she meets saying that 'In the air the British and American fighter aircraft are defending Rangoon itself efficiently. Men and machines are greatly superior to those of the enemy.'[14] By contrast, in her book, reporting on the same situation, she says, 'The Japanese had tommy guns where the English had rifles, and hundreds of planes versus dozens of planes: the British sky was almost empty.'[15] She is convinced that Rangoon would soon fall despite the optimistic noises of the army—because without air support a disaster was inevitable. Her summary was damning: 'In Burma an ill-equipped colonial army had to cope, at the same time, with a fanatical enemy and with a partly disloyal native population.'[16] These comments may have been made in hindsight after the defeat, but they seem rather to reflect a skilled and experienced journalist's ability to sum up situations quickly and perceptively at the time. Other correspondents, who spent longer than the few days Curie was in Burma, must have felt similarly gloomy about the military prospects, but there was no way that they would or probably could report such views. It was not that they gave deliberately misleading accounts, for instance reporting a defeat as a victory, but that they avoided what might be considered defeatist accounts.

For all these reasons, one can understand why the correspondent's accounts were challenged at the time or avoided later on by historians. However, once the context and limitations of their work are understood, their writing and images can be seen to have value as historical evidence.

This study is arranged thematically, so that the broader issues of the role of war correspondents can be brought out rather than following a more strictly chronological arrangement. This does inevitably involve some repetition in order that chapters can be coherent accounts in themselves. Individual chapters will also focus on particular journalists who made a special contribution within that thematic area. Although Burma cannot boast of having the most famous war correspondents, such as an Ernest Hemingway, Martha Gellhorn or Ernie Pyle reporting this campaign, it is important to recognise the extent to which individual personalities shaped the reporting, and how reporting the war further shaped their lives.

Chapter One will establish a background to the campaign in Burma, looking at the geography, politics, society, constitution and military preparations, while judging how much the correspondents understood of these issues. A short summary of the stages of the military campaign is given in order to create a context for their writings.

Chapter Two looks at contemporary criticisms of the role of the Governor of Burma, Sir Reginald Dorman-Smith, and the way that the journalists took up these issues, predominantly but not entirely, in their memoirs after the retreat.

Chapter Three focuses on the work of the first cohort of reporters who mostly arrived in Burma during December 1941, just as the Japanese started bombing Rangoon. It explores the role played by two experienced journalists, Leland Stowe and O'Dowd Gallagher, who came into conflict with the authorities at an early stage.

Chapter Four establishes how the correspondents functioned while in Burma under the Services Public Relations Organisation which became established in January and February 1942. It looks at the constraints on their reporting, most importantly the censorship restrictions they operated under, and also at the limited role of women correspondents in the campaign.

Chapter Five is devoted to the work of the only photo-journalist present in Burma, George Rodger, who worked for *Life* magazine. It looks at his coverage of the American Volunteer Group of airmen, the so-called Flying Tigers, his coverage of the Battle of Shwegyin in March 1942 and his distinctive approach to reporting on the campaign.

Chapter Six also deals with the visual coverage of the war, in this case the work of two British newsreel cameramen, Alec Tozer and Maurice Ford. It raises issues which are particular to the difficulties of filming the war in Burma.

Chapter Seven returns to the main role expected of the correspondents: the reporting of the fighting at first hand. It contrasts the achievements of correspondents like Bill Munday, Tom Healy, Wilfred Burchett and Jack Belden in making dramatic reports direct from the battlefield with the failure of the earlier correspondents to do so.

Chapter Eight looks at how the story of the largest group of victims of the British defeat in Burma, the civilian refugees, the majority of whom were Indians, was reported. The journalists' coverage of this issue was not really their finest reporting, but, ironically, many of them also became refugees, forced to find whatever way out of Burma they could find in the final weeks of the campaign.

Chapter Nine focuses on the battle for public opinion after the retreat ended. There was something of a public relations war between the army and civilian government to apportion blame for the defeat, and the journalists played their part in this. One of the most surprising contributions was the government support given to one of the correspondents, Alfred Wagg, to publish his account of the campaign in a way that was more sympathetic to Dorman-Smith and the civil government.

The Conclusion/Epilogue evaluates the role of war correspondents and the value of their writings to historians. It also looks at what happened to the correspondents after the Burma retreat, raising questions about the cost, both physical and psychological, of war reporting.

1

BURMA 1942

THE WAR CORRESPONDENTS' PERSPECTIVE

One of the difficulties that all correspondents faced in wartime was that they were often instructed to move to new theatres of conflict at short notice and, therefore, had little time to research the countries that they now reported on. This often resulted in a lack of context in their reports. Burma, for instance, was a country that few westerners had much knowledge of, and was often seen wrongly as an appendage of India. Snatches of Kipling's poetry reverberated in the heads of correspondents though they found the reality of Moulmein or the road to Mandalay far less attractive in wartime reality than his poetic licence might have led them to believe. It was important for the correspondents to be able to judge the political mood, especially the attitude of the Burmese to the Allied and Japanese protagonists respectively. This inevitably involved some knowledge of the geography, history, politics, sociology and religious make-up of the country.

Probably geography was the easiest aspect of Burma for the correspondents to comprehend. As they flew into it or took part in RAF bombing raids they could see the peculiar kite-shaped country, broadest in the north where it bordered India, Tibet and China, and narrowest in the south where its long, thin Tenasserim Peninsula bordered Thailand, leading to Malaya in the far south. The topography changed from thick mountainous jungles in the north, through a dry plain in the centre and rich, rice-producing deltaic areas surrounding the capital Rangoon, which lay some twenty miles from the sea at the mouth of the mighty Irrawaddy river. Four main rivers cut through the country from north to south: the Irrawaddy with its northern tributary the Chindwin, the Sittang and the Salween. In strategic terms these rivers were expected to be important barriers to a Japanese invasion from the south and east, though the last two were not navigable for any distance and were much reduced in size during the dry season. Roads and railways ran parallel to the rivers, and were separated by a low, forested mountain range, the Pegu Yomas. The correspondents had plenty of experience of the roads as they often had to drive hundreds of miles to reach a battlefront and then return to file their stories for onward dispatch. Wilfred Burchett wrote that 'to visit all fronts before returning to send a story entails 2,000 miles of travel, due to the lack of an inter-connecting road network here'.[1] One railway line followed the Irrawaddy northwards some 150 miles from Rangoon to Prome. The main railway connected Rangoon in the south with Mandalay in the north, where it split. The north-east line continued to Lashio where it met the Burma Road which led on across steep mountainous territory into China. The north-western line reached its furthest limit at Myitkyina. The British had built a number of airfields across Burma. Lashio airfield was a stopping-off point for flights between China and India and the point of entry for many of the correspondents. Myitkyina airfield was the last, desperate point of departure for some civilian refugees, wounded soldiers and the Governor of Burma himself in the first week of May 1942.

It was more difficult for the journalists to understand Burma's history and the impact of British colonial rule. Some saw Burma as being a racially divided society, along the colonial lines of preferences given to Europeans over indigenous peoples as was apparent in the earlier experience of civilian evacuation in the Malayan Peninsula for instance. There was a tendency to think in terms of the European community as gin-swilling, racist, pukka sahibs living a high life, oblivious to the threatening realities of war which were fast reaching them. O'Dowd Gallagher, the South Africa-born correspondent of the *Daily Express*, had seen something of this type of expatriate society in Singapore and

Malaya, and he wrote very disparagingly of the 'smugly ignorant complacency' of the *burra sahibs*, or big-businessmen, of Burma. Unfortunately for any claim to social-scientific sampling, his single example of bad colonial behaviour was a member of the Mingaladon Golf Club who objected strongly to the invasion of his club by boisterous American Volunteer Group (AVG) pilots and war correspondents.[2] Leland Stowe also disparaged the apparent complacency of the European community in Burma, describing them as 'sleepwalkers among the bombs', people who seemed to go about their lives as if the war did not exist.[3] What these journalists seemed to fail to understand was that the attempt at maintaining normality was, in part, a defiance of the disruption caused by the Japanese. This was the sort of behaviour that was admired by commentators in the London Blitz but which triggered a very different response in colonial Southeast Asia. In fact, the businessmen were instructed by government to maintain business as usual because it was vital to the Allied war effort that Burma continued to produce essential commodities such as oil and rubber.

Thomas Healy, an Australian journalist writing for the *Daily Mirror*, and arriving only shortly before civilians were evacuated from Rangoon, reflected on the reasons that the British, despite the material improvements they had brought to Burma, had never really won over the Burmese people to their rule. He commented on the way that the reliance on non-Burmese capital, whether British, Chinese or Indian, had left the Burmese poor in an increasingly rich country. At the same time, he would have concurred with Gallagher's reading of the racial superiority and complacency of many British expatriates in Burma. He dined in the exclusive Upper Burma Club, situated in the heart of Mandalay Fort:

> The conversation at the dinner table was extraordinary. It was so remote, so other-world, that I began to be afraid for Burma. Were these people typical of the British residents of the country? One recognised at once the little niche they would have occupied at home, in England or Scotland. They were middle to lower-middle class. But here they were rudely ordering servants about and speaking in what they believed to be aristocratic tones.
>
> 'I say, did you notice? The sherry was poor tonight,' said the languid young man.
>
> 'It was Australian, I suppose,' said the very plain woman who held her knife as if it were a pen.

'… been my servant for years. I kept him because he was so good with the dogs,' a dowager was saying. 'Now, when I need him most, he abandons me. Some servants have no sense of loyalty.'

'Mohameddans are so aggressive sometimes, don't you think?'

I felt like asking them whether the Mohammedans were as aggressive as the Japanese now thrusting into their adopted homeland. After all, the war was only 450 miles away.[4]

Of course, not all the British in Burma behaved in this stereotypically Forsterian way, but the journalists were picking up on the lack of rootedness of British rule in Burma. This was given backing by a number of contributors to the post-mortem on Burmese attitudes to British rule and to the war undertaken by the Government of Burma in exile at Simla after the retreat was over.[5] It was not so much a matter of the exclusiveness of the clubs that was considered most important but rather the lack of inter-racial socialising more generally, and the air of superiority and separation which the Burmese sensed among Europeans in Burma, from officials through to businessmen and police. Leland Stowe, perhaps the most distinguished of the correspondents in Burma, writing for the *Chicago Daily News*, also emphasised the negative impact on Burma of colonial exploitation:

> For more than one hundred years, enormous fortunes were reaped in Burma by the British. Burma has produced and still produces a fabulous wealth in oil, teakwood, silver, rubber, and rice. It is extremely difficult to find traces of this great native Burman wealth in the lot and the lives of more than 14,000,000 Burmese natives. You do not find well-built and attractive schools in Burma's towns and villages. You do not find many hospitals or clinics… The vast natural wealth of Burma … has been drawn out of the country for the enrichment of a small band of foreign capitalists who have no interest in the land and the people who are the source of their fortunes.[6]

Upwards of seventeen million people lived in Burma at the outbreak of war, of whom over one million were Indians and some 200,000 were Chinese, and fewer than 12,000 were Europeans.[7] There were very few Europeans in government services, only 116 European officers (including Anglo-Burmans and Anglo-Indians) out of a total cadre of 812. These figures suggest a colonial regime that was stretched in terms of manpower. Eighteen infantry battalions defended the country in 1941, of which sixteen were Burmese and only two were British. George Orwell's novel *Burmese Days*, based on his experiences as a police officer in Burma in the 1920s, seemed to epitomise the isolation from the Burmese people that colonial rule induced in some of its officers.

Burma was considered by some to be a particularly lawless country. Leland Stowe wrote that

> thievery and murder had been extraordinarily prevalent in Burma for many decades. The murder rate in Burma was said to be the highest of any country in the world. Poverty explained that to some extent, but the Burmese were generally credited with being excessively quick with a knife. We were warned never to show any money wherever we went because you could be killed as quickly for a five-dollar bill as for a purse containing five hundred.[8]

Most war correspondents carried weapons to defend themselves while travelling through Burma, although as non-combatants they were not supposed to. The reality was that most Burmese posed no threat to the correspondents and indeed treated them hospitably. However, particularly in some areas where *dacoity* (gang crime) or support for the Thakins (extreme Burmese nationalists) was thought to be prevalent, correspondents travelled warily. It is likely, however, that they misinterpreted or exaggerated some so-called 'fifth column' activity among the Burmese.[9]

It seems that the correspondents generally expected that colonial governments would have complete control of decision-making, especially in time of war. They failed to take into account the devolved nature of power under the Government of Burma Act of 1935, which separated Burma from India, and meant that the governor shared power with elected Burmese ministers. Although Sir Reginald Dorman-Smith, who took over as governor in May 1941, had control of key areas such as defence, and a veto power over all other matters, he was very reluctant to use those latter powers and wanted to involve his ministers in all matters as far as possible. He was sensitive to the fact that the nationalist movement had grown in strength during the 1930s and that serious rural revolt and communal violence had taken place in recent years in Burma. He was also aware of the very limited forces he had at his disposal for maintaining law and order in time of war, and the very real problems that any disorders would cause for army operations. Dorman-Smith was much criticised by journalists for his failure to implement martial law in Rangoon, but he defended his policy on the grounds that he already had all necessary powers, and that martial law would only alienate those Burmese politicians whose support he needed. Frank Donnison, a Burmese civil servant and no fan of Dorman-Smith, supported this policy: 'General supersession of the constitution would have invited charges of bad faith in regard to British policy of conferring a real measure of self-government upon Burma and would have been the quickest way to forfeit the cooperation of the Governor's ministers and the goodwill of the politically-minded.'[10]

Judging by their analyses published in newspapers at the end of the retreat from Burma and in their later books, the war correspondents were well aware of the problems that the British faced in defending Burma from Japanese invasion in 1942. Since their surprise attack on the American Pacific naval base at Pearl Harbor on 8 December 1941, the Japanese had made remarkably rapid progress through Hong Kong, Thailand, Malaya, the Philippines and the Dutch East Indies. The British defence strategy, which was based on being able to provide emergency naval support to the key naval fortress of Singapore, was literally blown out of the water with the sinking of the two capital ships which were supposed to fulfil this task, the *Prince of Wales* and the *Repulse*, on 10 December off the east coast of Malaya. The *Daily Express* correspondent, O'Dowd Gallagher, was rescued from the *Repulse*, and would live to be one of the earliest correspondents to arrive in Burma later in the month.

The correspondents were well aware of the lack of any priority given to the Burma campaign by the British government. This was partly because a Japanese attack on Malaya and Singapore was considered very unlikely, but, in any case, regional defence was intended to be focused on Singapore and its 'impregnable' naval base. Churchill wanted to concentrate British resources on defence of the homeland and on the vital strategic area of North Africa and the Mediterranean. Only two British battalions were kept in peacetime Burma: the 1st Gloucestershire Regiment and the 2nd King's Own Yorkshire Light Infantry (KOYLI), that is about 1,700 men. There was a regular Burmese army, the Burma Rifles, of less than 4,500 men, and a Burma Frontier Force, mostly Indian

16

and Gurkha troops, of under 8,000, and auxiliary and territorial forces from the local populations of approximately 3,000.[11] The Burmese army was largely composed of men from the preferred 'loyal' tribes, Karens, Kachins and Chins, with relatively few Burmans recruited.[12] It was 'a force useful for colonial missions of chastisement but utterly unfit for defending a country larger than France against invasion by a modern army supported by armour and aircraft'.[13]

Jack Belden of *Time-Life* was damning in his account of the Burma retreat of the colonial nature of the British strategy for Burma:

> On the eve of the invasion of Burma the outcome was a foregone conclusion … the British met the Japanese invasion without plan, morally undermined by a fatal policy, and organised for an ancient kind of frontier warfare.

> The British Army in Burma was a garrison force, a colonial army of occupation unprepared to fight a war against a powerful invader. It possessed a tradition of victory only over unruly natives, and it had to continue its police work at the same time that it opposed a new adversary. Its racial mixture did not permit the moral homogeneity that distinguished its opponent. Indian, Karen and Kachin soldiers were fighting merely for pay and not for any great cause. Even if the British cadres and officers had an intense belief in their cause at home, they were moved to no high patriotic pitch in defending the colonies abroad.[14]

Another complaint that the reporters made of British strategy in Burma was that the meagre forces were spread too thinly, 'scattered across the country like gendarme forces, waiting to be struck one by one and beaten'.[15] Belden said that the army had been hamstrung by the civil governor's insistence on keeping the normal garrison forces in Lower Burma in place.[16]

The air force was also under strength. There were two squadrons of the Royal Air Force (RAF), one of light Blenheim bombers and another of old-fashioned Brewster Buffalo fighters. These were augmented for the time being by the AVG pilots flying twenty-one modern Curtiss P40 fighter aircraft, who were training for service in defence of China, but widened that remit to defend Rangoon and the connections to the Burma Road to China. The Allied airplanes were greatly outnumbered by Japanese fighters and bombers. They were, however, to provide the correspondents with some of their most personal and positive stories of the campaign.

Correspondents knew nothing of the tussles between Churchill, the War Cabinet, General Wavell and the Australian prime minister, John Curtin, about what strength of reinforcements could be sent to Burma after the war with Japan began. It seems clear to historians now that Wavell was given unfulfilled promises by Churchill, which contributed to him refusing the largest part of the armies that the Chinese offered him to defend Burma in December 1941. It also seems likely, though, that Wavell himself misled his commanders on the ground in Burma and the Governor of Burma about the amount of reinforcements he was prepared to send to Burma.[17] Wavell believed that the Axis Powers planned to force the British to overstretch their limited military resources by directing them to the periphery, which would leave the key areas of the Middle East and Central Asia open. He therefore wanted to limit the numbers of troops sent to Burma to just enough to maintain its defence successfully. He also believed that Rangoon did not have the capacity as a port to bring in large numbers of troops and equipment, especially after the Indian dock-workers fled the city after the air-raids at the end of December.[18] The problem was that Wavell did not take his commanders or Dorman-Smith fully into his confidence on the matter of reinforcements and a false optimism was allowed to persist, which correspondents were encouraged to promulgate. In his dope sheet of filming for British Paramount News on 1 February 1942, Maurice Ford reported that 'troops by the thousand have been arriving here ... there ... and everywhere in Burma'.[19] It was true that the 46th Infantry Brigade had just recently arrived in Rangoon but as General Hutton wrote: 'it consisted of young troops and had been destined for Iraq where it was intended it should complete its training. It was not really fit for further active operations without further training and had no experience in jungle warfare.'[20] Ford filmed the arrival of Gurkha soldiers of the 48th Infantry Brigade on 1 February, who did indeed look very impressive. However, the promised 18th Division was diverted to early captivity in Singapore and two promised African brigades never materialised.

Some of the correspondents, particularly those who had previously been in Chungking, believed that if General Wavell had taken a more positive attitude to Chinese troops entering Burma as soon as possible, they might have been used to defend the Shan States in the north-east and thus allow British troops to be used further south in defence of Rangoon.[21] However, Chinese troops did not arrive in any numbers until after the fall of Rangoon. Most correspondents, when writing their post-mortem on the retreat, emphasised this delay in bringing in Chinese troops as a major factor, and British authorities prepared responses to these criticisms in the knowledge that they had received a good deal of support in the US.[22] Wavell argued that there were logistical and administrative reasons for the delays in bringing in the Chinese troops that had been originally agreed with Generalissimo Chiang Kai-Shek, the Chinese nationalist leader, but by 19 January he had instructed Hutton to accept any Chinese troops that were available.[23] Without substantial reinforcements, it was probably impossible to hold Rangoon, especially after the fall of Singapore on 15 February which allowed the Japanese to send more troops to Burma and to threaten Rangoon from the sea. Obviously, the British Empire was seriously overstretched and the priorities remained in Europe, North Africa and the Middle East. It was not just with hindsight, however, that it was recognised that saving Rangoon and Burma should have been a greater priority than pouring more troops into Singapore after the middle of January 1942.[24]

Because the correspondents lacked the ability in the first weeks of 1942 to spend any meaningful time outside the Rangoon area, they focused their attention on the heroic story of the RAF and AVG defence of Rangoon. The problem was that this gave a misleading impression of the relative air power of the Allies as against the Japanese. Once Tavoy and Moulmein fell, there was no radar or effective warning system for the fighter aircraft, which would give them assured time to get in the air in time to take on the enemy bombers and fighters. The AVG and RAF were forced to leave Mingaladon and the airfields in southern Burma and were pushed further north, eventually reaching Magwe, where their planes were caught on the ground and suffered heavy casualties in Japanese raids on 21 and 22 March. The final airfields used were Lashio for the RAF in the far north of Burma and Loiwing in China for the AVG. Wavell had determined that RAF priorities had to be in defending India, and in the later stages of the campaign Allied troops fought without any air cover, which was demoralising.[25] The fact that the correspondents had to leave Rangoon for Maymyo, 450 miles to the north, after the order was given for non-essential civilians to leave on 20 February, meant that they missed direct reporting on the crucial battle of the campaign which took place at Mokpalin and the Sittang river crossing on 22–23 February. It seems that the military deliberately kept the disastrous loss of men and equipment caused by the Sittang Bridge a secret for about a fortnight. Neither did the correspondents know of the high level arguments between Hutton and Dorman-Smith on the one side and General Wavell in overall command on the other. Hutton and Dorman-Smith judged that the Japanese threat to Pegu and the main roads north from Rangoon warranted evacuating Rangoon in good time, and thus avoiding another Singapore scenario where large numbers of troops and civilians were captured by the Japanese. Convoys bringing reinforcements into Rangoon port should be turned back. Wavell saw it very differently and believed that the military leadership in Burma was stuck in a defensive/retreating mode and that there was still time to bring in more troops which would allow offensive operations to be possible. Wavell countermanded the evacuation process and brought in a new commander General Alexander to replace Hutton. Unfortunately, the staged evacuation plans which had envisaged a relatively short interval between non-essential civilian evacuation and the final stages of scorched earth evacuation were now extended by more than two weeks. The result was that there was a chaotic period in which all the key institutions, banks, newspapers, fire services etc. were removed from Rangoon, leaving a vacuum which was rapidly filled by looters, released convicts and lunatics. This was the Rangoon that a number of correspondents recorded with some disgust.

Meanwhile, the Japanese came ever nearer to the capital. A couple of maverick reporters, Tom Healy and Bill Munday, broke away from their conducting officers and managed to report their very close involvement in the battle of Pegu, some fifty miles north-east of Rangoon. Their reports, along with those of Rodger and Tozer from the recapture of Shwegyin on the Sittang river, were welcomed as rare positive stories from the Burma campaign. In reality, they were hollow victories and masked the embarrassing fact that British troops evacuating Rangoon had only narrowly escaped capture at Taukkyan by luck and by dint of the Japanese desire to race to enter the capital.

The correspondents managed to report on the gallant resistance of the Chinese at Toungoo, some two hundred miles north of Rangoon, but from that point they were forced to decide whether to report the Chinese on the eastern side of the country or to follow the British forces on the western side retreating towards the oilfields of Yenangyaung and to Mandalay. Once the oilfields at Yenangyaung were destroyed to prevent them falling into Japanese hands, the game was really up as there was a limit to the fuel supplies to the Allied forces trying to defend Upper Burma. The Japanese, on the other hand, could bring in extra divisions through Rangoon for a final push towards the Indian frontier. Some correspondents were already choosing to leave Burma before the end of March as it was becoming increasingly difficult for them to follow the fast moving fronts and send their dispatches home. The Japanese bombing of Mandalay in early April, which cost many lives and knocked out the telegraph station which the correspondents had relied on up to this time, made life even more difficult. Dispatches would now have to go out by air, and the airfields themselves were becoming more difficult to reach. As it became clear that the British and Chinese armies were preparing to withdraw from Burma, correspondents had to choose not only how long they would stay but which exit route they would take. Journalistic considerations were still in play. Some chose to fly out to Calcutta where they could file reports more easily, or at least that is what they thought. Others took the longer routes to Calcutta, by foot, river or jeep over high mountain ridges and though disease-ridden jungles and valleys. It was a race to beat the Japanese but also to avoid being bogged down in muddy tracks as the monsoon set in around the middle of May.

Whether reporters took the mountain routes or left though airfields such as Lashio, Shwebo or Myitkyina, they would have come across the plight of thousands of civilian refugees, mostly Indian, but also European, Anglo-Indian and Anglo-Burmese, who were desperate to reach safety in India. Correspondents reported on these and on the troops who were also forced to cross the mountains into India. When they arrived in India, in the safety of the grand Calcutta hotels they would swap stories with rival correspondents and glean new ones from the European refugees, who were only too happy to embellish them if necessary.

THE GOVERNOR OF BURMA AND HIS CRITICS

He was an aloof and blimpish character, typical of an ineffably awful Old Harrovian…
Ronald Hyam, *Britain's Declining Empire: The Road to Decolonisation*, 2007

Dorman-Smith's Reputation

In time of war, correspondents tend not to criticise the fighting forces or even the generals, but rather focus their concerns on politicians and, in the case of the empire, on colonial governors.[1] Correspondents in Burma were frustrated with the lack of facilities for visiting the battle-front and transmitting their stories to their newspapers and magazines. This frustration fed on rumours provided, often second-hand, by civilians and soldiers caught up in the retreat, and sometimes resulted in reports criticising the governor and the civil administration of Burma. The lack of an effective publicity or public relations organisation allowed the criticisms to flourish unchallenged.

Governor Sir Shenton Thomas had proved to be a target during the defence of Singapore, so it was not surprising that Sir Reginald Dorman-Smith, who had only been inaugurated as Governor of Burma in May 1941, should have come under the scrutiny of the war correspondents.[2] The two governors faced very similar problems. Some correspondents arrived in Burma already having a low view of British administration and defence capabilities in Southeast Asia. The correspondents from the US and Australia tended to be sensitive to the class-based and hierarchical nature of the British governing elite, and Dorman-Smith, an Old Harrovian with a penchant for describing the Japanese as 'little blighters', in some ways seemed to fit the picture of ineffective colonial governors.[3] The early experience of the Japanese bombing attacks on Rangoon on 23 and 25 December, resulting in the mass exodus of the Indian civilian population, led the journalists to question the efficacy of civil defence and evacuation procedures.

Contemporary criticism of the governor's handling of the crisis of December 1941 to May 1942 was widespread amongst both soldiers and civilians, and was reflected in journalists' reports and books of the time. The military historian Jon Latimer says that the governor was disparagingly called 'Dormant-Myth' and 'Dormouse-Smith' by contemporaries.[4] Those negative opinions have tended to hold sway ever since.[5] However, the record needs to be re-evaluated and Dorman-Smith and his public relations officers provided a wealth of material after the end of the first campaign to support a more balanced view, much of it aimed at countering the journalists' criticisms.[6]

Dorman-Smith had not been first choice for the appointment of Governor of Burma, and he is sometimes dismissed as having no military experience and a poor ministerial record in the Chamberlain government. Neither of these criticisms is really correct. He had served with the Indian Amy for a short time after the First World War and, when Minister of Agriculture in 1939–40, he had shown a strong capacity for forward planning, making sure that farmers were given financial support to turn pasture over to arable land, and to stockpile tractors ready for the war.[7]

As with a number of the generals and officials drafted into Burma either shortly before the Japanese invasion or during it, Dorman-Smith inherited an appallingly poor hand on his arrival in Burma in May 1941. The previous incumbent, Sir Archibald Cochrane, was the first governor to operate the new constitutional system under the Government of Burma Act (1935) whereby Burma was separated from India administratively and Burmese ministers took responsibility for most departments of government, save defence, financial affairs and foreign policy. Cochrane was the first politician to be made governor, and some civil servants resented the loss of the appointment of one of their number. Cochrane was poor at involving his Burmese ministers in decision-making, and has been described by R. H. Taylor as 'a some-what dour individual who kept power and information to himself'.[8] He had a low opinion of the capabilities of Burmese politicians. Whilst the British government was keen to give aid to the Kuomintang govern-ment in China in their war with Japan, Cochrane feared Chinese migration into Burma and, even more, feared provoking Japan. The result was that he did not allocate enough resources to the develop-ment of good communications with China either via the new Burma Road, completed in December 1938, or by building a Yunnan-Burma railway.[9] Unlike his predecessor, Dorman-Smith enjoyed his relations with his Burmese ministers, especially with his prime minister U Saw, who was regarded by the governor as a loveable rogue, disreputable and unreliable, crafty and corrupt, but also 'amusing, manly, warm and human'.[10] Unfortunately, Dorman-Smith's support for U Saw's mission to London to press the case for post-war independence for Burma seriously backfired when U Saw was caught, when returning from London, allegedly contacting the Japanese consulate in Lisbon shortly after the Pearl Harbor attack with a view to leading a rebellion in Burma. U Saw was exiled from Burma for the duration of the war, and Dorman-Smith was forced to appoint a new prime minister, the con-servative Sir Paw Tun. Dorman-Smith saw his role as taking his cabinet with him as far as was possible in what Taylor has called an 'experiment in tutelary democracy'.[11] As evidence of this, he did not use his powers to veto ministers' decisions and, when at war with the Japanese, he was sensitive to the need to maintain a belief that the British would not go back on their aim of moving Burma towards the goal of responsible self-government within the empire. He took his ministers with him on his tours of the country and made sure that Sir Paw Tun was with him when he inspected the armed forces.[12] Altogether, Dorman-Smith was far from the Colonel Blimp figure that he is sometimes depicted as.[13] His short career with the Indian army (15th Sikhs) did, as he said later, enable him 'to get to know, to like and respect Asiatics'.[14] As Bayly and Harper point out,

> He was an Irishman with family lands on both sides of the border and he remained a citizen of Eire… His nationality did give him an interestingly ambivalent view of empire and nationalism. He claimed to sympathise

with nationalist aspirations though his political conservatism meant that it was only pukka, old-style Burmese and Indian politicians he could really tolerate.[15]

Civil Defence and Air-Raid Precautions in Rangoon

The two areas where Dorman-Smith and the civil government were most criticised by journalists were the apparent failures in civil defence of Burma's main city Rangoon, and the subsequent failure of plans for the orderly evacuation of the civilian population.

After losing his ministerial role when the Chamberlain government fell in 1940, Dorman-Smith helped to set up the Home Defence Executive in Britain, which acted as liaison between the armed forces and the various government departments. He had first-hand experience of civil defence and home security organisation. He needed all these planning skills in Burma, as the country lacked adequate defences and a proper civil defence organisation in the case of enemy bombing of towns and cities. A start had been made on Air Raid Precautions (ARP), including plans for evacuating non-essential civilians from Rangoon to specially built camps in the northern outskirts of the city, whence they could be moved on to central and northern Burma, or returned to Rangoon if the Japanese were repelled.[16] Dorman-Smith argued the urgent case for sending a civil defence expert from London, someone who had practical experience gained in the Blitz, and was pleased, if surprised, that London sent out one of their best civil defence experts, Richard de Graaff-Hunter.[17]

Hunter arrived on 23 August 1941 to take up his role of Commissioner of Civil Defence. He recognised immediately that it would take at least two years to prepare a proper ARP system for the country but he knew he had only months to do so. He was shocked not only at the lack of personnel and equipment, but also the failure of the evacuation plans to recognise the importance of keeping essential personnel in Rangoon as long as possible so that supplies could be kept coming into the port. Hunter argued that, despite the difficulties, a month before the bombing of Rangoon on 23 and 25 December 1941, a basic ARP organisation existed with the necessary personnel, communications and sheltering arrangements for most of the Rangoon population.

Image 1: Richard de Graaff-Hunter, courtesy of Sarah de Graaff-Hunter

However, there was a severe lack of equipment, especially fire-fighting appliances. Unsurprisingly, the people of Rangoon did not behave as the government had planned. When the Japanese first bombed the capital on 23 December, many people stared at the sky to watch the aircraft before they realised, too late, the need for shelter. The large number of casualties, over 2,000 people killed, led to a mass exodus of mostly Indians from Rangoon, but instead of going to the evacuation camps on the outskirts of the city, they went much further north along the road to Prome, some 150 miles away. It was then very difficult to persuade workers to return to the city, but the success of the RAF and the AVG in forcing the Japanese to avoid daytime raids, combined with inducements, led to some returning during January 1942.

When it became obvious that Rangoon would have to be evacuated on 20 February, ten mobile civil defence units were sent further north to help after Japanese air-raids had taken place.[18] According to Hunter, these units remained intact until the end of the retreat. However, it is clear that when the Japanese had control of the skies from March onwards, they could bomb Burmese towns at will. Journalists reported seeing the string of burning towns that resulted from the predominantly wooden buildings and the lack of equipment to deal with fires. Mandalay underwent particularly dramatic destruction in the bombing at the beginning of April, and burned for weeks. Madame Chiang Kai-Shek was so horrified at seeing dead bodies floating in the palace moat at Mandalay that she berated British officials for the failure of civil defence and her husband wrote to Prime Minister Churchill to complain. The Chinese leader and his chief of staff General Stilwell had a very poor view of British resilience in the face of Japanese aggression and there is little doubt that their views were picked up by journalists covering the war. Stilwell's involvement in Burma came after the evacuation of Rangoon and was coloured by his hostility to the British 'Limeys', as he called them, and general frustration at the lack of properly integrated command structures in Burma. His class-consciousness and dislike of fighting a war to restore British colonialism in Asia was certainly reflected in the writings of a number of journalists, not only American ones. They were constrained and frustrated by censors in Burma but were able to put their thoughts in book form when they returned to the US.

Civilian Influence on Military Strategy

Dorman-Smith was dealt an almost impossible task when taking charge of a country that was regarded as a backwater of empire, and that was wrongly regarded as protected by its geography from potential enemy attack. Military assessments, reaching right to the top of the British government, discounted the likelihood of a Japanese attack and defence forces were kept at a minimum. Even when Japan did invade in late December 1941, no priority was given to sending reinforcements to Burma, despite urgent requests from Dorman-Smith and the military commanders. Rangoon was seen as of secondary importance to 'fortress' Singapore, mistakenly in the view of the governor, and some well-informed contemporaries. The speed of the Japanese invasion and the success of Japanese tactics meant that, right through the first four months of 1942, the British and their allies were on the retreat, with no clear military plan until an exodus to India was finally decided at the end of April. Military tactics involved spreading troops thinly across the country rather than focusing them on key strategic positions from which to defend the capital Rangoon. This raised criticisms of the governor's contribution to military decision-making, some of which the journalists picked up on. There have been suggestions that Dorman-Smith influenced such decisions in three key areas. The first was on the strategy to spread armed forces across Burma in an attempt to defend as many towns as possible, particularly in the southern approaches towards Rangoon. Jack Belden insisted in his book *Retreat with Stilwell* (1943) that, with only two divisions under his command, General McLeod wanted to concentrate his forces: 'But he could not. The civil government insisted that the normal dispositions of garrison forces in Lower Burma not be changed. With his hands tied by officials, McLeod was doomed to fight without a chance, to leave his forces scattered and to wait as a man waits to commit suicide.'[19] Later, Major-General J.G. Smyth, commanding the 17th Indian Division at Moulmein, argued in favour of a consolidated defence falling back to the Sittang river as the best chance of defending Rangoon. However, he was overruled by the new GOC General Hutton, who favoured a policy of forward defence, in other words defending southern towns like Tavoy and Moulmein as long as possible. According to Smyth, Dorman-Smith was responsible for this policy of defences being spread out because the governor was afraid for Burmese morale if the southern towns were just evacuated.[20] Although Dorman-Smith may well have held this view, it is unlikely that he was able to persuade Hutton against his wishes. He had very good reasons to try to hold on to the southern defences, including the need to hold airfields and communications posts which would be vital for the defence of Rangoon.[21] The governor was in any case not in command of the army in Burma.[22]

The second criticism of Dorman-Smith's alleged military contribution was the refusal to allow Chinese forces into Burma in the numbers offered by Chiang Kai-Shek on 22 December 1941. Correspondents were not initially pointing the finger at Dorman-Smith for this decision, but rather at General Wavell and overall British imperial priorities. The two journalists who were most likely to be well-informed were Jack Belden and Wilfred Burchett, who were both present in the Kuomintang capital Chungking at the time and managed to interview Wavell. There is no evidence that they were aware at the time of what was actually agreed at Chungking. However, American military representatives, including General Brett, were present and it is likely that Belden, who was close to the American military, was soon informed. Belden suggested in his book that one of the reasons for the British reluctance to bring in Chinese troops was the fear of the civil authorities that it would be difficult to get them out of the country when the war was over.[23] It does seem likely that Dorman-Smith told Wavell of the fears held by his Burmese ministers that the Chinese had territorial ambitions in Burma, and that if British reinforcements were available, they would be a better option.[24] Once again, however, there is no evidence that Dorman-Smith's views decisively influenced Wavell's decision to allow only a limited number of Chinese troops into Burma. The decision was taken on a number of grounds: his preference for using promised British and Commonwealth reinforcements, his belief that it would take too long to get Chinese troops into the country and to be properly supplied, and, finally, a distinct under-rating of Japanese capabilities.[25]

Civil-Military Relations, Martial Law and the Evacuation of Rangoon

The final issue was partly military and partly civil, and involved the arrangements and timing for evacuating personnel from Rangoon. Reporters took most of their information from military sources in the absence of an effective government publicity machine: particularly after the retreat, the military deliberately shifted the blame on to the civilian government at various levels.[26] During the retreat itself, there were few comments critical of the Burma government published in the British press. One exception was an article in *The Times* on 20 March which argued that 'while the present is no time for recrimination, it will be necessary to hold a searching enquiry into the reasons why Rangoon had to be abandoned'. The author was most likely M. J. Pritchard, a stringer or part-time correspondent, who was also working for the *Statesman* newspaper of Calcutta. The reasons he gave for the evacuation were primarily military but he also pointed to 'psychological reasons', namely the lack of advanced information given to the civilian population so that they would not panic under the bombing. He also blamed the 'surprise' evacuation order of 20 February for causing another panic and concluded that Rangoon 'was given over to the military too late to stop our retreat'.[27] Thomas Healy's article in the *Daily Mirror*, published a week earlier, was a stronger attack on the civil government. The article was headlined bluntly, 'Poor Leadership Betrayed Rangoon'.[28] Particular criticism was targeted at the lack of effective and honest propaganda, but there was also an emphasis on the failure to organise labour for the docks. The correspondents obviously felt that Dorman-Smith should have handed over control to the military at an earlier stage.[29] Later, the governor defended himself by arguing that the military had not asked to take over and did not have enough manpower to do so. As far as martial law was concerned, he argued that he had enough powers to deal with looters and 'fifth column' elements.

In fact, during the battle to save Rangoon, relations between the governor and the army were good. It was outside of Rangoon that ill-feeling arose. Dorman-Smith obviously felt that the army's defence of southern Burma had been poor, to say the least. The army, on the other hand, complained of local officials deserting their posts, while hard-pressed local administrators complained that they were given misleading or untimely information by the military.[30] In his unpublished memoirs, Dorman-Smith says that civil-military relations were good, but there is no doubt that he felt the need after the evacuation to try to put the government's side of the case to counter the army's publicity.[31] He makes the very good point that it was military complacency about a Japanese invasion of Burma, and the army's conviction that it could hold Rangoon, that determined his efforts to try to keep essential Indian labour in Rangoon and to avoid a mass civilian exodus obstructing the military effort. 'If we had only been concerned to think of our own civilian problems, then a different story might have been told,' he wrote, 'evacuation might have started at an earlier date... But our job was not to concentrate our energies on getting away from danger. Our duty was to keep essential services operating so long as they could usefully serve the military forces.'[32]

Field-Marshal Slim, in his very well received memoirs of the Burma campaign, *Defeat into Victory*, argued that the civil authorities delayed proper arrangements for the evacuation because they were afraid of the impact on morale:

31

When it became evident that war was imminent, the civil authorities were reluctant to organize evacuation schemes, refugee control, intelligence machinery, the militarization of railways, or anything in the nature of a Home Guard. There was a fear, which seems often to afflict other administrations than the Burman, that if the people were told unpleasant things about an unpleasant situation they might become depressed and panic. As a result, no one was prepared for war and the series of British reverses was a stunning surprise… If the families of Indians, Anglo-Indians, and the Anglo-Burmese in government employ could have been evacuated to India at the start of the campaign it might have caused some despondency among the local population, but it would have increased the reliability of the Burmese military and civil services very considerably.[33]

With hindsight, Slim was making a good point, but it must be remembered that he only joined the campaign after the fall of Rangoon in March 1942 when he was given command of Burma Corps. He did not, therefore, have first-hand knowledge of the evacuation plans for Rangoon, but could only comment on the impact he saw on non-British troops and support staff, who were badly affected by the knowledge of what was happening in the retreat to their families and their compatriots. The military dictated the timing and method of evacuation from Rangoon, and later from central and northern Burma. General Hutton had started that process, after consultation with the governor on 20 February 1942 'due to [the] serious situation [on the] Sittang river and inevitable loss of Rangoon'.[34] Dorman-Smith, in an emotional telegram to Secretary of State Leo Amery, told him that he proposed to leave Rangoon on 1 March. However, the orders for final evacuation of the city were postponed on the orders of the commander-in-chief General Wavell, who was determined that the army should stop retreating and go on the offensive.[35] He wanted to give time for armoured reinforcements to reach Rangoon. This delay was nearly disastrous. Although the armoured brigade was able to disembark, the whole of Hutton's army was nearly trapped in Rangoon by Japanese encirclement; it was only by chance that they escaped on 7 March. Rangoon fell to the Japanese on the following day. Wavell had completely misread the situation, partly as a result of the overstretched Allied command structure which based him in distant Java until 23 February when he was moved to India.

The humiliating retreat from Burma was primarily a responsibility of British government decisions, taken before and during the war, resulting in a lack of manpower, jungle training and equipment. The command structure was constantly being changed and as commanders such as General Slim were prepared to admit, some poor strategic and tactical decisions were made.[36] It is pretty clear that, from the beginning of March 1942, the governor had only a limited say in the process of retreat from Burma once Rangoon fell.

O'Dowd Gallagher criticised Dorman-Smith for failing to raise morale in the capital by showing himself more in the city, touring the bombed areas, for instance.[37] There was some basis for this criticism and in many ways it seems unusual that such an extrovert character as Dorman-Smith did not use his presence in Rangoon more often. However, Dorman-Smith insisted that he did go and talk to people directly and the contemporary newsreels bear this out to some degree. He is shown, for instance talking to Indian refugees returning to Rangoon.[38] However, the governor argued that he preferred to go into the city at night-time so that people's work would not be disrupted by official protocol. This was perhaps a missed opportunity to stamp his authority on the defence of Rangoon. He did also have the opportunity of making radio broadcasts, though these would have reached a limited number of people. It is not clear how good he was as a radio performer. His broadcast of 8 December 1941, immediately after Pearl Harbor was attacked, was a rather embarrassing transposition to a Burmese topography of Winston Churchill's more famous oratory of 4 June 1940: 'We will fight till we win. We will fight on our hills, in our plains, in our cities, in our towns and in our villages. We will defend our land whatever the cost may be.'[39] Correspondents were particularly critical of the governor's speech on 8 February 1942. He had handed responsibility for delivering a speech to a deputy to read in order 'to dispel rumours about the [imminent] evacuation of Rangoon and its occupation by the military'. His absence from the broadcast, however, inevitably led to rumours that the governor had fled the capital and he had to return to the studio the next day to assure listeners that he and the British were resolute in staying in Rangoon.[40]

This only underlines the lack of a proper government public relations or propaganda organisation. As usual, Gallagher voiced this lacuna:

As the Japanese army drew nearer to Rangoon the radio adopted as a preface to its news broadcasts a sentence: 'Here is the news—do not listen to the rumours.' This was soon changed by a cynical, unconvinced public to 'Here are the rumours—we haven't got any news.'[41]

It was ironic that in his last night at Government House in Rangoon, Dorman-Smith, who had a low opinion of most of the war correspondents, was joined by two late arrivals, James Hodson of the *Daily Sketch* and Philip Jordan of the *News Chronicle*. Hodson described the governor as being 'full of fight'.[42] Dorman-Smith got on well with them and gave the two correspondents a lift in his car and flight to Magwe where he was to meet with Generals Wavell and Hutton. This allowed them exclusive interviews with the generals.[43] It is worth noting also that after the retreat, Alfred Wagg reporting for the *Daily Express* had prepared a list of criticisms of the governor's actions during the retreat, but was won over by Dorman-Smith's charm and explanations.[44]

Reflecting on the loss of Burma, Dorman-Smith recognised the fundamental weakness of the British position there. It was not just that they had been unprepared and completely under-resourced but also that they had lacked the support of large parts of the Burmese nation. Partly, that was the fault of poor propaganda, a failure to point out the dangers of Japanese expansionism early enough. The Japanese had proved more effective in their propaganda, persuading the Burmese that they meant them no harm but would stand together as Asians against Western colonialism. However, it was deeper than just poor propaganda. Dorman-Smith realised that British rule had not rooted itself in any depth amongst many of the Burmese people. 'It is definitely disappointing,' he told Leo Amery, 'that after all our years of occupation of both Lower and to a lesser degree Upper Burma we have not been able to create that loyalty which is generally associated with our subject nations. But I fear that we must accept the fact that we have not ... induced that sort of loyalty which will withstand adversity.'[45] The British had not recruited ethnic Burmans in the armed forces until too late. Many of these soldiers had deserted when they realised the Japanese were occupying their family homes. Dorman-Smith did not approve of the use of the words 'traitor Burman' and denied the existence of any large-scale fifth column in Burma.[46] In many ways he was flying in the face of widespread evidence to the contrary, but he understood why many Burmese had at the very least stood aside as the combatants destroyed their country. He stood up for his ministers and argued that none of them were Quislings who went over to the Japanese. He estimated the size of the Burma Independence Army as no more than four thousand, and he regarded this force as mostly made up of the young political radicals, the Thakins. From his perspective, it was important that Americans did not get the impression of the Burmese as being intrinsically hostile to British rule. Such a belief would make it much more difficult for the returning Allied forces to win over the local population and, of course, for the British to retain their role in Burma. Dorman-Smith clearly believed that the British would return to Rangoon, but by the time this happened in 1945 the widespread support for the Thakins, their leader Aung San, and their demand for immediate independence would make his task of restoring British rule virtually impossible.

Dorman-Smith's refusal to recognise the widespread nature of Burmese fifth column activity was a peculiar blind-spot which the correspondents referred to time and again. He maintained his view after the retreat, and indeed even after the war was over. It did not derive from a blimpish conservatism but rather from an empathy with the ordinary Burmese viewpoint that this was not their war and that they gave priority to the safety of their families when security was collapsing all around them. He focused his blame on what he considered to be a minority of 'traitor' Thakins. At the end of the war his failure to understand the depth of support for the Thakins and the demand for immediate steps towards Burmese independence would cause him to lose the governorship.

Mistakes were undoubtedly made in the governor's response to the situation caused by the rapid Japanese advance in Burma, but it was a military defeat that lay at the heart of the crisis. The military defeat stemmed from the British government's unwillingness over many years to give the defence of Burma the priority that it deserved. Dorman-Smith's lack of experience as a colonial governor counted against him as did his suave, upper-class appearance, which contributed to the prejudices of American journalists and the US military alike. As Dorman-Smith later pointed out, appointments to colonial governorships were not popular with career politicians or family men, so it was not unusual for political appointments to this position to be new to the role. He had less than a year to prepare Burma for a Japanese attack which many military experts believed would never take place. In fact, both he and Leo Amery recognised as early as June 1941 the danger of Japanese bombing of Rangoon and the impact it would have on the civilian population and took action to improve the ARP provision.[47] Even so, it was too little too late. When the invasion did take place, Japanese successes were so rapid that it was almost impossible to implement anything except crisis management measures. In the circumstances, Dorman-Smith's policies were much more defensible than have been depicted by historians. His emphasis on maintaining civilian morale and avoiding panic was sensible in view of the crucial need to keep Rangoon docks operating as long as possible and to maintain the supply route of the Burma Road to China.

EARLY BIRDS OR 'VULTURES'?

Sir Reginald Dorman-Smith described the war correspondents arriving in Burma in 1942 as 'rather like vultures'.[1] This image was not fair to the journalists and revealed the essentially defensive attitude of the Governor of Burma. It was certainly not an apposite description of the first few correspondents to arrive in Rangoon in December 1941. They might be better described as refugees. Harold Standish (*Sydney Morning Herald*/London *News Chronicle*) and Darrell Berrigan (United Press) were fleeing from Japanese-controlled Thailand, whilst O'Dowd Gallagher (*Daily Express*) was an early migrant from Singapore and Leland Stowe (*Chicago Daily News*/London *Daily Telegraph*) had left Chungking in order to be able to publish a set of articles critical of the Chinese nationalist running of the Burma Road.

Leland Stowe and the Burma Road Story

Leland Stowe arrived in Rangoon on 16 December. He was probably the most distinguished of the reporters covering the Burma retreat, having established a powerful reputation as a foreign correspondent for the *New York Herald Tribune* since 1926. Born in the last year of the nineteenth century, Stowe was blue-eyed, silver-haired, pipe-smoking and distinguished-looking. He was already a Pulitzer Prize-winning foreign correspondent in 1930 and when he visited Nazi Germany in 1933 he wrote articles predicting its future territorial expansion. His articles were not published, however, so he wrote them up in a book, *Nazi Germany Means War* (1933). This was a tactic he used again when he faced wartime censorship in reporting the Burma retreat, because his subsequent book, *They Shall Not Sleep* (1944), allowed him to tell a very different story from his newspaper articles published at the time. In Burma, Stowe was writing for the *Chicago Daily News*, which had a deserved reputation for the strength and depth of its foreign news coverage. Over fifty North American newspapers subscribed to its foreign news service. Stowe had switched employers because his *Herald Tribune* editor considered him too old to be a war correspondent. Lee Stowe, as he was known to colleagues, proved his previous editor entirely wrong, covering tens of thousands of miles reporting war in numerous countries in the coming years. He managed to report world exclusives on the Nazi attacks on Finland and Norway in 1941 and would probably have won a second Pulitzer Prize but for the fact that it was decided that the 1941 annual award should be a collective one for all American war correspondents. Stowe's criticisms of the bungled British campaign in Norway are reputed to have contributed to Prime Minister Chamberlain's demise. After reporting in the Balkans and Greece, he returned to the US in February 1941 and wrote *No Other Road to Freedom*. He was then sent to report from China.

Stowe disliked his base in the nationalist temporary capital, Chungking, and resented the censorship imposed on him, but his attitudes to nationalist China were, like those of many Americans, very ambivalent.[2] In October 1941 he had travelled part of the Burma Road, the 770 mile-long route from Lashio in north-east Burma to Kunming in south-west China. Lashio was the rail-hub which connected to Rangoon, 561 miles away to the south. Altogether it was nearly 2,000 miles by road between Rangoon and the Chinese nationalist capital, Chungking. The road had been completed in 1938 but was closed by the British under Japanese pressure for three months in 1940. The closure had antagonised the Chinese who depended on it for supplies from the outside world, even more so when their other main supply route was closed by the Japanese invasion of French Indochina in September 1940. Stowe knew, therefore, how vital the Burma Road was for it brought vital American Lend-Lease supplies from the port of

Rangoon up to China to maintain its war effort. Now it had become obvious that only a fraction of those war materials were reaching their intended destination.

Stowe drafted a set of articles outlining the corruption and inefficiencies that were stopping a large proportion of the war materials that were in Rangoon port reaching their destination in China. He declined to publish the stories immediately because he felt that he needed more evidence. Corruption on the Burma Road was well-known to the correspondents in China but Stowe believed they had not reported on it, largely out of a fear that it would undermine Chiang Kai-Shek's war effort. He also argued that Americans had taken on a romanticised and unrealistic view of China, probably because of the long American missionary presence there, and also because there was a certain guilt in America about western failure to support China in its long war with Japan. In any case, he viewed it as his duty to report the reality of conditions on the Burma Road. When he felt he had enough proof, Stowe faced the problem that Chinese censorship would not allow him to publish his views; he would have to leave China to try and publish elsewhere. Singapore was already covered by another correspondent for his paper, so Burma was the only choice. His editor had instructed him to stay in the China sector, but Stowe conveniently took that to include Burma as China had allowed the American Volunteer Group (AVG) pilots to train there and they were likely to play an important role in combat with the Japanese very soon.[3] He left for Rangoon on 16 December 1941 with the intention of reporting on the AVG but also so that he could publish his devastating critique of the running of the Burma Road. He was to stay in Burma for almost three months, not leaving until 12 March. It was almost as if Stowe was determined to win another Pulitzer Prize, his Burma Road material was so thoroughly researched and his arguments backed with really telling evidence. He wrote a series of seven articles and had them approved by the Burma censor. The *Chicago Daily News* trumpeted the stories in its 30 December edition with an unprecedented half-page advert, proclaiming 'BURMA ROAD SCANDAL EXPOSED by World-Scooping Leland Stowe'. Stowe was pictured looking thoughtful with pipe in hand, poised over his typewriter. Only the last three articles were actually published over two days, 30 and 31 December, before publication ceased on the intervention of higher authorities. T.V. Soong, the Chinese ambassador and Chiang Kai-Shek's brother-in-law, had complained to the State Department.[4] The first article had laid out the accusation about the operation of the road very bluntly:

> Ever since its opening in September 1938, it has been a national scandal and a national disgrace... Because the Burma Road has been dominated for years by racketeers and war profiteers, always partially operated or controlled by the same kind of gentry, some 10,000 Chinese soldiers have gone without rifles, hand grenades or munition... The amount of these materials actually required each month inside of China represents less than one-sixth of the monthly capacity of the Burma Road. In actual fact, however, the Chinese have moved only one-twentieth of the monthly quota of these needed raw materials over the road for the past 10 months.[5]

The second article stated: 'The responsibility must rest unfortunately with the Kuomintang dictatorship which has tolerated these abuses for years, and upon the profit-seeking appetites of many Chinese businessmen, politicians, government officials and employees.'[6] Stowe was careful to exonerate Chiang Kai-Shek, whom he admired but believed was too taken up with other matters to focus on the Burma Road failings.

On 11 January, Stowe was summoned urgently to the governor's residence in Rangoon, where Dorman-Smith explained that, though the articles were 'undoubtedly justified', he would like them stopped so as to avoid antagonising the Chinese.[7] The conversation, according to Stowe's recollections, seems to have been amicable and he agreed to desist, in any case knowing that the published articles had probably already had the desired effect. The Chinese did indeed respond and, at least on paper, took on board some of the criticisms that Stowe had made. Lend-Lease tonnage transported over the Burma Road reached its highest levels over the next two months.[8] This was one of the most notable examples of the correspondents apparently having an immediate impact on policy.[9] It seemed, however, that Dorman-Smith's intervention only heightened Stowe's resentment of what he regarded as censorship of information vital for the war effort, and henceforth his relations with the Burma authorities deteriorated. In his book Stowe wrote: 'Any serious observer must admit that official refusal to publicize numerous instances of Allied "mistakes and inefficiency" again and

Image 2: O'Dowd Gallagher of the *Daily Express*, from Alfred Draper, *Dawns Like Thunder: Retreat from Burma, 1942*, Barnsley: Pen & Sword, 1987, p. 116

again has greatly delayed corrective measures and has merely served to encourage a dangerous false optimism among our home publics.'[10]

O'Dowd Gallagher and Conflict with the Burmese Authorities

Eve Curie described Stowe as 'one of the most charming colleagues' whom she had met on her whole round-the-world war-reporting trip, and it seems surprising that he, of all the correspondents, should have tangled so much with the authorities in Burma.[11] Perhaps the problem was that he had teamed up with the much more aggressive South African correspondent for the *Daily Express*, O'Dowd Gallagher. Both men had arrived in Rangoon just at the time when the Japanese began their heaviest bombing raids on the city, those of 23 and 25 December.

It was also at a time when the public relations set-up in Burma was not yet properly established, so that correspondents faced the problems of uncertain censorship and non-existent travel arrangements.

O'Dowd Gallagher is described by Paul Preston in his book on war correspondents in the Spanish Civil War: 'Unshaven and scruffy, he was a hard-drinking half-Irish, half-South African, who had proved that total disregard for appearance was no impediment to attracting streams of women.'[12] He was, though, the most experienced of the war correspondents, having reported for the *Daily Express* not only from Spain but also in the Abyssinian War before the Second World War started. He was one of the few correspondents allowed to go to France in May 1940 with the British Expeditionary Force but was recalled after his paper was so infuriated with the rigid censorship imposed that it suggested that it would be better for the government to inform the public through dropping information leaflets out of aeroplanes. This was not to be the last of Gallagher's brushes with authority.

Gallagher reported in North Africa before being sent to Singapore when it was being threatened by the Japanese. He was famously on board the battle-cruiser *Repulse* when, along with the *Prince of Wales*, it was sunk by Japanese aeroplanes off the Malayan coast. Although Gallagher was rescued, together with the CBS broadcaster, Cecil Brown, the experience of this British military blunder and his subsequent encounter with colonial society in Singapore hardly enamoured him to British imperial ways. Cecil Brown was subsequently banned from broadcasting from Singapore because his reports were deemed detrimental to public morale. It seems that Gallagher also clashed with the strict Singapore censors; in any case his final dispatch from there, published on 17 December, was headed 'Singapore is Silent'. It continued:

> There is a complete absence of news from the Malayan fronts today. The communiqué usually issued about midday was not given out. The Services Public Relations Office had nothing to communicate. All that reporters were told was, 'Sorry, we have no news for you'. Just that simple statement. Result is that Singapore buzzes with rumours. The fact is that the Public Relations Office is not giving facilities for the widespread publication of news.[13]

Gallagher left Singapore for Rangoon just before Christmas Day 1941. If he was dissatisfied with the Public Relations Office on the island, he was to find it virtually non-existent in Burma, still waiting for a proper establishment and budget. Lacking transport and other facilities, Stowe and Gallagher concentrated their reporting on the air battle over Rangoon. This was sensible because the defence put up by the combined aircraft of the RAF and the AVG against overwhelming numbers of Japanese bombers and fighters was one of the very few positive stories of this stage of the Burma war. Mingaladon airbase was only about twelve miles from the centre of Rangoon. Gallagher and Stowe moved to the Rangoon Golf Club to be closer to the aerial action.

There were multiple clashes between the two reporters and the Burma authorities. Censorship was obviously one issue, but there were also complaints about delays in transmission of their dispatches, and of unfair priority being given to agency reporters. So serious were these that at one point Gallagher sent a telegram to his editor on 24 January:

> Most reluctantly I must ask you to recall me or accept my resignation. Working conditions are intolerable, and I cannot continue the abortive wrangling in efforts merely to write matter calculated to help the war effort. I am constantly confronted by deadening frustration caused by the mishandling of the propaganda machine by officials, some of whom are self-confessedly unqualified.[14]

The immediate issue concerned enforced delays in reporting a story of British air successes until the RAF had confirmed the information in its official communiqué. It is likely that Gallagher was hiding deeper reporting frustrations because neither he nor Stowe seems to have had much trouble in reporting speedily on the successes of the Allied pilots in defending Rangoon. His message of complaint was, of course, intercepted and Dorman-Smith informed. The governor telegraphed Secretary of State for Burma Leo Amery: 'If you could rid us to [sic] Gallagher and Stowe we would be grateful.'[15]

Dorman-Smith soon withdrew his request but it was clear that relations with the two correspondents were in a pretty poor state. What is interesting, therefore, is the complete contrast in the published articles which the two journalists wrote during the campaign and what they wrote in their later books. Because of censorship, both Gallagher and Stowe had to avoid any criticisms of the governor, the civil service or the army command in their dispatches. Indeed, their reports often go out of their way to put a positive spin on issues which they must have viewed very differently in private. Their books, on the other hand, are almost contemptuous in their criticisms of the decision-makers in the Burma retreat. They contrasted the failures of the 'chiefs' with highly favourable comments about the ordinary soldiers, junior officers, Anglo-Indians, Anglo-Burmese, dock-workers and of course the RAF and AVG pilots.

A good example of the positive spin used during the campaign is an article by Stowe that appeared in the *Chicago Daily News* on 3 January entitled 'Rangoon Loses War Jitters as Allies Rout Jap Fliers'.[16] This was written at a time when the correspondents were critical of the lack of shelters for Rangoon's residents in the air-raids of 23 and 25 December. They knew that the raids had led to the mass exodus of the Indian workforce that was essential to the running of Rangoon and its port. The temporary shelter camps that had been prepared on the outskirts of the city had been bypassed by the Indian refugees who walked on northwards towards Prome, some 150 miles away, in the hope of finding a route from there to reach the Irrawaddy and return to India. The newspaper article was written almost as if it were a press release by the governor in response to these criticisms, and it was prefaced with the statement, 'Passed by the Governor of Burma', which must surely count as a form of journalistic sarcasm. The article explained why Rangoon relied on slit trenches rather than underground shelters—the ground was marshy. The thousands of Indians who fled the city had either now returned after they realised that the air forces could see off the Japanese or were persuaded to return from Prome by commissioners sent by the governor. A picture was given of Rangoon returning to normal. Stowe, who had argued for the better use of Lend-Lease trucks to take war goods to China, now claimed that there were plenty of trucks which could be used for civilian evacuation, if needed to compensate for the lack of shelters. In his book, discussing the same first week in January, Stowe commented on the refusal of the Chinese to hand over any but a small proportion of the trucks and Lend-Lease equipment to their British allies.[17] The ground defences at the Mingaladon airfield were in a parlous state, while the AVG planes had been reduced to fourteen, many of which were badly shot up, and the RAF was down to about eight Brewster Buffaloes in a condition to fly.[18] Stowe concluded gloomily: 'The first weeks of the Burma war clearly foreshadowed everything that happened afterward; so much so that those of us on the spot knew from the beginning what the inevitable end must be.'[19] It is clear from Stowe's contemporary notebooks that this was not a matter of writing from hindsight; he was predicting the imminent fall of Burma not long after he arrived there in mid-December.[20] Yet, in his articles Stowe repeatedly emphasised the unique offensive capabilities that Burma provided the Allies. On 16 January, in an article headline 'Allied Forces Mark Time In Burma For Push', he said that reinforcements were being built up in Burma all the time and he doubted whether the Japanese had the ground and air forces to attack Burma and the Malay Peninsula at the same time, for some time to come. This was only one month before Singapore surrendered to the Japanese and only five weeks before the British suffered their most serious defeat at the Sittang river, which made a Japanese advance on Rangoon inevitable.[21]

Gallagher also reported the story of the return of the refugees to Rangoon and concluded it with praise of the governor, writing, 'Sir Reginald Dorman-Smith, who at 42, continues to maintain a cheerful energy in face of the problems of the job'.[22] This was ironic at a time when Dorman-Smith was widely criticised in private by the correspondents for not implementing martial law and the requisitioning of labour.[23] It seems likely that, in response to the strict censorship restrictions in the war zones, newspapers were able to suggest criticisms of government in indirect or coded ways. For instance, on 14 January the Daily Express reprinted an article from the current issue of Life magazine by the banned CBS broadcaster Cecil Brown. Brown's report, entitled 'The City of Blimps', was an attack on civilian apathy in Singapore but was also scathing about the efforts of the Services Public Relations there to suppress accurate information while propagating a ridiculously positive gloss on a rapidly deteriorating situation.[24] These were just the sort of criticisms that reporters like Stowe and Gallagher would almost certainly have liked to have made about their experiences in Burma.

The war reporting in Burma of both Gallagher and Stowe was really disappointing for such experienced correspondents. Their tangles with authority led them to play a rather restricted role, apparently biding their time to write more fully once they had left Burma. They had decided to leave Rangoon for Mandalay a couple of days earlier than the main civilian evacuation which took place on 21 February.[25] All the journalists missed reporting in person on what was one of the most decisive setbacks of the campaign, the ignominious withdrawal by British forces from the Sittang river on 23 February. The newspapers reported the bare facts from army communiqués that the railway bridge over the river had been blown up to stop the Japanese crossing it and that British troops had withdrawn to the east bank, but they did not know that hundreds of British soldiers had been stranded on the wrong side of the river by the premature demolition and were forced to swim for their lives across a half-mile wide, fast flowing stretch of water. Many lives and a good deal of equipment were lost and the Japanese now had the route to Rangoon open before them. This debacle, which has been closely examined by military historians ever since, was only brought to the attention of the British newspaper readership through second-hand accounts. The earliest was by J.L. Hodson of the *Sunday Times* on 1 March. Hodson had only arrived in Rangoon with Philip Jordan of the *News Chronicle* on 25 February when the other correspondents had already left the city. They were able to obtain interviews with Dorman-Smith, Lieutenant-General Hutton and Air Vice-Marshal Stevenson and were thus able to learn something of what had happened at the Sittang Bridge. Even so, Hodson's report paid minimal attention to the premature blowing up of the bridge and put a positive gloss on the story. He described it as 'a kind of Dunkirk' and focused on the high number of Japanese casualties and the fact that more British troops were able to re-join their regiments than expected. It was not until a week later that Philip Jordan's much more graphic description of the traumatic experience of the British troops was published.[26] The army had managed to suppress the real nature of this military disaster for some two weeks. It highlighted the importance of having reporters on the battlefront as eye-witnesses to history. James Lunt, who served with the 1st Burma Regiment during the retreat, wrote later that 'If the battle fought on the River Sittang on 23 February 1942 did not lose us Burma, it certainly lost us Rangoon—which in the end came to the same thing. It must therefore rank as one of the most decisive battles fought during the decline and fall of the British Empire.'[27] It is clear from his notebooks that Leland Stowe was picking up piecemeal, second-hand information on the debacle at the Sittang Bridge, some of it from American military mission personnel and some from soldiers who were actually there. He clearly regarded this story as a potential scoop relating to a turning point in the campaign but did not publish it, perhaps saving it for his imminent departure for India.[28]

Lieutenant Colonel Foucar, the Services PRO, was annoyed that Stowe and Gallagher filed dispatches from Mandalay before the press department had caught up with them there, and threatened not to include them in a party of correspondents leaving for the front. In fact, they were both included but most of the group turned back at Pyinmana, when the conducting officer, Captain Rogers, could not get information confirming that the road south was safe. Healy and Munday decided to continue south without a conducting officer and managed to obtain some of the best battle stories of the campaign at Pegu.

Neither Gallagher nor Stowe, therefore, got really close to the fighting, preferring to base themselves in the golf club at Rangoon or in the hill-resort of Maymyo for the most part, and to report on the one really positive story of the campaign, the heroics of the fighter pilots. This meant that many of their stories were second-hand accounts from civilians and soldiers caught up in the retreat or from the American military mission in Burma.[29] It was not that they did not face danger: anyone staying near Mingaladon airfield, as they did, was under threat from constant Japanese bombing. Gallagher overcame the reluctance of press officers to allow him to join an RAF bomber mission over Bangkok, and on 6 March both correspondents visited the Chinese troops at Pyinmana, seventy miles north of Toungoo, where the main battle in central Burma would be.[30] Their air force stories became repetitive, however, and gave a misleading view of how the war in Burma was actually going. It seemed to be deliberate editorial policy to hide the bad war news at the end of articles which told a different and much more positive story altogether.[31] Their editors often had to fill in their articles with the real military news from the news agencies, in the middle or at the very end of their articles. Ironically, it was their friend and fellow American Darrell Berrigan who provided some of this information for the United Press agency. He suffered from cerebral malaria while in Burma but was still harried by his bosses for more war news.[32]

When the air force was pretty much forced out of Burma, Gallagher and Stowe decided to leave. Stowe had been planning ways of leaving

Burma as early as 14 January, complaining that there was nothing new to file, and he was clearly feeling the loneliness of the war correspondent's life, receiving little or no news from home.[33] He did at least manage to stick it out in Burma for another two months. A day before he left the country on 12 March he wrote in his notebook that he felt 'rather tired and stale—need a change & bit of rest'. His spirits lifted on the day that he flew when he read in a Calcutta newspaper that Churchill had announced the Cripps Mission to discuss future constitutional arrangements, and that this would take place not long after he arrived in India. Typically, he commented that the mission was only two and a half years late, but at least he must have thought that he could, for a time, return to his real expertise as a foreign correspondent.[34]

Stowe's greatest contribution in Burma had been to raise the whole issue of the problems involved in getting America's generous Lend-Lease supplies through to China. He researched the issue thoroughly and almost certainly was effective in bringing pressure on the Chinese to allow reforms to the system. He kept a tally of the number of ships in Rangoon harbour and the amount of equipment that was waiting to be unloaded and, if necessary, assembled. It seemed madness to him that the Chinese initially refused to let the British use any of the Lend-Lease materials for their own defence of Rangoon, particularly as the Chinese could not actually transport or use much of the material. His reporting of the AVG contribution was also meticulous. He kept a tally of AVG strikes and losses, and in a situation in which it was very difficult to obtain accurate figures, he tried to make as fair an assessment as possible. He was actually asked by the AVG commander, Colonel Chennault, to check the AVG strike facts, and Chennault had instructed his pilots to talk freely to Stowe and to provide any evidence he required.[35] The downside to Stowe's record of the campaign was the very strong anti-British bias that permeates his notebooks. With the exception perhaps of the RAF, it is very difficult to find him saying anything evenly slightly favourable about the British civilian and military leadership in Burma. He continually complained of the snobbism, racism, deep-down conservatism and lack of will to fight that he thought characterised the British elite. He kept his strongest bile for the following people: the governor, whom he calls 'Dormouse Smith',[36] 'a politician, vain, anxious be praised, trying hard to be what he ain't—by no means a strong or decisive man';[37] Major Cook,

Director of Information, a 'pompous, conceited, pipsqueak';[38] and General Hutton, who 'should never been appointed'.[39] Clearly, part of Stowe's hostility to the British leadership was based in American anti-colonialism, a distaste for fighting to prop up an empire that was seen as both morally indefensible and also on its last legs. There was also a clash of cultures in that American drive is compared with British inefficiency and complacency. Stowe's views were fed by his proximity to members of the American military mission in the China-Burma-India theatre, men like General John Magruder and Colonel Frank Merrill, who gave him information that was often critical of their British allies. Of course, there was probably a good basis to many of Stowe's criticisms of this humiliating retreat, but it does seem when one read his notebooks that he was storing up evidence which would confirm his prejudices. He made no attempt to try to see things from the British perspective or to interview the key figures that he condemned so strongly.[40]

Stowe's notebooks are also very revealing about working relationships with journalist colleagues. At the point at which he was leaving Burma he revealed his deep frustration with his travelling companion, O'Dowd Gallagher:

> For 1st time in 21 years of reporting, shall be glad to have working arrangement (usually collaboration) with colleague ending—& pray to God never have to renew it. This guy [Gallagher] simply doesn't understand share & share alike—has held out on me repeatedly—after I've passed on such information as 2½ brigades cut off [at Sittang Bridge] etc. He can't be wrong never admits it. Goes on principle his stuff must always go first... Sick & tired his moods & silk-tongued contrast. His philosophy—if you call it that—bitter, destructive, mocking, negative—Bad taste in mouth.'[41]

Stowe completed his Burma notebooks with a detailed analysis of the reasons why Burma was lost, written when British troops still had some two months of fighting there. Of the four pages, one was devoted to the responsibilities of the Burma government, and another to fifth column activity. Only one or two points reflected the superiority of Japanese troops or tactics, most focused on poor British leadership.[42] When he reached India, Stowe was able to publish only a very tame version of his thoughts on the reasons for the Japanese successes in an article for the *Chicago Daily News* of 23 March. He focused on the many striking similarities with the Nazi campaign in Norway, but as Norway had no jungle, and was not under colonial rule, it was difficult to push the analogies too convincingly. He ended the article by effectively acknowledging continued censorship in Calcutta: 'It is only fair to say that the complete story of the Burma war must be reserved for historians, but many of its lessons must be the subject of serious study now.'[43]

At least Stowe was able to make a much better analysis when *They Shall Not Sleep* was published in 1944, whereas Gallagher's book, published in September 1942 as *Retreat in the East*, seems very rushed.[44] The latter book received very mixed reviews. Winslow L. Christian of Stanford University, reviewing the American edition in the *Far Eastern Quarterly*, remarked: 'Here are few dates, no documentation, considerable sentimentality, some hero-worship and hasty condemnation, frequent over-simplification and too many facile conclusions.'[45] The essence of Christian's argument was that although books like Gallagher's could convey better than anything the feelings that retreat involved, they did not have the wider political and strategic perspective which explained why the Burmese defences were so under-prepared and the troops so outnumbered. Christian did point out, however, that the American editors had omitted the very particular praise that Gallagher had made of the bravery and skill of British soldiers in Burma, which had been included in the British edition. A reviewer who came from a rather different political perspective was George Orwell. Orwell did, of course, have a very good knowledge of colonial society in Burma, having spent five years as a police officer there in the 1920s. He took a much more favourable view, describing the book as 'a valuable piece of reporting'. Orwell's review for the *Observer* was not actually published because his editor was concerned that its negative comments about the behaviour of the British in Singapore and Burma would only add to current American unease about fighting for Britain's outdated empire. It was a pity that the review did not receive an audience because Orwell thought it highlighted three issues which were not general knowledge and which needed investigating. These were:

1. That fresh troops were landed at Singapore, long after it was known that its fall was inevitable, when Wavell had wanted them diverted to Burma;

2. The reluctance of the British to allow in Chinese troops initially;
3. Racist distinction in the treatment of refugees.[46]

These were all matters that Gallagher had not reported in his dispatches to the *Express*, but had a strong basis of truth. They will be discussed in later chapters.

The gross discrepancies between the contemporary newspaper reports and the later published books were mostly due to the strict censorship that they obtained in Burma at this early stage of the campaign. Later on, some of the journalists were able to successfully challenge the censorship and it was eased, allowing for a fuller and somewhat more informative, if not always entirely reliable, coverage of the infantry warfare.

4

ORGANISING THE WAR CORRESPONDENTS IN BURMA

All correspondents who wished to report from the front had to be accredited by the local Services Public Relations Office (SPRO). This not only provided authorisation to report at the battlefronts but also, at least in theory, facilitated the means to do so by providing transport, accommodation, food rations, a uniform, dark-room and facilities for censoring and transmitting dispatches. The problem was that these offices took time to set up when war with Japan began and had to be provided with funds, staffing and equipment. Government propaganda in Burma before the war was in a very poor state. An official report written in July 1941 by a visiting services publicity officer, J.C.R. Proud, pointed to the amateurish nature of propaganda efforts. Publicity in Burma was divided between the Defence Department and the Burmese ministers, linked by the joint secretary, Home and Defence Departments, U Kyaw, who was hopelessly overworked, and actually ended up editing press reports himself. Proud also reported a lack of suitable journalists to do the necessary work of countering Japanese influence and breaking down 'indifference and defeatism in the minds of the local Burmese population'.[1] As a result, Dorman-Smith asked for a trained journalist to be provided by London. In his view, there were no suitable journalists in Burma, and the Ministry of Information (MOI) eventually provided Charles Newham, who had

had a distinguished journalistic career in India.[2] Newham arrived in Rangoon at the beginning of December 1941 and served as the MOI representative in Burma until March 1942.[3] It seems that like de Graaff-Hunter, Newham was not well received by his colleagues in Burma. He left for India in frustration at not being able to implement his recommendations.[4]

Before Newham had arrived, it had been decided to appoint Captain E.T. 'Tommy' Cook, the governor's aide-de-camp (ADC), to head the English section of the Defence Department's publicity as director of News Services. Dorman-Smith explained that Cook had good journalistic and administrative experience and got on well with the Burmese: 'that Cook is about to marry my daughter I do not consider to be any great drawback!'[5] The nepotism involved did, however, matter to some journalists, and the fact that Cook had rather draconian views on how the press should be expected to follow the government line did not help either.[6] Around June 1941, Major Hewett of the Burma Rifles was deputed to provide publicity materials for the army. He started by producing newssheets for army personnel serving in Burma. This was expanded in September to include bi-weekly radio broadcasts and pilot officer Kenneth Wallace-Crabbe, an Australian who was serving with the RAF in Malaya, was brought in to expand the work of the SPRO. Even so, it was not until the war with Japan was over two months old and correspondents had come into Burma in increasing numbers, that the SPRO was officially authorised on 12 February 1942. A week earlier Major Hewett had been replaced by E.C.V. Foucar, a local lawyer, as director of the SPRO.[7] Foucar had some journalistic experience and had acted as a stringer for a couple of British newspapers, so that Leland Stowe's rather condescending description of him as a detective story writer who had been commissioned a lieutenant-colonel was rather wide of the mark.

The Burma SPRO, therefore, had dual functions of maintaining publicity both for the armed forces in the country and for overseas use, and dealing with the war correspondents and their professional needs. The latter activity came to dominate and was the domain of Kenneth Wallace-Crabbe who was promoted to the rank of squadron-leader. Although Foucar's deputy, he effectively ran the practical work of the office. Wallace-Crabbe had experience as a journalist on the *Melbourne Herald* and got on well with the war correspondents. At forty-one years of age,

Image 3: Lt Col E.C.V. Foucar, SPRO, from the Foucar family collection. The photo was taken in Dehradun, India in May 1942 after the retreat

Image 4: Kenneth Wallace-Crabbe, deputy PRO, in RAF uniform in Delhi, 1944, courtesy of Christopher Wallace-Crabbe

⸴e was older than most of the journalists, and, as a forthright and more egalitarian Australian, he probably found it easier to win their respect.[8]

Foucar expressed the skills required in dealing with the war correspondents very well:

> A War Correspondent is very much of an individualist. He is exceedingly jealous of his privileges and is always with an eye wide open for an exclusive 'story'. He is very apt to resent anything which he considers has been done either to his own detriment or to favour some other War Correspondent. His profession requires all this of him, and if he is not excessively alert and aggressive in professional matters he is not a good War Correspondent. The result is that the handling of War Correspondents in the mass by the authorities calls for the exercise of constant care and much tact... In only one case was it found necessary to take disciplinary action and to withdraw the official Pass.[9]

The main issues of contention between the SPRO and the correspondents would have been obtaining access to the front, censorship of their dispatches and the difficulties and delays in having their stories sent to their newspapers. These problems were interconnected and from the journalists' point of view obstructed their ability to carry out their jobs properly. As Foucar indicated, journalism was a competitive business and it was crucial to get good stories and to have them transmitted as soon as possible, preferably before any of their rival papers could receive them. The greatest prize would be to post an exclusive story, one that no other paper was able to report. Hence the frustration that journalists felt when their stories were delayed or they perceived that rival organisations were being given more favourable treatment. One problem was that the censors often wanted the reporters to wait for official communiqués to be issued on particular battles before allowing the correspondents' reports through. As the reporters often felt that they knew more about what had happened than Army HQ, this was particularly annoying. O'Dowd Gallagher and Leland Stowe were involved in a number of serious disputes with the SPRO over censorship and delays in transmission of their dispatches.

Censorship

The most frustrating delays resulted from the long-winded censorship arrangements, especially after the evacuation of non-essential civilians from Rangoon took place. Journalists had to present their dispatches to three authorities in Burma: first the SPRO and then the civil and the military censors.[10] In Rangoon, where each of the censors was in close proximity, delays were not great, but when the journalists had to leave Rangoon for Maymyo, some 450 miles away, on 21 February, delays were more severe. In Maymyo, dispatches had to be taken from the SPRO office three miles away to the army censor and then needed a forty-mile drive to Mandalay for approval by the civil censor. It was helpful if correspondents could be present when censorship took place as they could discuss the reasons and sometimes find a compromise. More often than not, it was not possible for them to do this. For a time, the correspondents allocated one or two of their number to take all their dispatches from Maymyo to Mandalay, but this arrangement broke down, apparently when one of them was accused of ensuring his messages took priority when he delivered them in Mandalay.[11] Wireless communication had never been available to war correspondents and so unreliable landlines had to be used.[12] When the Mandalay telegraph office was destroyed in the bombing in early April, other means had to be found for transmission of messages. This usually meant trying to get the messages out by aeroplane to India or China.

The press censorship regulations operating in Burma stated that:

> The object of press censorship in war is to control the publication in print, whether at home or abroad, of information which is likely to assist the enemy or to be prejudicial to the national security and well-being. This control will be exercised in Burma partly by preventive measures but mainly by the voluntary and loyal cooperation of the press.[13]

Most of the censorship restrictions in Burma applied to information about troop movements, weapons or any information that the enemy might find useful. Although the reporters accepted these restrictions, they found some difficult to understand. For instance, place names were deleted in case they gave information to the enemy, whereas the correspondents knew that the Japanese had better maps of Burma than the Allies, having purchased them systematically before the war. But certain other restrictions listed below had potential for conflict as to how they were interpreted, for example:

> v. Matter calculated to impair the efficiency, morale or discipline of or to prejudice recruiting for His Majesty's forces (e.g. disparagement of those

in command of His Majesty's forces) or to create or encourage disaffection in any section of the population in any part of the British Empire.

vi. The disclosure of the intentions or supposed intentions of our forces or of our allies in either attack or defence.

viii. Such information regarding subversive movements, agrarian or industrial unrest, and communal disturbances as might be calculated to raise the morale of the enemy.

Regulations v and vi meant that it was difficult for the correspondents to comment on the wider strategic context of the Burma campaign, although their later books would show that they had a good appreciation of this. It meant that military correspondents writing from their desks in Fleet Street had greater freedom to analyse broader strategy, whilst the correspondents on the spot tended to describe the immediate action in the theatre, whether from the front or from Army Headquarters.

Regulation viii brought conflict between the authorities and the correspondents over the scale and role of so-called fifth column activity among the Burmese. The correspondents continually described the actions of a minority of Burmese in helping the Japanese, either by guiding them along hidden routes, through acts of sabotage or outright armed warfare on the side of the Japanese. The Burma government was very aware of the comfort these reports could give to the Japanese, how they could feed American anti-colonial feelings, and also make it difficult for the Allies when they returned to recapture Burma. It is likely that, though the correspondents probably exaggerated the scale of fifth column activity, the government undoubtedly downplayed its role. This is discussed in more detail in Chapter Seven.

Censorship was an area of much frustration for the journalists. On the one hand, they recognised the need for censorship and to some extent welcomed the fact that some of the responsibility for protecting the public and the people at home was taken off their shoulders. However, they really hated what they regarded as unnecessary or nitpicking censorship and would do all they could to challenge it in whatever way they could. Sometimes their appeals worked, as in the case of Tom Healy and Bill Munday's reports of the fighting at Pegu. This was usually because a higher authority saw the benefit of allowing more detailed coverage of the successes of British troops and personnel at a time when Chinese and American criticisms of continual British retreats were considered damaging both at home and abroad. Sometimes reports which would normally have been censored slipped through by chance, but normally censors leant towards caution because this was the safer option within the job. The chief civil censor, Colonel Raymond, was particularly restrictive, arguing, 'I don't pass anything unless I first see a report of it in the newspapers. Then I can safely let a message repeating it go out.'[14] He once told Leland Stowe: 'I always ask myself if my dear devoted daughter in England would be alarmed by this. If she'd be alarmed, however true, it shouldn't be reported.'[15]

Sometimes correspondents tried to evade Burmese censorship by trying to have their dispatches sent directly through China or India. This was very much deprecated by the authorities.[16] However, there were also cases where dispatches which had been approved by the censors in Burma were queried by the censors in India, which was not supposed to happen.[17] Whatever the regulations were, some correspondents were more successful than others in getting round them. This is difficult to explain. Before the SPRO was established in February 1942, it seems that the governor's office participated in the censorship. The correspondents were aware of mounting criticisms of the government for failing to establish compulsion on labour in the docks so that Lend-Lease equipment could be released for use, but held back from reporting it. However, the editor of the *Rangoon Gazette*, E. W. R. Stone, published an excoriating article which had as its headline: 'Faith in our fighting men: but save us from the non-belligerent dopes'. Leland Stowe and O'Dowd Gallagher decided that if Stone could publish this story then they could follow suit. Yet Colonel Raymond refused even to look at their dispatches and directed them to Government House. The governor's secretary, Bernard Ottwell Binns, refused to show the dispatches to the governor, knowing that Dorman-Smith was furious with Stone and was threatening to pre-censor his paper.[18] It is easy to see how censorship of this type restricted the correspondents quite severely in reporting the truth about how the war was being conducted. Yet it is difficult to understand how someone like O'Dowd Gallagher, an aggressive journalist of great experience, seemed timid in his newspaper reporting of the retreat. His book *Retreat in the East*, which was the first of the correspondents' books to be published in September 1942, was highly critical of the Governor of Burma and especially of the evacuation process from Rangoon. Yet he was entirely supportive of the civil government in his articles for the *Daily Express* at the time of the retreat, to a point of being over-sanguine and misleading about the way the war was going. Censorship did seem to relax somewhat over time and other correspondents such as Tom Healy and Bill Munday, writing for the *Daily Mirror* and the *News Chronicle* respectively, were able to write far more interestingly and directly of their experiences than Gallagher was. This was partly the result of challenges to the censorship system that the journalists made and partly due to a realisation that over-rigorous censorship was not doing the British war effort any favours.

Women War Correspondents

For a large part of the Second World War, women correspondents were barred from the fighting front by both British and American armed forces. The British armed forces did not officially accredit women war correspondents until late 1944. The Americans took a somewhat more lenient attitude from 1943 but, even so, editors often expected women correspondents to report only on how civilians fared in war zones or how military hospitals treated soldiers.[19] Individual women reporters managed to challenge the ban and by the end of the war women such as Martha Gellhorn, Lee Miller, Margaret Bourke-White, Claire Hollingworth and Marguerite Higgins had played an important role as war reporters.

Eve Curie, the daughter and biographer of her famous mother Madame Curie, the Nobel Prize-winning scientist, was one of the women to challenge the restrictions. She was sent on a global reporting expedition by the *New York Herald Tribune* and Allied Newspapers (London) which lasted from November 1941 to April 1942. During her travels she was able to reach the fighting front on three occasions, in the Soviet Union, Libya and Burma. She seems to have managed this by dint of her mother's reputation and by her own personal charm and intelligence. In Libya she reached the front thanks to her friendship with Randolph Churchill, son of the British prime minister, who introduced her to the RAF there. Even so, her presence caused great consternation in the accrediting authorities in North Africa. Curie managed to pay a very short visit to the frontline in Burma in mid-February 1942, *en route* to China. It seems that the army may have realised too late the gender of the newly arriving journalist. In any case, she was treated as a VIP by Wallace-Crabbe, deputy services PRO, when she arrived in Rangoon on 14 February.[20] At the railway station, seeing the crowds of Indian refugees, she already sensed that things were not going well: 'I smelled at once this ghastly odour of defeat, of retreat, of fear, that I knew only too well, that was attached forever to the Europe of 1940 and had obsessed me ever since the fall of France.'[21] She was given war correspondent status and provided with Unni Nayar of the Indian army as her conducting officer to travel the same afternoon to the front defending the Bilin river. Her gender obviously came as a surprise to the army, who had made no special arrangements for her. She realised that her presence was just one more problem for the soldiers to worry about: 'A good rule for war correspondents, and certainly for women correspondents, is: Never descend on battle headquarters in the midst of a retreat. Officers who withdraw don't like to have reporters around.'[22] The next morning she interviewed Major-General Smyth. Despite the confident front put up by the general, Curie was not convinced. She could see that the British troops were poorly prepared and armed for the type of warfare they were now fighting. Worst of all was the lack of air support. 'In Burma,' she concluded, 'an ill-equipped colonial army had to cope, at the same time, with a fanatical enemy and with a partly disloyal population.'[23]

Curie's pessimistic writing reflected a keen analytical mind which had broad experience of reporting war from across the globe. In only a short visit to Burma she had picked up on many of the key issues: the racism, 'decayed snobbery' and conservatism of the British in Burma, the lack of preparation for war, military failings and the poor transport links. The quotations above are all taken from her excellent book, *Journey Among Warriors*, which was published in 1943 and inevitably involved some degree of hindsight, though how much is difficult to tell. Needless to say, her newspaper reports displayed none of that gloomy realism. The *Daily Sketch* which published some of her reports in Britain was proud to boast of her being the only woman war reporter in Russia and now in Burma. Instead of her later comments about the importance of the lack of air power, her article insisted that 'our air pilots and machines are greatly superior to those of the enemy'. She told a partial truth about the air war over Rangoon but it covered a greater deception about the state of the war in the rest of Burma.[24]

Curie was not the only woman correspondent in Burma. Later, Clare Boothe Luce, wife of Henry Luce, the owner of *Time-Life*, would make a short visit to Maymyo and Mandalay but, although she wrote a good deal in *Life* magazine on her experiences in Burma, she was not accredited as a war correspondent and declined the chance to visit the front.[25]

5

GEORGE RODGER AND *LIFE* MAGAZINE
PHOTO-JOURNALISM

George Rodger was thirty-three years old when he arrived in Rangoon at the end of January 1942. Like many other photo-journalists he was largely self-taught as a cameraman, and became a war correspondent more or less by accident. He had worked for the BBC's *Listener* magazine and freelanced for the Black Star Agency. He was unable to volunteer for the RAF on the outbreak of the Second World War as he was considered to be in a reserved occupation. He took photographs of the London Blitz and it was these that brought him to the attention of the American *Life* magazine which took him on as a freelance photographer. His contract allowed him to provide his photos to other illustrated magazines such as *Picture Post* and *Illustrated*. These magazines were an important source of visual information about the war in the pre-television era and *Life* alone had a circulation of more than three and a quarter million, which probably meant a readership of many times that number.[1] By the time Rodger reached Burma, he was already very well-travelled in various war zones, especially in Africa and the Middle East.[2] Yet it was his coverage of the British and Chinese armies in Burma that was to make his name and secure him a permanent contract with *Life*. In Burma Rodger developed his distinctive combination of text and picture. Indeed, his biographer Carole Naggar calls him the inventor of the package story, and emphasises how he

63

always wrote his own full captions and lead-in texts.[3] *Life*, however, treated his Burma work as photographic support material and never gave him a writer's byline, though eventually he was awarded a seven-page spread for his war photos in the 10 August 1942 edition.[4] Sometimes his captions were used verbatim but the accompanying articles were either written by editors or by other correspondents such as Clare Boothe or Jack Belden [See Appendix 2 for a list of Rodger's contributions to *Life* magazine]. This is a pity as Rodger was a very good writer, as is apparent from his Burma memoir, *Red Moon Rising*, published in 1943.

When Rodger arrived in Rangoon on 26 January, a number of correspondents had been there for several weeks waiting for the rudimentary Services Public Relations Organisation (SPRO) to become established and to provide them with the means to reach the fighting front. There were particular problems for Rodger as a cameraman. He was required to have his photos developed before being censored and then transmitted to London or New York. Finding the right chemicals to develop the film was very difficult in the wartime conditions in

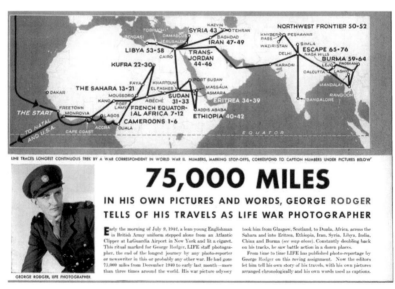

Image 5: '75,000 miles' [George Rodger], *Life*, 10 August 1942, p. 62

humid Rangoon, but with the help of Squadron-Leader and Deputy Public Relations Officer Wallace-Crabbe, Rodger managed to send off his first assignment.[5]

The Flying Tigers

Along with the other journalists, Rodger found his best stories initially by covering the fighter pilots based at Mingaladon airfield, close to Rangoon. However, there was a particular importance to Rodger in photographing the American Volunteer Group (AVG) pilots, the so-called Flying Tigers, and their exploits. Firstly, they provided really photogenic subjects, and one of the few success stories in the Burma retreat. Secondly, unlike the RAF pilots, they could be named and their background stories printed, so that they fed the American appetite for news of their 'boys in the Far East'. Perhaps most importantly, they fitted the requirements of *Time-Life* to show the support that the United States was giving to the Chinese government through the volunteer air force scheme and through Lend-Lease provisions sent via Rangoon and up the Burma Road to China.[6] Americans had obviously focused primarily on the Pacific War since Pearl Harbor, but they needed to be shown the wider global war in which they would increasingly be called on to participate. Henry Luce, owner of *Time-Life* and son of a missionary to China, wanted to see America give more support to Chiang Kai-Shek and the Chinese nationalists, and *Life* correspondents were almost always in line with this editorial policy. Rodger achieved this with the stories he focused on and the photographs he took rather than through written commentary. He modestly saw himself as 'a war photographer and no journalist', and aimed to report 'as non-committally as possible, only of what I saw'.[7] Of course, this photographic neutrality was an impossible ideal: Rodger's published work was probably more supportive of the Allied war effort in Burma than that of the other war correspondents considered here.

Unlike the journalists, Rodger had to be used to long delays in having his stories published, and in fact his 'Flying Tigers' story, which was developed and censored at Rangoon, only managed to reach the United States for the 30 March 1942 edition.[8] Many of his other stories were very much delayed in transmission, and appeared sometimes months after the event.[9]

He took the trouble to include photos of the sixteen pilots in the squadron, and gave each of them a background story from their hometown through to their hobbies, and, if they were married, referred to their wives too.[10] One of the pilots, Tom Cole, was shot down and killed and Rodger made sure that he had his photograph included.[11] This was all good publicity at a time when in fact the war was going badly for the Allies in Southeast Asia.

Rodger was not alone in devoting a lot of copy to the story of the Flying Tigers. O'Dowd Gallagher reported on the American airmen as

Image 6: The Flying Tigers, a group of American volunteers (AVG) at Mingaladon airfield near Rangoon, with Curtis P-40 Tomahawk fighter, 1942, George Rodger/Magnum Photos

soon as he arrived in Burma and made an effort to give attention to the British and Commonwealth pilots too. He devoted four chapters of his book to their story.[12] His companion Leland Stowe reported that on 23 December 'the first American and British aviators to fight in a common engagement as official allies in the Second World War fought side by side over Rangoon today...'[13] Of the Christmas Day Japanese bombing raid, Stowe wrote that it represented the 'first whopping and crushing defeat that the Japanese Air Force has suffered in four and a half years of war', and he compared it to the Battle of Britain.[14] Stowe began keeping the score of Japanese losses as a result of their first two major bombing raids of Rangoon and concluded that a minimum of 149 Japanese aircrew had been killed as against only six for the AVG and RAF. He was confident that he had carefully checked his figures. When Stowe came to write his book *They Shall Not Sleep* in early 1944, he attempted a more rounded picture of the AVG and its achievements. He admitted that he had not been impressed with the pilots when he first met them in September 1941. He regarded them as arrogant young Americans, only interested in the generous pay and bonuses for each Japanese plane shot down.[15] However, he came to appreciate the way that they had been trained by their commander Colonel Claire Lee Chennault and estimated that the AVG were responsible in the first six weeks of fighting from Mingaladon airfield for shooting down 130 Japanese planes, of which at least half were bombers with crews of eight men. Thus he calculated a Japanese loss of personnel of 585 as against seven for the single AVG squadron which opposed them, usually with six or seven planes. He reckoned on a remarkable strike rate of five Japanese planes for every single P-40 Tomahawk that they shot down.[16] More recent studies, such as that by Jerome Klinkowitz, have cast doubt on these figures.[17] Klinkowitz writes that these figures were grossly exaggerated: 'Nowhere near 130 Japanese planes were shot down and no Japanese bomber carried a crew of eight.'[18] There were great difficulties in estimating such scores in the sort of conditions that applied in the aerial dogfights over Burma. Pilots from all countries tended to overestimate the number of kills they made, and in the case of the AVG there was a large financial incentive to claim their successes. This is not in any way to diminish the remarkable achievements of both RAF and AVG pilots, who were completely outnumbered by their Japanese opponents and, certainly in the case of the RAF, were flying outmoded planes. Klinkowitz believes that the damage caused to Japanese bombers by the AVG and RAF delayed the Japanese capture of Rangoon by three months, which allowed the Allied troops time for a more organised retreat.[19] In any case, stories of the exploits of the pilots were used repeatedly by journalists throughout the campaign, as they provided one of the few positive stories during the military retreat.[20] The correspondents obviously became closely attached to the individual pilots and mechanics with some of whom they lived and messed. After hearing of the death of one of his favourite pilots, Rodger expressed a rare anger at the American authorities 'who left their boys to fight crack Japanese pilots with nothing but suicide crates to fly in'.[21]

One problem for the war correspondents in Burma was that communications were often very poor and Rodger received no instructions from New York as to what to cover next.[22] He decided to go north to cover the very ambitious plans to build a new Yunnan-Burma railway designed to relieve traffic on the Burma Road. He travelled with Alec Tozer, the British Movietone News cameraman, in separate jeeps, and they reached right into China after many adventures *en route*. Again, this story was very much in line with Luce's requirements. The Burma Road, ultimately linking the port of Rangoon with the Chinese headquarters at Chungking, was by now the only supply line by which American materiel could reach nationalist China. When he reached Yunnan province in south-west China, accommodation was very difficult to find and often involved sleeping rough after a day's arduous driving. On the Burma-China border his guide found him accommodation in a two-storey barn described as a new hotel, but the place was so crowded and noisy that it was impossible to sleep so the two correspondents began to type up their diaries to the bemused interest of the Chinese residents:

> But we were the only white people there and were carefully watched all the time. Every little thing we did excited curiosity. As soon as we set up our typewriters, the other inmates crowded round us and watched the keys fascinated. One who could read a little English, leaned over my shoulder and translated the words as they formed, for the benefit of the others. I wrote: 'Chinese crowd around me reading what I write.' They thought this a hell of a joke, roared with laughter, slapped me on the back and shook me by the hands. Tozer smiled superciliously from across the table.[23]

The Burma Road journey met Henry Luce's requirements in showing American support for the Chinese war effort. However, it was a risky venture as it was forbidden to photograph on the Chinese sections of the Road and there was a constant danger that Rodger would be arrested and have his camera and film confiscated. One is struck by the fact that battle zones were not necessarily the most dangerous places for war correspondents: driving along the winding Burma Road, with precipitous drops on the side and faced with oncoming Chinese truck drivers oblivious to other traffic, was certainly very frightening. It was also risky in journalistic terms as it was very time-consuming to make such journeys which took Rodger and his companion, the Australian correspondent Wilfred Burchett, away from the battlefronts with no real idea of how long it would take to get their stories back for censorship and transmission. It was rather less of a problem for Rodger than for Burchett, as the former was working for a weekly pictorial magazine that could cope with delayed stories if necessary. Yet the pair nearly missed reporting the fall of Rangoon, and only arrived when the city had been almost totally evacuated of civilians, within a few days of the departure of the troops and the final round of demolitions.

In early March, as Rodger and Tozer drove down to see the final days of Rangoon, they came across thousands of Indian refugees streaming in the opposite direction, desperate to find safety. It was obvious that many Burmans disliked the Indians and would not help them. Rodger described the treatment of Indian refugees who had walked 180 miles from Rangoon without food and shelter:

> When they arrived at a river bank, after walking for hours over the hot dusty roads, they found Burmans armed with dahs—their square-ended swords—on guard to prevent them from quenching their thirst until they had paid an anna for a cupful of the tepid river water. They were charged exorbitant prices for food, and in places they had met Burman police who had held them up on the road and demanded one rupee before allowing them to continue. I found one of these illicit tolls in operation. A bamboo pole was slung across the highway and footsore, weary Indians were being charged a fee before they could pass by a band of Burmans, some of whom wore the uniform of the native police. I drove the Burmans away at the point of my gun and let the Indians through, but one of them told me he had already had his last rupee taken from him and had nothing more with which to buy food.[24]

This passage reminds the reader that many of the war correspondents in Burma carried guns to protect themselves, which they would not normally be allowed to do in other theatres of the war. They were prepared to use them too, sometimes to intimidate potentially hostile Burmans, but also, in Rodger's case, to warn 'crazy' Chinese truck drivers to keep to their side of the narrow mountainous roads. The journalists were not passive onlookers of the war but mucked in when needed, for example acting as stretcher-bearers for the wounded or taking messages between the different commands.

In March, just as Rangoon was being lost to the Japanese, Rodger was invited to photograph a battle which was taking place on the east bank of the Sittang river to recapture the town of Shwegyin. Rodger saw it as 'a chance I had been waiting for. A chance to get some real action pictures and show the people at home what fighting was like in Burman jungles.'[25] He was accompanied by Wilfred Burchett and the newsreel cameraman Alec Tozer. Rodger was using light Leica and Rolleiflex cameras.[26] He admitted that 'neither of us had got a single picture' of the main advance on Shwegyin, and it was too dangerous to try to stand up and take good photos as Japanese snipers were very active.[27] Indeed, he tells of a close encounter with death:

> As I crept along a bullet zipped past my ears. I thought it must be coincidence and kept on going. A second bullet that missed me by only an inch or so proved it was no chance shot and I lay down flat on my stomach at the bottom of the ditch trying to figure out where the sniper might be hiding. A third bullet skimmed over my back and nicked a Sikh who was crawling just behind me. He leapt up with a roar and ran forward to where our ditch led into a drain-pipe. Straddling the pipe he poked his tommy-gun inside it and released the trigger. The Jap who was hiding in it squealed as he died and the Sikh stood up and saluted me, a broad exultant grin spreading across his sweating features.[28]

This was part of a Sikh assault on one of the houses in the village from which Japanese snipers were firing. Rodger says that he 'got a few pictures of the mad rush ... but there was no time to stop and focus properly or choose a good view-point for it would be certain death to stand still out in the open'.[29]

There is a conflict between Rodger's exciting account published in his later memoir and his repeated statements that he found it impossible to take photographs of the battle. This is resolved by reading Rodger's diary which showed that the three correspondents missed the actual battle, which took place early on the morning of 11 March, while they only arrived at the Army Headquarters near Nyaunglebin a day later on 12 March. Here they interviewed Major-General Bruce Scott and Lieutenant-General Alexander, the newly arrived commander of the army in Burma. They reached Madauk, on the east side of the Sittang river too late on the same evening to cross over to the west side until the next morning, 13 March. Rodger confirms that he 'got good series of action photos' in the morning before returning to Maymyo on the same day.[30] Thus, the photos that Rodger took were of re-enactments of the battle, which the army must have agreed to stage in order to give Rodger and Tozer the rare chance to report a British offensive victory in the Burma campaign. The Shwegyin battle was not important in itself as the troops were ordered to withdraw almost immediately afterwards, but it did have a propaganda value.

Burchett let the cat out of the bag in his account published in *Bombs Over Burma*:

> We came back next morning and the battalion commander repeated the action for the benefit of the photographers. Houses and shops were still burning, and with a realistic background the Sikhs put on a terrific bayonet charge, that gave the photographers all the action they wanted.[31]

E.C.V. Foucar, the director of Services Public Relations in Burma, confirmed that 'our troops willingly went through the performance again, and in due course pictures of the Shwegyin battle were shown on the screens of the world'. He described this as 'an incident that amused us'.[32]

Rodger, however, makes no mention of reconstruction in either his published accounts or in his private diaries and correspondence. His account in *Red Moon Rising* and the photos which appeared in *Life* magazine correspond accurately to the photos that are in his archive, but they do not explain his emphasis on the impossibility of taking photographs of the real battle, especially of the quality of the one shown in Image 7. However, the British magazine *Illustrated* also published three of Rodger's photos of the Shwegyin battle in its edition of 20 June 1942. One photo, which is not listed in the archive, looks staged. The picture

(Image 8) shows Indian troops turning sideways on to the house and pointing their bayonets to the ground. The caption reads, 'Charging an Advanced Japanese Post on the Outskirts of the Town. Indian troops bayoneted the defenders before they could escape. Then the attackers swept on to their next objective.' No Japanese are shown in the picture, and the soldiers would at least have had to take covering action against snipers who would be more probably placed in the houses. This photograph does not tally with the newsreels of this incident which show the Sikh soldiers running directly up to the house rather than stopping to bayonet any Japanese soldiers. It is ironic that earlier in the same edition of *Illustrated* a comparison is made between British truthfulness in treating photographic images with German readiness to fake them.[33]

In Rodger's archive there is a signed enlarged print of *Life*'s Shwegyin photo (Image 7) marked 'Indian troops re-enact their attack on a Japanese outpost'. The evidence is therefore conclusive in relation to the newsreel and photos of the Indian troops attacking the building at Shwegyin: it is a re-enactment. It is likely that the other film of troops

Image 7: Sikhs of the Indian Army attack Shwegyin on the far bank of the Sittang river, March 1942, George Rodger/Magnum Photos

Image 8: 'Indian Troops Bayoneted the Defenders Before They Could Escape', *Illustrated*, 20 June 1942, pp. 18–19

crossing the river is also part of a re-enactment staged for the cameramen. It is perhaps understandable why Tozer and Rodger decided to take the only opportunity they had had in the Burma campaign to actually present the re-enactment as reality. Yet it is difficult to understand why Rodger should have concocted such a detailed story around it for his book, *Red Moon Rising*. He was known to be totally opposed to falsifying photographs, arguing that they had to be 'meticulously factual, honest and true—no staged effects, no Western Desert mock-up, no falsity'.[34] It is also difficult to understand why the British army, at this critical stage in the campaign, should have been prepared to spend time re-enacting parts of the assault on Shwegyin.

After Shwegyin, Rodger and Burchett moved further north, hoping to cover the Chinese troops on the Toungoo front. They found that the Chinese were in the process of retreating too. By now, Japanese bombing raids were obliterating Burmese towns, whose houses were mostly built of wood and very vulnerable. At Pyinmana, they were relieved to find that Dr Seagrave's hospital had not been engulfed in flame like the rest of the town but was working on tirelessly under the most difficult conditions. Gordon Seagrave was a Baptist missionary and surgeon who was born in Burma and had set up hospital in the Shan states. In 1942 he joined the US Army Medical Corps and moved his hospital to

Pyinmana to serve the Chinese 6th Army. Many journalists called by to report on his remarkable work, perhaps captivated too by the young Burmese nurses who worked for him devotedly. Travelling further, Rodger and Burchett came upon the horrific sight of the village of Thazi, almost completely flattened by Japanese bombing. They used their jeep to ferry the wounded to a dressing station outside the village. Rodger wrote:

> I shall never forget the next hour that passed—the heartrending cries of the wounded; the screams of those who were caught in the flames, and the animal-like look of gratitude in the eyes of those who we were able to rescue... We dragged out a small child and a Burman girl whose leg was severed just below the knee, and loaded them into the jeep... The girl's dangling leg, held only by tissues, was obviously distressing her. It would be impossible for any surgeon to save it so I cut it off with my knife and sat beside in the jeep, holding up the dismembered stump with my thumb on the main artery to stop the bleeding, while Burchett drove the gruesome load to the dressing station.[35]

Anyone reading Rodger's harrowing account would be disabused of the idea that war photographers are conditioned to ensure that their professional duties override their common humanity.

If the devastation that Rodger had seen in towns and villages travelling north from Toungoo was bad, much worse damage was inflicted on Burma's second city Mandalay, which was bombed by the Japanese on Good Friday, 3 April. Strong winds had fanned the flames and caused utter devastation. 'Charred bodies sprawled in the streets and rotting corpses floated among the lily-pads in the moat surrounding the rose-red walls of Fort Dufferin... Every temple had gone; the bazaars and shops had gone, and the homes of 150,000 people; Mandalay itself had gone.' With some exaggeration he concluded: 'What took a thousand years to build took but an hour to fall.'[36]

Maymyo

Rodger and Burchett were relieved to leave Kipling's fabled city and to drive some forty miles north-east to Maymyo in the hills. Maymyo had been the correspondents' base since the fall of Rangoon. It was a typical hill station, the quiet summer retreat for the British governing elite from the heat of the Burmese plains. Now it was the rear headquarters of the British armed forces under General Alexander as well as the civilian administration under Sir Reginald Dorman-Smith. The Baptist Mission compound housed the American General Stilwell, 'Vinegar Joe' as he was popularly known for his outspoken and often acerbic treatment of friend and foe alike.[37] It was a suitable headquarters for the son of a missionary who had served in China and bequeathed a long-standing interest in that country to his son. Stilwell was commander-in-chief of forces in the China-Burma-India (CBI) theatre, and chief of staff to the Chinese generalissimo, Chiang Kai-Shek. He was an American commander with American staff officers but no American troops. The interrelationship between the three allies was to prove difficult to say the least, and became more fraught as the Japanese reached closer to Mandalay. It is likely that the American correspondents, certainly Berrigan and Belden, stayed close to the American headquarters and its public relations team.

Some of the war correspondents were considering leaving Burma at this point. The telegraph station in Mandalay had recently been destroyed and they had relied on it for transmitting their stories and pictures back to their home offices. Now they would have to find a way to get their material to the airport at Lashio, about a hundred miles away, and hope that from there it would survive the hazardous air journey across the Himalayas to India. Most were convinced that the Allied forces in Burma would soon be defeated and the surviving armies would have to make the difficult journey back to India to re-group or join the Chinese army defending the Burma Road.

Clare Boothe Luce

George Rodger was joined in Maymyo by two other *Time-Life* correspondents, Clare Boothe and Jack Belden. Clare Boothe was married to the owner of *Time-Life*, Henry Luce. This gave her the ability to make short visits to various war zones but not to the fighting fronts, where women correspondents were still banned, particularly in General Stilwell's area of command. Having reached Maymyo with General Stilwell she was soon able to meet up with the generalissimo and his American-educated wife, Soon May–ling. On 5 April she joined Rodger and Burchett to go and see the very badly damaged city of Mandalay. It seems as if the men were keen to bring the smartly dressed Boothe down to earth by showing her the realities of the aftermath of Japanese bombing. In the 'sea of desolation,' says Rodger, 'her trim figure in well-cut slacks and snow-white shirt seemed out of setting.'[38]

In fact, Rodger was to be impressed with Boothe's resilience and capability, and he was not alone. Stilwell's aide, Frank Dorn, commented that while bombs fell nearby, she 'casually snapped pictures as calm as if she were at a Sunday outing'.[39] Next day, she set up a photo opportunity for Rodger with Chiang Kai-Shek, Madame Chiang and Stilwell. Stilwell had no love of reporters but Madame Chiang managed to get him to relax and smile.[40]

Rodger would have another opportunity soon after this to see Clare Boothe's bravery when Maymyo was bombed by the Japanese. She was offered a helmet as she sat in a slit trench while Maymyo took a heavy bombardment, but rather than wear it she sat on it, believing that it

Image 9: Chiang Kai-Shek, Madame Chiang and General Stilwell, Maymyo, April 1942, George Rodger/Magnum Photos

would not save her in case of a direct hit. She photographed the rescue of some of the casualties but only a couple of days later she was flying out to Chungking in China. She had diplomatically turned down offers of seeing the front, saying that 'my feet would swell from walking, my lips crack with the sun, I'd get fatigued, and in the end you'd curse me and say "why the hell did we bring a woman?"'[41]

Boothe's style of reporting was rather flirtatious and gushing. She described General Alexander as 'a small, handsome, vigorous and charming man', and commented that his 'pale robin's egg flannel bush jacket ... brought out the color of his clear English eyes'.[42] George Rodger she described as 'a good looking young Englishman, with a browned face and sunburned, very long English legs'.[43] Dorman-Smith told Maurice Collis the amusing story of his meeting with 'The Blonde Bombshell Mrs Luce' at Maymyo: 'At the end of the interview all she had to say was "How wonderful it was to find a virile Governor." I can assure you that she had no opportunity to test my virility!'[44]

If Boothe was impressed with the physical characteristics of the English men, she was less enamoured with their leadership roles in the Burma campaign. She obviously believed that Stilwell, leading the Chinese troops, should be in overall command in Burma, and that this would mean a more aggressive strategy. She wrote on 12 April:

> In the past weeks Chinese patience has been sorely tried. The Chinese feel that the only apparent British answer to Jap tactics of infiltration is defiltration everywhere. Also Burma is designated as a British theatre of war, whereas the map and the events of the past two months show that Burma is now, logically, a Chinese theatre.[45]

Her report for *Life* gave a potted summary of the reasons for the poor showing of the Allies and showed a distinct sympathy for the criticisms of the British contribution made by both Stilwell and the Chinese.[46] It must have galled Rodger to listen to the complaints about British military failures which were held by the Chiangs and by Stilwell.[47] Boothe ended her report with a pessimistic judgment that both the British commander, Alexander, and the correspondents believed that Burma was now lost. Of the reporters, she put their view that 'Burma was being lost, not in the Sittang and Irrawaddy valleys but in New Delhi, London and Washington. Burma, they felt, was the result of inertia in India, obstinacy in England, ignorance in America.'[48]

Boothe was right about the pessimism among correspondents, many of whom were preparing to leave the country because of the practical difficulties of filing reports in this period of rapid retreat. They also feared being trapped by the rapid Japanese advance. The main consideration now was which route they would take to leave. Some decided to leave by plane from Lashio, calculating that they would be better able to file reports from Calcutta or Chungking rather than chance the long trek over the mountains into India. Others, like Burchett and Rodger, could see a story in the very difficult journey through Nagaland to India. Indeed, they had already pioneered part of the route by jeep in their earlier coverage of the building of the Yunnan-Burma Railway.[49] The problem was that it would take a long time to get stories back to New York, by which time they might well be too out-of-date to be used.[50]

Red Moon Rising (1943) is very well-written and shows that Rodger could have been a very good travel writer. Large parts of the book amount to a travelogue rather than a war diary. Lacking instruction from his editor in New York, he obviously regarded himself as having freedom to travel to different parts of Burma and along the Burma Road into south-west China. Some of the travel seems to have been recuperative— a chance to recover from relentless coverage of the horrors of the retreat—for instance, to Kalaw in the Shan States and to Lake Inle where he photographed the famous leg-rowers who were fishing on the lake. There is evidence from his letters to his future wife Cicely that Rodger was physically and mentally exhausted at times during the Burma campaign and was seriously thinking of returning home.[51]

Rodger's book differs from those of other war correspondents in that it makes almost no criticisms of the way the retreat in Burma was handled. He clearly did not regard himself as a reporter in that sense. As he wrote in his book:

> There were men in Burma, fellow-correspondents and official observers, more fitted than I to refight the battles, to criticise the strategy, and to forecast future effects of the campaign on the general picture of global war. Therefore, I, as a war photographer and no journalist, leave to them the recording of history and write, as non-committally as possible, only of what I saw.[52]

Rodger's photographs are best when they are depicting people, whether the streams of Indian refugees flooding the roads out of

Rangoon, or Chinese soldiers being treated by Dr Seagrave's field hospital. He loved to photograph the tribespeople of the Shan states and of the Kachin and Naga hills, especially their elegant women. His love of the tribespeople, whose fate in the Burma war concerned him deeply, led on to his work after the war, especially in photographing the Nuba people of Africa.

When Rodger arrived in India and tried to write up his story he was dismayed to find that the censors would not allow him to write about the retreat. Like other war correspondents, he believed that it was important for a true account to be published and for lessons to be learnt:

> Surely this was the time that a complete presentation of the British case was most needed. Something should be done to relieve the confusion in the minds of the people who had nothing but rumours brought in by refugees and ambiguous, over-glossed reports in the papers on which to base their opinions. Now that the Japs were on India's frontier something should be done to bolster up the already-tottering faith in British ability and willingness to defend India.[53]

When he left India for New York, he was feted by *Time-Life* as one of their top staff photographers. He had a chance to recuperate and to finish writing *Red Moon Rising* which he had started when in India, but it was not long before he was back at the battlefront. He covered the Allied landings in Sicily and mainland Italy, as well as the D-Day Normandy landings. He photographed the liberation of Paris and was one of the photographers who had the traumatic task of photographing the victims of the Bergen-Belsen concentration camp. His long experience of war had left him scarred and it is not surprising that he did not continue as a war photographer. In 1947 he was a founding member of the Magnum Photos cooperative and he revelled in the freedom this work gave him, the opportunity to travel the world and, especially, to return to Africa.

6

NEWSREEL CAMERAMEN

ALEC TOZER AND MAURICE FORD

During the retreat from Burma in the spring of 1942 there were only two newsreel cameramen, both British, filming as the Japanese invaded. The problems they faced were compounded by the speed of the Japanese advance and the unpreparedness of the official publicity organisations to provide them with some of the necessary facilities for their work. The resulting film record is somewhat disappointing in terms of the lack of coverage of direct engagement with enemy forces. It also gives a misleadingly optimistic impression of the likelihood of Allied troops being able to repulse Japanese aggression. The newsreels, and the accompanying documentary evidence, have been neglected by historians until recently.[1] Yet they provide valuable evidence of how news was filtered for wartime audiences and the structural constraints on providing the public with an entirely accurate view of how the war was progressing.

Of the two British newsreel cameramen, both Londoners, Maurice Ford, was the more experienced, having joined the cinema industry in 1927 at seventeen years of age, and had filmed for British Paramount News since 1936.[2] By the time war broke out in September 1939, he was regarded as one of their leading cameramen. He made a name for himself with daring night-time filming of the City of London under

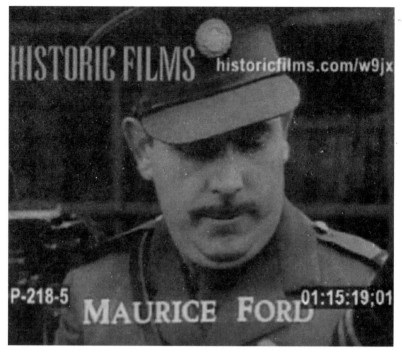

Image 10: Maurice Ford (British Paramount News), 1940, www.historic-films.com

German aerial bombardment in the Blitz of October 1940.[3] He had filmed war-work in South Africa in July 1941 but Burma was his first frontline assignment.

At twenty-seven years of age Alec Tozer was three years younger than Ford; newsreel filming in wartime was a young man's game.[4] He was only a recent recruit to the newsreel industry: his first film for British Movietone News was made in 1939. However, by the time he reached Burma in 1942 he was already a very well-travelled war correspondent, having covered stories in North Africa, Kenya and the Middle East. He was a short, wiry man with a swarthy complexion and wavy black hair, characteristics which once resulted in him having been mistakenly identified as an Italian prisoner of war.[5] He had a mischievous sense of humour, which was almost certainly needed as a way of dealing with the horrors of war that he witnessed.

Image 11: Alec Tozer (British Movietone News) in war correspondent's uniform, courtesy of Mrs Anna Patterson

The cameramen operated under a wartime pooling arrangement, sharing their stories with the three other British newsreel companies.[6] Both men were highly experienced and had already witnessed their fair share of wartime dramas on various fronts. Burma, however, was to present very particular problems for them. There was a lack of facilities for the newly arrived war correspondents, which made it difficult to reach the fighting front initially. Even when they were able to reach the frontline, conditions made it difficult to take good pictures as much of the fighting was very mobile and often took place in jungle environments. Even so, the surviving newsreels, cameramen's dope sheets and production documents provide a valuable source for historians, which has been underused.[7]

Alec Tozer arrived in Burma sometime in January 1942. He was among a group of three correspondents who were allowed to make a short visit to the front on the Salween river at the very end of January.

They arrived in time to witness the British retreat from the strategic town of Moulmein and then to rush back to Rangoon to have their stories censored and dispatched. It seems that Tozer was unable to take any satisfactory combat film and that most of the time the correspondents had spent trying to get transport.[8] The little film he took was not shown in Britain until 30 March with a commentary apologising for the delay.[9]

Maurice Ford's first dope sheets for British Paramount are dated 25 and 28 January 1942 and suggest that he is filming background footage, mostly in the Rangoon area, while waiting for direct access to the fighting. As Richard Osborne argues in his close analysis of Ford's films made while he was in Rangoon at the end of January and during the first three weeks of February, there is no intimation in Ford's dope sheets for these films that Allied forces would soon be defeated.[10] On the contrary, a picture of calm determination in the face of Japanese bombing is presented. Ford, who filmed in the London Blitz, presents a picture which British and American audiences would appreciate, with shots of street posters such as 'Rangoon Must Not Burn. Join the AFS', 'Don't Desert Your Homes but Protect and Guard Them' and 'Join the Civil Defence Service'. These posters had a particular resonance as many Indian families had fled Rangoon in the wake of the bombing, and Rangoon's civil defence arrangements were criticised as grossly inadequate.[11]

Ford's dope sheets are very colourful and give a strong sense of the narrative he wished to convey. To some extent, he worked under instruction from his editor in London but, at a distance in wartime Burma, he obviously had a great deal of initiative to pursue his own stories. That did not mean, however, that Ford's film or his version of the story would reach the British public in the form he intended. The British Paramount editor would decide what material could be shown within the well-established format of the seven-minute bi-weekly British wartime newsreel. Newsreels were shown as part of a cinema entertainment programme at a time when audiences were reaching peak numbers, and when newsreels were seen by the government as probably the most effective way of conveying images of war to the public.[12] They were subject to censorship both in the country of origin and in Britain. In practice, however, newsreels self-censored because they understood that their role within the cinema programme was to avoid alienating audiences and to support the main films. Newsreel editors also realised the power of government to control access to locations and to film stock, and anyway naturally saw themselves as contributing to the patriotic war effort.[13] Under a wartime agreement between the Newsreel Association of Great Britain, the Ministry of Information and the War Office, the newsreel companies dropped some of their normal peacetime competitive practices in order to avoid unnecessary duplication of manpower and resources. The Association nominated selected cameramen from the companies to film in particular war zones and then to make their resulting film available to all five companies. This was known as the rota system, and was the cause of certain tensions when companies wished to be allowed to show some exclusive material from their own cameramen. There was also concern about the same newsreel film being shown repetitively to regular cinema audiences.[14] Although the companies received the same film material, they made different editorial decisions about which parts were shown and what was said in the all-important commentaries, as we shall see in the case of the Shwegyin attack film taken by Alec Tozer. Other considerations meant that audiences would only have seen a small proportion of the film taken in Burma by Ford and Tozer.[15] The most important factor was that the films took a long time to reach audiences in Britain, sometimes four weeks or more, in which time the stories would have become out-of-date and probably not worth showing. Also, because the Burma story is largely one of Allied defeat and retreat it may not have been deemed good material to burden audiences with at a very difficult time in the war. More likely, the film would be edited and given a positive gloss through the all-important commentary. The danger, however, was that the public would not be prepared for the outcome of the campaign and, as with the loss of Singapore in February 1942, it would contribute to a sense of being misled by government and media.[16]

Along with other journalists covering the war in Burma, Ford and Tozer focused on the battle in the skies over Burma until they could obtain the required permissions from the armed forces and transport to cover the front. This was difficult filming as it was obviously challenging to film aerial combat in tropical light conditions. Maurice Ford did his best and even filmed aerial dogfights and anti-aircraft battery scenes at night-time.[17] This filming also provided the most positive coverage of the

Burma campaign as British army positions in the south of Burma were being surrendered very rapidly. The American Volunteer Group (AVG) pilots, in particular, provided very good stories and lively images with their easy American camaraderie and bravado. The AVG were only too willing to have their pilots and their home affiliations publicised. Maurice Ford's earliest film was taken on 30 January and showed both AVG pilots in their planes and a Japanese aircraft crashing near the airstrip at Mingaladon, as if to emphasise their successes.[18] Ford sent two shipments, filmed between 29 January and 8 February, which he admitted were 'entirely personality' stories. He feared that the AVG pilots might soon be taken over by the US Air Force and then lose their bonus payments, which did indeed happen later in the year. In any case, he argued that the British government should show its appreciation to men who had proved themselves to be 'among the finest pilots in the world'.[19] Ford was careful to balance his coverage of the AVG with film of the RAF pilots too, and his best chance came when he filmed the crews of Blenheim bombers on 22 February. He sent seven rolls of film to Paramount showing the RAF pilots preparing for a raid. Some twenty pilots are named in his dope sheet, with details of their roles and nationality. The diversity of the pilots is remarkable: they come from Britain, Australia, Canada, Southern Rhodesia, Ireland, Denmark and India.[20] Ford actually flew on this bombing raid over Martaban and the BPN newsreel celebrating his work in Burma shows him climbing into a bomber accompanied by large amounts of bulky camera equipment—he must have been a mixed blessing as a passenger.[21]

There is no doubt that Ford wanted to provide positive stories for the newsreels back home, and to make Britons relate to what was happening to people in Asia. Even when filming the bomb damage in Rangoon, he writes in his dope sheet, 'Thank you London for giving these people spiritual courage to carry on, for wherever I go I hear words of praise to my homeland from these people who are now also bearing the heavy burden.'[22] He describes Burma as 'a country of innocent peace-loving souls'.[23] Sometimes it required a degree of imagination to conjure up a positive view of what was happening in Burma under the rapid Japanese advance. In his dispatch of 1 February 1942 he reports that 'troops by the thousand have been arriving here ... there ... and everywhere in Burma.'[24] In fact, the governor, Sir

Reginald Dorman-Smith, and the army command had been desperately pressing London for reinforcements, which, though promised, never seemed to appear, at least not in the numbers that would have made a real difference. Ford also portrayed business as usual at Rangoon docks, despite the fact that most of the Indian population had fled the city after the first air-raids, and only a portion of the Indian workforce in essential services had been persuaded to return. Ford reported that

> these dockers are showing the country how not to run away... Work is going on, troops are quickly being placed in secreted defence lines and when the time comes for these fellows to push back the yellow slugs, they will do it, I feel, perhaps very soon ... but certainly faster than the Japs took to gain their occupied territory.[25]

This underlines the point that the newsreel stories were designed to be more positive than that of the newspaper correspondents with whom the cameramen worked closely. As Nicholas Pronay has argued, the newsreels

> were run by their parent-companies as a break-even advertising unit to keep their names before the cinema-goers and to keep off others who would undoubtedly have filled their time span on the screen ... there was more than the normal degree of commercial pressure upon them to give the public what it, or rather what the cinema-owners said, it wanted.[26]

The newsreels were an adjunct to the standard film programme and there was obvious pressure not to alienate the cinema audience by a diet of bad news from the fighting fronts.

A fascinating example of how newsreel stories could be transformed back in London is the film of the Burma Road that Ford was making at the same time as his AVG stories in early February 1942. Ford filmed the distinguished American war correspondent Leland Stowe typing up a story for the *Chicago Daily News* which read, 'For three and a half years the Burma Road has been operated chiefly as a racket. It has been both national scandal and national disgrace.'[27] This series of articles, which actually dated back to the turn of the year, had proved to be diplomatic dynamite and further publication of the articles had been halted.[28] Ford's story, filmed on 1–2 February 1942, threatened to re-open the wound and he must have recognised that the story would not be used. He was, however, genuinely annoyed and wanted the corruption and waste of British and American shipments to China to be recorded: 'If the story is not used ... as I can quite imagine ... it will not be ... I am sure these pictures should be kept as a permanent record.'[29] In fact, when the Burma Road story was shown in the newsreels it had been transformed from a story of Chinese corruption and mismanagement into a positive one of British and American Lend-Lease material waiting at Rangoon docks, of these goods making the remarkable journey to China, and of Chinese troops being welcomed across the border into Burma.[30] By the time these reels were shown in Britain and the US, they were pretty much out-of-date anyway. The Movietone newsreel of 12 April praised the Yunnan-Burma railway project, which was to supplement the road to China.[31] This project had actually been filmed by Alec Tozer two months earlier. By the time the film was released, this railway scheme had been stopped in favour of the more urgent Ledo Road project, which would allow a new route from India through northern Burma to replace the Rangoon link, which had, by then, been lost to the Japanese.[32]

Filming actual scenes of fighting was very difficult for the newsreel cameramen. Burma fighting was very mobile and much of it took place in wooded or jungle areas or at night, making it difficult, if not impossible, to film. At least the cameramen were soon able to obtain American Lend-Lease jeeps which they shared with other correspondents. Alec Tozer teamed up with an old friend, the stills photographer George Rodger, who was working for *Life* magazine. They travelled with another journalist, the Australian Wilfred Burchett, who was writing for the *Daily Express*. They spent quite a lot of time travelling the Burma Road into China and filming the last days of Rangoon rather than actual fighting. Their chance came in March 1942 when, with a conducting officer, Captain Stevenson, they were allowed to film British attacks across the River Sittang. These attacks were intended as diversionary, to take some pressure off British troops as they evacuated Rangoon and moved northwards. They had a propaganda value as they showed Indian troops counter-attacking the Japanese in a campaign that had largely shown retreats and rearguard actions.

Shortly after the fall of Rangoon on 8 March, Tozer and Rodger filmed a company of Kumaoni troops of the Burma Frontier Force advancing across the River Sittang as part of the attack on the town of

Shwegyin, which had been captured by the Japanese.[33] In the previous chapter it was established that the journalists did not arrive in time to cover the battle and that the film must be part of a re-enactment staged by the army for the photographers on the morning of 13 March. Unfortunately, we do not have a copy of Tozer's dope sheet which would allow us to verify this. There were clear instructions from the British Movietone editor Gerald Sanger to completely avoid passing off films of manoeuvres as authentic battle scenes, and, if forced to use 'reconstructions' due to the unavailability of authentic film, to make it very clear to audiences that this was the case.[34]

There are two short versions of the newsreel which are worth comparing. While the Movietone edition of 30 April 1942 includes shots of troops crossing the River Sittang and a section showing 'our troops going through the town', it does not claim to be showing actual battle footage. Pathé's edition of the same date is fuller and shows Sikh troops advancing to recapture the town of Shwegyin, climbing over a fence and, according to the commentary, 'Once over the wire barricade an enemy sniper brings down one of the attackers'.[35] It is the last section of the Pathé newsreel which seems most obviously faked as no other film of such close combat casualties was made in this first Burma campaign.

Other films from the 1942 retreat from Burma do show apparent army action and engagement with the enemy but seem to be best described as film of training activities or 'reconstruction'. Maurice Ford filmed Gurkha soldiers 'running thru [sic] jungle ... cutting down trees with Kukri knives', and this was shown as part of the Gaumont British newsreel of 28 May 1942.[36] Unfortunately, the clip looks more like a training jog through a banana plantation. More film is devoted to the Gloucester Regiment, focusing on named, smiling British soldiers, and shows mortar firing on what we are told are Japanese troops 'in trees and bushes'.[37] Maurice Ford is shown running with his camera to keep up with the action as British troops advance through a village. The results give a 'training-ground' image to the British forces, especially when compared with much more impressive film of the devastation caused by Japanese air-raids on Burmese towns and villages. The clip ends suitably with a sunset over Burma: by the time the film was shown British forces had been forced out of the country altogether. This underlines the difficulty that cameramen had in taking film of direct engagement with the enemy at this phase of the campaign. The messages conveyed by the newsreel were very mixed and somewhat misleading. 'Rearguard' had become a rout and the film of long lines of refugees in bullock carts and on foot fleeing Burma is very telling.

The newsreels provide first-hand evidence on certain important issues, although they have to be used with caution. For example, newsreel commentaries and pictures depict Burmese 'fifth columnists', a term which neither the army nor the civilian government liked to use. George Rodger asserted that half of the fighters the army faced in Shwegyin were in fact Burmese, and Alec Tozer's film of the fighting there ended with a short clip showing a captured fifth columnist being led by a soldier of the Burma Rifles. This is contrasted tellingly with film of Dorman-Smith meeting with loyal Shan chiefs.[38]

It is difficult to find firm evidence of fifth column activity from the visual evidence alone. For instance, Maurice Ford's film 'General Yu and Ships leave Rangoon' includes a short clip of what he described as 'fifth column blokes ... with handcuffs on their wrists' being taken from Rangoon by boat on the river Irrawaddy'.[39] Quite how Ford knew the men were fifth columnists and not merely convicts being sent away from Rangoon at this time is not clear. Fifth columnists were more likely to be shot on the spot at this time of great tension in the city. However, this scene was not included in the long compilation film of Ford's coverage of the Burma retreat, even though it had passed military censorship in Burma.

Criticism of the fighting forces was unknown among the correspondents during the campaign. Some journalists made critical comments about the Government of Burma and its civil servants, but even this was rare before the campaign was over. In civilian circles and amongst the war correspondents themselves, there circulated widespread criticisms of Governor Dorman-Smith, especially at the time of the evacuation of Rangoon. The newsreels, on the other hand, were not just uncritical, but were positively optimistic and supportive of the war effort in all aspects. One particular criticism which was made of the governor was that he did not show himself in public at the time of crisis in Rangoon. However, Alec Tozer's film shows him examining bomb damage, supervising Air Raid Precautions and, with the Burmese premier, Sir Paw Tun, meeting refugees returning to Rangoon, and talking with a man whose wife has been killed.[40] In fact, the governor was keen to avoid any sense of panic in Rangoon and the newsreels assisted in giving the impression of a calm response to the Japanese bombing there. He also wanted to show that the civil government remained in place and that he was working with the co-operation of Burmese ministers like Sir Paw Tun. It was important, therefore, to show that he was working closely with the military and that the latter had not taken over control, through the use of martial law for instance. Again, the newsreel cameramen supported this image. Maurice Ford filmed 'intimate friends' shots of the governor, his wife and youngest daughter with Sir Paw Tun, and cameraman Ford drooled in his dope-sheet that 'Dorman-Smith may prove a great man by the end of this campaign … watch him … he is making great strides… You know it is blokes like these give us guys "heart to carry on".'[41] The image was reinforced by pictures taken by Ford on 14 March of Dorman-Smith towering over General Alexander in the grounds of Government House in Maymyo, followed by pictures of the Burmese ministers.[42] The reality was rather different. General Alexander's ADC wrote later that he found Dorman-Smith 'unimpressive' and very reliant on the military, who, in any case, made the ultimate decisions about evacuation of Burma.[43] By the time these pictures were taken, the governor was becoming powerless to influence events.

Also in this newsreel were shots of Chinese military and civilian representatives. By this stage, Chinese troops, who had been somewhat reluctantly allowed into Burma by General Wavell, were playing a crucial role in the defence of the country, under the command of the US General Joseph Stilwell. The newsreels took a very positive view of the Chinese contribution, talking of 'the gallant soldiers of ancient China … Remote, unsmiling, tough little men.'[44] The commentary described Chiang Kai-Shek, head of the Chinese nationalist government, as a 'brilliant leader' and became positively utopian, announcing that 'this is not international warfare but world revolution; the powers that value the standards of decent conduct against those that value nothing except greed and conquest'.[45] Furthermore, the Chinese troops were shown bartering for food supplies with local market-traders, something they apparently lost interest in doing during the more brutal phases of the retreat from Burma. The favourable treatment of Chinese nationalists under Chiang Kai-Shek followed the line pursued by the British and American media at this time. There may well have been an element of guilt at the failure to give material support to China in her conflicts with Japan in the 1930s, and a desire to make amends.[46]

The final phases of the retreat from Burma were not covered by the newsreel cameramen. The last film that Alec Tozer took was of the 'scorched earth' destruction of the oilfields at Yenangyaung which took place on 15 April but was not shown in the newsreels until June, well after the final evacuation.[47] He escaped over the Naga Hills into India by jeep. Tozer was one of the few correspondents to cover the Burma war at both the beginning and end of the campaign with the recapture of Mandalay and Rangoon in 1945.[48]

Maurice Ford's last film was shot on 6 April when he filmed Chiang Kai-Shek and Madame Chiang arriving at Lashio airport.[49] This may well have been Ford's opportunity to leave Burma. It did not make sense for the cameramen to hold on in Burma or to film the retreat across jungle and mountains into India. Opportunities to have their film censored, approved and flown back to Britain were becoming more difficult to find and, in the words on the canisters, film was 'Useless if Delayed'. The Gaumont British newsreel commentary of 8 June had Stilwell's famous words on reaching India—'We have been run out of Burma and it was humiliating as hell'—deleted. Instead, the retreat was described as a 'valiant rearguard action' which 'gave invaluable breathing space to our war effort in the Far East'.[50] This was very much the view that the British army wanted to be propagated.

In conclusion, the newsreels gave the general public a rather misleading and over-optimistic view of the campaign in 1942 in Burma. The two cameramen did not show themselves as politically aware as the war correspondents whom they often travelled with. This suggests that their approach was driven essentially by the role that they saw the newsreels performing within the cinema, which was to be uplifting and non-controversial. The newsreel companies tended to be conservative politically, aware of the need to meet censorship requirements, and wished to avoid alienating international, especially American, audiences. However, the cameramen had performed their duties in very difficult circumstances in Burma. They, along with other war correspondents, had risked their lives in pursuit of stories as they drove through very uncertain territory, not knowing when the Japanese might outflank them. Perhaps inevitably, in filming the retreat in jungle conditions, they often took better action film of Japanese air-raids and their impact on civilians than they did of British offensive actions. They had started to overcome the many technical and logistical difficulties of filming the fighting in Burma and provide historians with an under-valued insight into a doomed campaign.

7

REPORTING THE BATTLES

The main task of the war correspondents was to report war directly from the battlefront, but, as we have seen, this was not always possible to achieve in the rapidly changing situation in Burma in the spring of 1942. The journalists had to wait for permission to visit the front and then usually had to be accompanied in groups by army conducting officers. This procedure did not suit many of the journalists who preferred to use their initiative and travel freely by jeep to reach the front and to interview the soldiers and commanders in the field. Their initial forays to the front south-east of Rangoon proved pretty unsatisfactory. At the end of January 1942, three correspondents left Rangoon for a short visit to the front on the River Salween where the army was defending the key town of Moulmein on the south bank and Martaban on the north bank. The three were Roderick Macdonald (*Sydney Morning Herald* and *News Chronicle*), Dan De Luce (American Associated Press) and Alec Tozer (British Movietone News).

Macdonald had arrived in Rangoon on 27 December, soon after the heaviest bombing of Rangoon had taken place. He was a Scot whose family had emigrated to Australia when he was a child. He had his early journalistic training in Australia in the early 1930s but spent a year in London working on the *Daily Express* before returning to Australia. In 1941 he was sent to report the Sino-Japanese war. Wilfred Burchett, a fellow Australian war correspondent, met Macdonald in Chungking and described him affectionately as having a broad horsetail type, fir moustache, and a prolonged pose of Byronic gloom. Roderick was always brimming over with 'inside dope', but was always so pleased with himself that he couldn't contain his news. After a few drinks he was always ready—with upraised, portentous forefinger and ponderous preface ... 'As a matter of fact, I am in a position to reveal...' to spill his story. Underneath his affectations and poses, Mac is a first-class reporter, with a keen nose for news.[1]

By this time, the army had been forced to make a series of retreats in response to vigorous Japanese assaults pushing up the Tenasserim Peninsula. Each time, the army had argued that it was making a strategic withdrawal to move back to more easily defended positions. The journalists reached the front by 1 February where they could see that the British had already been forced to withdraw from Moulmein. Maurice Ford nonchalantly started to film the Japanese troops across the river but was forced to make a hasty retreat when they shot at him.[2] It was an important lesson in the vulnerability of newsreel cameramen with their bulky cameras and tripods. It was a very quick visit to the front, and the reporters returned to Rangoon next day to have their reports censored and dispatched. Macdonald wanted to report the reasons for the Japanese successes, which were based around greater mobility and the use of encircling tactics forcing the British troops to withdraw. In fact, the full account of the loss of Moulmein would have made a very embarrassing story if it had been reported. The ease with which the Japanese took Burma's third city, the desertion of some of the Burma Rifles and the panicky evacuation of civilians were not reported. Macdonald tried to bypass the censor by treating the question of whether the army needed to withdraw as something that should be left to historians to decide. At first the trick seemed to have worked, as his two dispatches passed Burma censorship but then they were further censored in India, and the sections on whether withdrawal was needed and leaving the judgment to posterity were excised.[3] This external or secondary censorship should not have happened. However, Macdonald had managed to have his description of Japanese tactics published and also touched on the delicate subject of the Burmese people's response to the invaders and so-called 'fifth column' activity, subjects that were to prove much more sensitive to censorship later in the campaign.[4]

If this early foray to the front had proved something of a failure, there were three significant occasions when correspondents were able to report direct from the heat of battle, and in which they were closely involved themselves. One of these battles, the recapture of Shwegyin on the Sittang river, has already been discussed in Chapters Five and Six in relation to the photojournalist and newsreel coverage. Rodger and Burchett were able to interview General Alexander regarding the strategy at this stage. The battle was not significant in itself but acted as a morale-boosting story. The real journalistic coup came in the nearby fighting at Pegu, which was covered by Tom Healy of the *Daily Mirror* and Bill Munday of the *News Chronicle*. This story even reached Prime Minister Winston Churchill and it changed the way that battle reporting was allowed in Burma. The other major battle covered by the papers was that at Yenangyaung, where the British forces covered the 'scorched earth' destruction of the oil-fields and then tried to escape the enveloping Japanese armies. The Chinese army played an important part in their eventual escape. Three reporters provided the best coverage of this fighting at this late stage in the retreat. They were Darrell Berrigan of the United Press Agency, Jack Belden of *Time* magazine and Bill Munday of the *Sydney Morning Herald* and London *News Chronicle*. Their stories also provide interesting insights into the reporting of the role of the Chinese armies in this campaign.

William (Bill) Munday was a young Australian journalist whose boyish looks belied a fierce determination to get a story.[5] Munday arrived in Burma in the middle of February and would take over from fellow *News Chronicle* reporter Roderick Macdonald. He joined up with another newly arrived Australian reporter Tom Healy, who worked for the *Daily Mirror* in London. Australian reporters played a significant role in reporting for British newspapers both before and during the war.[6] Not long after they arrived in Rangoon, they were required to evacuate with other journalists to Maymyo, 450 miles away. There they harried the Services PRO, Kenneth Wallace-Crabbe, to let them go to the front. They had an advantage in pressing their case in that Wallace-Crabbe had previously been a reporter in Australia. Even so, their first venture proved frustrating since it was with a large group of reporters, accompanied by a conducting officer, Captain Rogers. The party reached as far south as Toungoo and Pyinmana, but the majority voted to return to Maymyo after they found these towns heavily bombed by the Japanese. Munday and Healy took matters into their own hands and headed south without a conducting officer towards Pegu, fifty-five miles from Rangoon and a key strategic point where the Japanese were aiming to cut the main railway line between Rangoon and Mandalay. Their gamble paid off as they obtained permission from the army to join the armoured troops at Pegu, which were preparing to break through a strong Japanese road block made up of logs and damaged vehicles. Munday's report appeared on 12 March and told how named regiments, the Hussars, Cameronians and the West Yorkshire regiments broke through the Japanese traps, and allowed British troops to pass through to central Burma.[7] The correspondents actually travelled in the tanks, their jeeps being brought through by the army. The next day the paper crowed that 'William Munday's cable in the *News Chronicle* yesterday on the Battle of Pegu was considered by many to be one of the greatest dispatches of the war.'[8]

Healy was also praised for his story on 13 March and had his picture on the front page, readers being told that Healy '[l]ives to tell battle story … he lived with death in the battle of Pegu and escaped with a tank column to tell one of the greatest descriptive stories that has come from the war in the East.'[9] Healy added spice to the story of breaking Japanese encirclement by telling of the execution of Burmese 'spies' by Cameronian soldiers who had been enraged to find six of their comrades with their throats slit.[10] As with most other correspondents in Burma, Healy carried a camera, a Rolleiflex, and took pictures of the firing squad. However, he was so ashamed by this that he destroyed the film.[11] His report emphasised his direct physical involvement in the action and his humanity, interviewing a member of the firing squad, acting as an observer spotting Japanese activity for the army and helping wounded soldiers. His comment 'that day I had looked on death more often than in my whole life' was no journalistic exaggeration.

On 14 March the *Daily Mirror* reported another exciting tale of the two correspondents participating in another breakout through a Japanese road block whilst being strafed and bombed by Japanese planes. Again, Healy added the personal touch that differentiated his reports from the more mundane reports based on army communiqués: 'A tank colonel and major came to us and the latter asked them to cable his wife and friend's wife to say Ralph and George are in very good health and doing fine.'[12] The *News Chronicle* made much of the humanity shown in Munday's dispatches, citing his words from the Pegu battles: 'I prayed hard that I might be allowed to see my wife and baby just once more.' It challenged readers to 'compare Munday's dispatches with those curt official communiqués which hide the self-sacrificing heroism of our brothers and sons'.[13] This admission of the emotional impact of war on the reporter was unusual at a time when a more macho image was generally favoured.[14]

It was only due to the dogged persistence of Munday and Healy that the Pegu stories were published quickly and in an uncensored form. The military censors wanted to wait two or three days for an official army communiqué to be published before they would allow the articles through. However, as Healy and Munday pointed out, this would mean that other correspondents could use the stories and take away the advantage of those who had risked life and limb to report the battles at first hand. Healy appealed to General Alexander, who agreed to immediate publication. Ironically, Army Intelligence did not receive communiqués on the Pegu fighting and had to rely on the journalists' reports to know what had taken place.[15] Once they were published, the newspaper articles were very well received in London. The War Office telegraphed that they 'have proved admirable stimulant home morale', and wanted more reports like them.[16] It was said that it was pressure from the prime minister himself that led to this request.[17]

Healy commented that the 'censor now seemed to allow us more slack'.[18] He certainly needed it because in between the fighting at Pegu the two correspondents had ventured down to Rangoon where the city was in its death throes and they had seen the continuing columns of refugees streaming northwards. Healy wrote a dispatch that was very critical of the failings of the civil government.[19] He was fortunate to find an Anglo-Indian (civil) censor at Mandalay who let the article through without any cuts. Healy thought that the censor had changed his mind the next day and refused Munday's attempts to send the same article to Australia, but in fact they did appear in the *Sydney Morning Herald* on 21 March.[20] His article for the *News Chronicle* reflected on the military reasons for the loss of Rangoon to the Japanese.[21] This type of analysis was a couple of months ahead of its time but probably got past the censors because it still argued that, despite these mistakes, the Japanese could not take central and northern Burma.

The other correspondents were aggrieved at Munday and Healy for scooping them by going off without a conducting officer. They were under pressure from their editors to provide similar copy.[22] A bigger issue, however, is why Healy and Munday were able to write so freely about military and civil affairs when other correspondents seemed unable or unwilling to at this stage. Healy argued that other correspondents preferred to stay away from the front and base their reports on army communiqués, but whilst this may have been true of a minority, most war correspondents were only too keen to be near the fighting and to scoop their rivals. The truth was that when correspondents criticised their colleagues they were often unaware of what the other correspondents were doing and where they were as they travelled by jeep around the different fronts. At the same time that Healy and Munday were reporting the Pegu battles, Rodger and Burchett were apparently endangering their lives to report the attack at Shwegyin, some fifty miles away. In any case, journalists had to judge whether they could actually get their dispatches back from the front to their editors in good time, given the very difficult communication problems in Burma after the loss of Rangoon. However, Munday was even able to make a story out of such problems in his report published on the front page of the *News Chronicle* on 4 April, saying that it was

> A Story to be Proud of ... three fighters roared down and shot my jeep from underneath me. I had driven from Prome to take my story on the 400 mile journey to the telegraph office of the censor... Miraculously neither myself nor the officer who was with me was touched... I continued my journey in a lorry loaded with gelignite which had stopped nearby when the fighters came down... I have hitchhiked two nights and a day to tell this story.[23]

Healy and Munday continued to work together but agreed to cover different fronts and then exchange their stories. This meant that Munday would cover the British front in the western side of Burma, whilst Healy would report on the Chinese front in the centre and east. They would rewrite their partner's stories and send them at the same time to their own papers.[24] This arrangement, which relied heavily on trust, seems to have worked well. Munday and Healy both reported on 21 March from

Toungoo, where the British and Chinese had been fighting together, but the two armies were now separating so that the British would defend the western Irrawaddy side and the Chinese the eastern and central sides along the Sittang. The battle for the strategic town of Toungoo was to be the first test of the Chinese army in battle with the Japanese. On 23 March Munday reported that he was 'the first correspondent permitted to enter the line which is now the Chinese operational area'.[25] It had taken until mid-March, after the fall of Rangoon, for the Chinese to become directly involved. It proved their fighting qualities but only served to show up the problems of the command structure as the Chinese generals ignored their supposed commander General Stilwell and took directions only from Chiang Kai Shek.[26] Correspondents wrote more favourably about the qualities of the Chinese army than perhaps it deserved. Munday described Chinese soldiers:

> Sturdy and tall, they are veterans of the type of warfare which the Japanese have been able to exploit to the full in Burma. They travel as light as the Japanese do, moving great distances on foot without fatigue. They are on level terms with the Japanese also in having no supply problem for, with ammunition and a few handfuls of rice, they are equipped to fight for days on end. The Chinese are popular with the Burmans, and their active participation in the war against the Japanese in Burma is doing much to rally pro-British feeling among the Burmans.[27]

The last sentence was particularly sanguine, but the Chinese were widely respected for their long struggle to defend their homeland against the Japanese and were now seen as the one hope to check Japanese advances in Burma.

The story of the involvement of Chinese troops in Burma is an important one. Many of the journalists believed that General Wavell's refusal to accept in full Chiang Kai-Shek's offer of both the 5th and 6th Chinese Armies when they met on 22–23 December 1941 was a serious error. The Burma correspondents did not start the story, which presumably originated in Chungking and grew out of Chiang Kai-Shek's loss of face over the issue, but they did help to perpetuate it over several months.[28] The generalissimo's annoyance reached the ears of President Roosevelt, who took it up with Winston Churchill in their meeting in Washington DC in January 1942.[29] What the correspondents did pick up on was the slowness with which Chinese troops actually entered Burma, and the way that they were treated in the beginning. The reporter who was closest to the story was Wilfred Burchett, who had recently been taken up by the London *Daily Express* for his reports from the Chinese nationalist capital, Chungking.[30] He came from a working-class Australian background, had experience helping the victims of fascism in Europe and was sympathetic to both the Chinese nationalists and the Chinese communists. He argued for the Allies to promise moves towards independence to the colonial territories in Asia so that they could be mobilised to resist the lure of Japanese promises of 'Asia for the Asiatics'. He admired the Chinese army's long and dogged resistance against the Japanese army, and especially admired the Chinese generalissimo Chiang Kai-Shek whom he described as 'a top notch soldier and strategist', who should have been made commander-in-chief of the whole Asiatic area.[31] Burchett persuaded the *Express* that he should move to Burma to cover the Chinese troops from the 5th Army which had been rumoured to have moved into the country sometime in January. At the end of the month Burchett reached Lashio and caught up with the Chinese General Tu who was commanding the 5th Army. He was horrified to find the lack of arrangements made for the Chinese command and soon realised that the bulk of the Chinese army was still waiting on the China-Burma border.[32] Burchett sent his story direct to Chungking, bypassing the proper censorship authority in Rangoon, and then took the opportunity to report his views on the poor treatment of the Chinese directly to the governor, Dorman-Smith.[33] Burchett felt satisfied that his intervention had had an impact as Dorman-Smith 'made notes and within a few hours a long cable was sent to Lashio ordering that everything possible be done to make Chinese officers and officials feel welcome in Burma'.[34]

One of the things that most annoyed Burchett was the low view that some Britons had initially of the Chinese army.[35] Both he and Belden had worked in China and wrote sympathetically of the Chinese soldiers. Belden wrote after the destruction of Mandalay by Japanese bombing:

> Soon after that, the main body of the Chinese Army reeled and staggered though the city. How pitiful were those sixteen- and seventeen-year-old soldiers who until recently had never known anything but the peace of a Chinese farm. One short month before, they had answered the call of their British allies and sped to the front below Mandalay, only to be cut to rib-

bons and come staggering back through one ruined and deserted village after another, without once pausing for rest. Now that the battle was over, they could not march home, but reeled onward to some unknown destination without friends, without succor, without comfort, and almost without hope.[36]

It was not just the bravery of boy-soldiers that impressed the correspondents. They were taken with the role of the young Chinese female soldiers. William Munday reported that

Their job is to comfort the wounded, taking the place, though they have no nursing training, of Red Cross nurses, of whom there are none on this front; to keep the Chinese soldiers in touch with news from home and other fronts and with world affairs; and to go among the Burmans and Indians—often dangerous missions—to explain through interpreters the disaster it would mean to them if the Japs were victorious.[37]

Berrigan and Belden at Yenangyaung

Four reporters provided detailed first-hand coverage of the British retreat through the valuable oilfields at Yenangyaung, south of Mandalay, in April 1942. They were the two American agency reporters Darrell Berrigan (United Press) and Dan De Luce (Associated Press), Jack Belden for the *Daily Mail* and *Time-Life*, and William Munday for the *Sydney Morning Herald* and *News Chronicle*. These were to be among the last journalists to leave Burma.[38]

What was supposed to have been a defence of the oilfields turned into the British army providing cover for the complete destruction of the wells and plant so that the Japanese could not use them. In turn, this became a desperate rearguard action and attempt to break a Japanese road block which would have trapped British troops in the waterless terrain, unable to re-join other British forces to the north. The story was one of heroism and good fortune, in which the British were ultimately saved by Chinese forces supported by British troops sent to rescue them. British forces, numbering some 7,000 soldiers, most of whom were exhausted from participating in the long retreat from southern Burma, were decimated by the struggle to get out of the rat-trap of Yenangyaung. Although the rescued 1st Burma Division was able to reach Mount Popa to recuperate, it was a broken force, having lost most of its heavy equipment, and most of the Burmese soldiers had deserted. The loss of Yenangyaung meant the loss of fuel supplies to the Allied armies and left open the road north to Mandalay, making the final retreat into India and China virtually inevitable. Because of the crisis on the British Irrawaddy section, General Stilwell had not only sent a regiment of the Chinese 38th Division to rescue the British but had also transferred his only motorised unit, the 200th Division, from Pyinmana to the Irrawaddy sector.[39] In doing so he had ended his hopes of an offensive from Pyinmana and, according to Colonel Claire Lee Chennault, admittedly no admirer of Stilwell, seriously undermined the confidence which Chiang Kai-Shek had placed in him.[40]

Darrell Berrigan was a Californian who, like Belden, had fallen into journalism almost by accident after landing up off a boat in Shanghai in 1939. He set up a United Press agency office in Thailand but managed to leave hurriedly as the Japanese took over in December 1941. Berrigan's dispatches for UP reached an international audience, and provided detailed first-hand coverage of the fighting. Berrigan was at his best reporting on the experience of ordinary British, Indian and Burmese soldiers. A good example is his reporting of the experience of an individual soldier, Private George Roberts, who was headlined in the *Mail* as 'Jolly George'.[41] Berrigan named the multinational force fighting a retreat at Yenangyaung:

> There were the Royal Inniskilling Fusiliers from Northern Ireland, the Cameronians from Scotland, the West Yorks, the King's Own Yorkshire Light Infantry (better known as the Koylies), the Gloucesters from England, Punjabis, Jats, Sikhs, Rajputs, Garhwalis and Gurkhas from India, Kachins and Chins from Northern Burma.[42]

If Berrigan's reports from Yenangyaung reached a more immediate audience in Britain, it was Belden's coverage for *Life* on 18 May which was the more colourful, and Belden also provided the fuller account in his book *Retreat with Stilwell* (March 1943) which gave a tactical analysis of the reasons that the Allied forces were being outmanoeuvred by the Japanese. Jack Belden was perhaps the most interesting character among the war correspondents in Burma, also one of the best at the job. Barbara Tuchman describes him as 'a great romantic and idealist ... moody, driven, alternately gay and despondent...'[43] Wilfred Burchett, who worked with him in Chungking, said he was 'morose, taciturn, tempestuous ... but good company as long as not before 11am!!'[44] He was the best informed of the reporters on the Chinese army as he spoke Chinese fluently, had reported since the beginning of the Sino-Japanese War for the United Press agency and had close personal connections to General Joseph Stilwell, then US military attaché to the Chinese nationalist government.[45]

Belden had an independent spirit and was determined not to be bound to headquarters with the other correspondents but to make off into the field to see war at first hand. He lost his job with UP in late 1938 for ignoring company orders and then freelanced for the *Daily Mail* and *Time* magazine until being hired full-time by the latter not long after he had flown into Burma in March 1942 with General Stilwell. At thirty-two, Belden had a reputation for wanting to be close to the fighting, and at Yenangyaung he certainly was, but it took a toll on him, especially the 100-degree plus heat and the lack of water. In his book *Retreat with Stilwell* he describes the physical and mental exhaustion and how helpless it made him feel:

> Here was I, the experienced war correspondent, the tough guy who had gone through five years of war in China, tramping from the plains of Peiping to the mountains of Shansi and the guerrilla areas around Nanking, undergoing every kind of hardship, subsisting on the barest kind of food, suffering every kind of danger, being surrounded and cut off by the Japanese four or five different times—here was I completely helpless, done in, almost without the physical guts to go on, while Berrigan, who had seen little of war, and Edwards who had never seen a battle before in his life, were marching about the road, making themselves useful, joking with the soldiers, watching the battle, and keeping their depressed spirits in decent check.[46]

However exhausted Belden felt, he was still able to write copious notes on the Yenangyaung battle for his dispatches to the *Daily Mail*, to *Life* magazine and eventually for nearly one hundred pages of *Retreat With Stilwell* (1943).[47] Belden prided himself as a journalist who immersed himself in the emotion of the battle by getting close to the soldiers. In his second book, *Still Time to Die* (1944), which he wrote in America while recuperating from leg wounds suffered in the landing at Salerno in Italy, he referred rather scornfully to those journalists who reported at a distance from the battlefield.[48] Whilst they might gain a clearer narrative of the battle and its results, they were reliant on army reports intended to clarify 'the fog of war'. They missed the confusion, the sheer exhaustion and unpredictability of the battlefield. Belden was too modest. He could record the battle at close quarters in great and colourful details but he could also analyse the tactics and the larger strategies of the campaign almost better than any other journalist. Within a few days he was providing the *Daily Mail* with a five-point analysis of the reasons for the Allied loss of Burma.[49] For reasons of military security, his more detailed analysis would have to wait until the retreat was finally over. In *Retreat with Stilwell* he pointed to the successful Japanese tactic of the road block at Yenangyaung, which was used to encircle the retreating British forces:

> It was the last and greatest that the Japanese put over in Burma, and in employing it they revealed to the full the heart and core of their tactical operations throughout the whole Burma campaign... At Pegu, Shwedaung, Prome, Toungoo, Bawlake—at all of those places, the names of which are indelibly etched in the souls of British and Chinese soldiers—Japanese infiltration parties or large units led by Burmese 'traitors' or 'patriots', depending on your point of view, slipped around Allied flanks and erected road blocks in their rear, and each and every time forced a withdrawal.[50]

Belden pointed out that this was not a new Japanese tactic; they had used it on the Chinese mainland as well. There was, however, a distinctly political nature to the large-scale road block in Burma, because it could only be undertaken with the help of local guides,

> who were undoubtedly well paid for their services and who often looked upon the Japanese as the liberators of their country. While the British were confined to the narrow strip of road leading up the Irrawaddy Valley, not daring to go into the villages except in well-armed parties, a Japanese column could disappear for as much as a week, march though the countryside, well supplied with food and water by the Burmese, and suddenly reappear at a pre-arranged point far in the British rear... Not only were the Japanese enamoured with their road blocks, but the Burmese people and the British troops became hypnotized by them... And toward the end of the campaign the mere utterance of those two words on the front was enough to make soldiers raise their heads in anxious alarm.[51]

Berrigan and Belden reported the British troops desperately breaking through the Japanese road block at Yenangyaung and being met on

19 April by a rescue party of Chinese troops led by General Sun Li Yen of the 38th Division. Belden was so relieved to see the uniforms and insignia of the Chinese army that he greeted them with their ancient war cry, 'Chung Kuo Wan Sui' or 'China Forever'. That war cry could have been the motto for Belden's journalistic career, so infatuated with the country and its people had he become. However, as we shall see, it also became the epitaph to his career as he came to be regarded by his publishers as too left-wing politically and too critical of his own country, America. Belden's politics can already be traced in the above quotation in which he gave the alternative description of Burmese 'patriots' rather than Burmese 'traitors' as the British army regarded those Burmese who assisted the Japanese in any way. Belden realised from his years of reporting on China that civilians would only resist an invasion if they had something to really fight for, and that this is what the people of Burma lacked. In Belden's mind, the British inability to call on the support of the Burmese people allowed the Japanese to project themselves as fellow Asiatics liberating them from colonial oppressors: 'As an avowed colonial power, they could no more launch a people's war, arm the population and fight a guerrilla struggle than they could give Burma her independence.'[52]

Belden's method as a journalist was to immerse himself at close quarters in the battles but then to trace back the causes of defeat to underlying structural problems in the social and political set-up. Retreats were not just misfortunes but had deeper underlying societal causes.[53] He was one of the most philosophical of war correspondents, quoting in the epilogue to *Still Time to Die* from his wide reading of writers such as von Clausewitz, Tolstoy and Marshal Foch. Belden's moody character, his essential insularity and a journalistic method that tended to scorn the work of other reporters did not endear him to many of his colleagues.[54] He was closest to Stilwell and his American headquarters staff, who relied on him for unalloyed information from certain battle fronts.

Collateral Damage

The term, 'collateral damage' is a modern way of describing the inevitable civilian casualties that occur in modern warfare, especially from aerial bombardment. When the Japanese had destroyed most of the RAF and AVG fighters at Magwe, the RAF withdrew to India and the AVG to China, and as a result the Japanese bombers had a free hand to target Burmese towns, whether military targets or not. Jack Belden described this 'wilderness of destruction' very well:

> Every town for a distance of two hundred miles on the two highways up the Sittang and Irrawaddy river valleys leading to Mandalay was by now completely burned to the ground. Pyinmana, Pyabwe, Meiktila, Magwe, Kyaukse and dozens of other pretty market towns, jungle cities and river marts set among groves of trees like oases in the desert heat of Burma had been wiped off the face of the earth and now no longer existed except as place names... Japanese planes, hurling down incendiaries from a low altitude had started this destruction. Burmese arsonists had come out and finished it... This was the special and most characteristic of the Burma War, the phase which distinguished it from campaigns elsewhere.[55]

The journalists were appalled at the 'wanton destruction' of the Burmese villages such as Thazi, which George Rodger and Wilfred Burchett passed through.[56] As journalists, they needed to record the horrendous scene but their priority was to get medical help to the victims and this meant dragging people from burning houses and transporting the wounded to a nearby dressing station.

Mandalay had been almost completely obliterated by raids starting on Easter Friday, 3 April. The raid killed 2,000 people. Rangoon had burned on for three weeks. Belden reported that

> Mandalay had an atmosphere all its own at the end. The profound calm and expectancy that spread over other Burmese towns just before they fell never appeared in the streets of Mandalay. There was absolute riot and terror in the air. The very streets seemed to breathe fear, horror and death. Nothing seemed under control...[57]

The Japanese used a lethal cocktail of incendiary, high-explosive and anti-personnel bombs. The last were thought to be particularly effective as they were said to have been designed to spread shrapnel at ground level, meaning that even those lying flat on the ground could be cut to pieces. Reporters in China had told of the Japanese use of mustard gas on the battlefield. In China such reports would be welcomed by the nationalists as a way of gaining international support. In Burma, however, it seems that the government did not want reports that spoke of Japanese atrocities; it feared that such stories would only lead to panic among the Burmese population and maybe demoralisation of the troops.

Some short reports of atrocities did get past the censor. The *Daily Mirror* and *The Times* of 31 March briefly told of the first reported Japanese use of poison gas in the Burma war at Toungoo on 25 March.[58] More disturbingly, the *Mirror* on 1 April reported Japanese deployment of germ warfare.[59] Both these reports came from Chinese communiqués and thus were not subject to Burma censorship and were unsubstantiated by the correspondents on the spot. Healy wrote in the *Daily Mirror* of the Prome Road battle in which he reported that the Japanese had bayoneted to death British prisoners.[60]

Fifth Column

One of the issues on which journalists clashed regularly with the Government of Burma was in their reporting of the activities of so-called Burmese 'fifth columnists'. Cedric Salter, the *Daily Mail* correspondent, had a tussle with the censor when he tried to tell of Burmans stretching steel wire head-high across the roads in an attempt to decapitate soldiers travelling in open-top jeeps.[61] The story, however, did appear on the front page of the 11 March edition of the paper.

Dorman-Smith did not approve of the use of the term 'traitor Burman' and denied the existence of any large-scale fifth column in Burma.[62] In many ways he was flying in the face of widespread evidence to the contrary. Historians Bayly and Harper follow the governor's line of argument that the military exaggerated the disloyalty of the Burmese as a way of excusing its own failings.[63] Yet the contemporary evidence from journalists and other witnesses is overwhelming. It is possible that they were on occasions misled, for instance when Japanese soldiers dressed as natives, or when agricultural practices such as burning stubble could be interpreted as providing guiding lights for enemy aircraft.[64] However, the correspondents were commenting on fifth column activity from early in the campaign, before the army needed to find a scapegoat to explain defeat. Dorman-Smith defended his ministers, refuted allegations that they were pro-Japanese and estimated the size of the Burma Independence Army (BIA) as no more than 4,000, regarding this force as mostly made up of the young political radicals, the Thakins. From his perspective, it was important that Americans did not get the impression of the Burmese as being intrinsically hostile to British rule. Such a belief would make it much more difficult for the returning Allied forces to win over the local population and, of course, for the British to retain their role in Burma.

The problem was that it was difficult to pin down exactly who was responsible for activities that were regarded as supporting the Japanese army. The BIA, which Dorman-Smith was focusing on in his calculations, was only the organised part of fifth column activities which the journalists saw. It was formed originally from the core of radical nationalists, the Thakins, who had received training from the Japanese in the year before Pearl Harbor. They participated in the initial Japanese surge through the Tenasserim Peninsula, picking up support from Burmese as they advanced. Bayly and Harper estimate that the BIA was about 15,000 strong by the time it reached Mandalay and about 18,000 in number by the end of 1942.[65] They observe: 'Most of the recruits were young students ... political activists with a sprinkling of working-class men and peasants', and that they received help from Buddhist monks.[66] They received support in areas like Tharrawaddy, just north of Rangoon, which had a history of rebellion in the past, and this was the area where Cedric Salter had reported their attacks on passing vehicles.[67] Not far away in Shwegyin, George Rodger reported that half the Japanese force defending the town were not Japanese but were in fact Burmese.[68]

So Dorman-Smith undoubtedly under-estimated the number of Burmese who took up arms, not so much in support of the Japanese as in the desire for Burmese independence. However, the journalists probably over-estimated fifth column activities, not because they were repeating army excuses, but because there were many other activities which took place outside and often against the wishes of the BIA. Opportunists, local criminals and others took advantage of the mayhem caused by Japanese bombing to loot and to burn. The correspondents did not speak the Burmese languages and would have found it difficult to gauge local opinion and activities. Some had a predisposition to be critical of the colonial power and to expect native hostility to it.

General Wavell probably put the issue in proper perspective when he wrote that 'the importance of the Fifth Column in Burma has been exaggerated; the number of actual rebels who took up arms against us or assisted the enemy was probably small. But the moral effect on the soldier of the knowledge that a proportion of the population was potentially hostile and treacherous was considerable.'[69] The same was probably true of the impact on the journalists as they crisscrossed a country which was alien to them.

Conclusion

The reporters' first-hand reporting of some of the Burma battles undoubtedly justified the risks they took in going to the front. The Malaya and Burma campaigns of 1942 were different from anything the British army had faced up until that point. The correspondents told of the special difficulties of jungle warfare and of fighting an enemy that used inventive tactics which took Allied soldiers by surprise. The downside was that the pressure of media requirements, the restrictions placed on them by their dependence on the military and the limits imposed by censorship meant that correspondents were rarely, if ever, able to report the realities of warfare. The dispatches which were most lauded by editors were inevitably those which romanticised the fighting, and which placed the reporter right in the middle of the dangerous action. The very nature of this reportage in Burma covered over or deflected attention from the reality of humiliating military setbacks and almost permanent retreat. To some extent, the correspondents could rectify this in their later books, when censorship was much reduced and they had time to assimilate and analyse what had happened in Burma.

8

JOURNALISTS AND THE EVACUATION
OF CIVILIANS FROM BURMA, 1942

The role of war correspondents in reporting the evacuation of civilians from Burma in 1942 is not a particularly distinguished one by the standards of modern war journalism. For the most part, the journalists concentrated on military stories, as might be expected. However, many of them were aware of the scale of the exodus—up to 500,000 civilians were thought to have left Burma in 1942—and of the tragic loss of life that was inevitable the longer it went on.[1] Many of the refugees had to walk though Burma, a country the length of France, and then climb across mountain ranges and pass through disease-ridden jungles, harassed not only by the Japanese but also, in the case of the Indian evacuees, by some of the Burman population too. Perhaps the journalists had already been hardened by seeing piteous lines of retreating refugees in the European war and elsewhere, although O'Dowd Gallagher, a very experienced journalist, wrote later that the plight of the Indian refugees leaving Burma was worse than anything he had seen elsewhere.[2]

The journalists' reporting of the civilian evacuation covers three main phases. Firstly, there was the highly controversial evacuation from Rangoon of civilians: Europeans as well as Indians, Anglo-Indians and Anglo-Burmese. This mass evacuation started spontaneously and was mostly unplanned when Rangoon was heavily bombed on 23 December 1941 and continued in waves until all non-essential civilians were ordered to leave the city within forty-eight hours on 20 February 1942. The luckiest evacuees were able to leave Rangoon by boat to India, and perhaps up to 70,000 travelled this way.[3] It was difficult for poorer Indians to pay the fares, especially after the government restricted deck passengers in order to try to keep labour in the capital. Some managed to leave Rangoon by twice-daily train services, but as time went on military requirements were given priority on the railways. Initially, many of these evacuees just wanted to reach safety in Mandalay, Maymyo or elsewhere in Upper Burma.[4] The journalists were caught up in these evacuation issues, partly because they themselves were annoyed at being required to leave Rangoon at short notice with other 'non-essentials', and to move some 450 miles up to Maymyo, the summer capital. In Maymyo, they listened to and reported the stories of aggrieved European evacuees.

The second phase was the reporting of the subsequent long trek, predominantly of Indian evacuees, who tried to reach India by land, sea or air over several months, including during the torrential monsoon period after mid-May 1942. As the reporters drove south to report the fighting they would come across long columns of refugees carrying babies and whatever worldly goods they could manage. Most were trying to reach the coast at Akyab from where they hoped to find boats to take them to Chittagong in India. Perhaps up to 150,000 escaped this way. Those fleeing from Upper Burma as the Japanese advanced in April 1942, were forced to take the most dangerous routes by foot through jungles and precipitous mountain routes into Assam in India and then on to Calcutta. The British, Indian and Burma governments had to respond to the growing grievances expressed by the Indian National Congress Party at the alleged racial discrimination shown during the Indian evacuation. After 4 May, when the governor left Burma, it was the responsibility of the Government of India to help the remaining refugees still in Burma and to provide support for refugees when they reached India.

The third and final phase of reporting covered the retreat of British and Chinese soldiers in May 1942 over the mountains into the safety of Assam and eventually Calcutta. The soldiers sometimes marched out alongside civilian refugees but at other times had routes designated exclusively for the military. By this stage, correspondents had already had to decide how they themselves should leave Burma. The majority took the option of taking any available flights out of airfields in northern Burma so that they could continue reporting the war from either India or China. However, some determined to take their luck with the refugees and retreating soldiers by taking the largely unknown and hazardous land routes over high mountains into north-east India.[5] The most famous of these 'escapes' was made by the American General Stilwell and his international assortment of followers, which was recorded by the journalist Jack Belden in his book *Retreat with Stilwell*.

Some of the most recent historical focus on the Burma war has been not so much on its military aspect than on this very large-scale exodus of civilians: Indians, Europeans, Anglo-Burmese and Indians who began to leave Burma as soon as the Japanese invasion started.[6] The most recent book by Michael Leigh is thoroughly researched and counters the previous tendency to focus on the European civilian evacuation, reminding us that by far the largest number of civilian evacuees were Indians:

> About 366,000 civilian evacuees left Burma in 1942 and of these about 350,000 (96%) were Indians. Only about 16,000 (4%) were Europeans, Anglo-Indians and Burmese... Between January and May 1942 Indians evacuated from Burma in large groups by road, rail, sea and air. They slogged along congested roads, struggled with hunger, thirst and disease and slept in filthy camps.[7]

Leigh cites the pioneering research by Professor Hugh Tinker, who, as a young Indian army officer, witnessed Indians fleeing into India from Burma. Tinker says of twentieth-century refugees that 'nobody directs the refugee to depart; no regular organisation assists him on his way; and when he arrives eventually at his destination, nobody really wants him to stay.'[8] This resonates today but is probably too harsh an assessment to apply to the experience of the Indian refugees leaving Burma, and especially of the help given to evacuees by officials and volunteers, but Tinker correctly recognises the unplanned and unorganised nature of much of the Indian evacuation from Burma. Any plans for civilian evacuation of Rangoon were completely overtaken by the speed of the Japanese military advance. Those refugees who took the overland routes to India often suffered inordinate hardships. Tinker sees the events of 1942 as the end of an era for the over one million Indians who had lived in Burma in the 1930s.[9] Leigh is very aware of the wider political repercussions of the evacuation of Indian refugees from Burma and argues that it 'undermined colonial rule in Burma, sparked unrest in India and reverberated around the corridors of power in Westminster'.[10]

The new civil defence commissioner, Richard de Graaff-Hunter, had arrived in Rangoon from London in August 1941 at the request of the governor, Dorman-Smith. He overturned the pre-existing civilian evacuation plan which had been drawn up by Wilfred Marsh, a former Police Service officer. Marsh's plan involved building camps on the outskirts of Rangoon, to which non-essential Indian civilians would be evacuated at the first signs of danger. From these camps, the 'non-essentials' could be moved on further north to greater safety. De Graaff-Hunter argued that it would be unworkable to divide evacuees into essential and non-essential workers in this way, with only the former staying put in Rangoon. He maintained that as soon as the non-essentials and their families left, there would be a panic and essential workers would leave too, resulting in the collapse of Rangoon's port.[11]

This difference of opinion at the top would prove very damaging. Dorman-Smith stuck by his new appointee and based his policies around the need to avoid upsetting morale in Rangoon by preventing any mass evacuation. As he later explained it:

> If we had only been concerned to think of our own civilian problems, then a different story might have been told about many items of this report. To take one example, evacuation *might* have started at an earlier date. But our job was not to concentrate our energies on getting away from danger. Our duty was to keep essential services operating so long as they could usefully serve the military forces.[12]

His plans were undermined, as he later admitted, by the sheer ferocity of the Japanese bombing of Rangoon on 23 and 25 December and the mass exodus that followed. As Leigh has argued, de Graaff-Hunter had some good ideas about reforming civil defence in Burma but he had neither the time nor the managerial skills to implement them.[13] He proved unpopular with existing Burma civil servants who had taken on the work of civil defence, and seemed arrogant and uncommunicative. The journalists were well aware of the flaws in the government civil defence and evacuation plans but could not write about them at the time. Maurice Ford's films for British Paramount newsreels gave a misleadingly positive view of the resilience of the population of Rangoon in the face of the Japanese air attacks, as if the London Blitz were being re-enacted.[14] O'Dowd Gallagher, who had arrived in Rangoon from Singapore on the first day of the bombing, gave no indication in his dispatches of the severity of the crisis at that time. His report on the bombing focused on the successes of RAF and AVG pilots in beating off the first Japanese raid but, whilst admitting that civilian casualties were thought to be heavy, he paid tribute to the behaviour of 'the Asiatic population who might understandably been panicky at the severity of the attack and its suddenness. They certainly moved hurriedly to the shelters, as is done elsewhere, but I and others did not see a sign of real consternation.'[15] It was not until he published *Retreat in the East* in September 1942 that Gallagher told a very different story about that day:

> Shelters were practically non-existent. The few that stood on the pavements, the cement not yet dry, were wisely avoided by all the cautious population: they were made of clay bricks. Well over a thousand people were killed in the first raid and the great trek began... Bewildered labourers abandoned the docks where lay scores of ships loaded with thousands of tons of war materials. Sanitary services broke down. Hotels, boarding-houses, flats, private houses, were emptied of their servants. Bus and tram-drivers vanished. All took the road to Prome and safety... The city came to an abrupt disordered standstill. Bodies of people killed in the first raid lay on the pavements for three days... Rangoon presented scenes of disorder more ghastly than I had seen in war cities in Abyssinia, both sides in the Spanish War, Shanghai in 1937, France in 1940, or the Middle East... The Governor himself told me he estimated that about 200,000 had gone. I said the figure was nearer 300,000... The civil population were given no vigorous lead by the Government ... [they] were left to sort out their own salvation.[16]

If Gallagher had to wait to make his criticisms public until after the retreat was over, another journalist, Thomas Healy, managed to publish an article critical of the Burma government only a week after the fall of Rangoon. The article appeared in the *Daily Mirror* on 14 March 1942 and was entitled 'Poor Leadership Betrayed Rangoon'. It is worth quoting his article quite fully as it stands out as a unique set of criticisms made in the middle of the retreat:

> ...it is a fact that lack of collaboration, lack of direction and flurried decisions directly weakened the capital and the morale of the people. The

Burmans—who are not strong-minded people—greatly needed resolute guidance in time of crisis, and they did not receive it... A sudden civil evacuation order, which was issued for a brief period before military control was established, made the city the prey of looters, rioters and fire-starters. Heading the civil evacuation from Rangoon was the Fire Service—which should have been ordered to remain on duty. The Civil Defence Service had been officially disbanded ten days before the civil evacuation and high officers in the Service freely admitted that—while a percentage of the wardens remained loyal—many ran towards the jungle.[17]

The fact that this article passed the censor seems to have been something of a fluke. Healy wrote that it had been seen by an Anglo-Indian censor (political) at Mandalay who let it through without cuts. But the next day the censor obviously had second thoughts as he refused the same copy that Healy's compatriot Munday was trying to send to Australia.[18]

The journalists, including Healy, Stowe and Gallagher, were infuriated by the fact that they too had to evacuate the capital by 21 February and leave for Maymyo, 450 miles from the front.[19] On 3 March, Leland Stowe saw several hundred bullock carts clogging the highway between Pegu and Toungoo. He described the occupants as 'natives': 'They looked like humanity's dregs—barefooted, dust-covered and covered in bedraggled, shapeless, sheet-like garments... They were dirty and hungry, exactly like the 4,000 lost children, like the lost tribes of Israel must have looked, I thought.'[20] Stowe's depiction of the Indian refugees tended to take away any real human identity from them.[21] All he could do was to encourage them to move on towards India: 'There was nothing we could do.'

One of the best newspaper reports on the plight of the refugees was written by Bill Munday and appeared in the *Sydney Morning Herald* of 18 March:

> I passed a great train of bullock carts, stretching one close behind the other for two miles. Women and children were plodding slowly on their way. Thirsty, they lifted thin arms in appeals for aid. Parched voices cried for water. 'Pani! Pani!' They pleaded, and men left their families to limp on as quickly as they could, wept and threw themselves down to press their foreheads on my shoes as they begged for a small share of the small supply of water, food, and bananas, which was all I was able to distribute among them. It was the most pitiful sight I had ever seen.[22]

Munday's report was very moving. It emphasised his personal response to the suffering of the refugees. It ended, however, by stating that the British and Burmese authorities were doing all they could to help but that the refugees were exacerbating the problem: 'Time after time, obsessed with only one thought—to get on their way—they have broken camp and upset plans, to take them[selves] in batches along roads where food was scarce and cholera rife.' Munday's response is entirely different from that of his travelling companion Tom Healy, who wrote bitterly later in his memoir of the plight of these refugees:

> Why hadn't their evacuation been properly organised? Why weren't they transported to safety if it was necessary to get them out of Rangoon? All this suffering could have been avoided if food and water stations had been established along the route. There was only one explanation: nobody was interested in their fate... Not even the government, apparently.[23]

One can only assume that Healy did not even attempt to have his refugee story passed by the censors, whereas his colleague Munday may have adapted his story to fit the government line and have it approved and dispatched.

As the civilian retreat continued and European evacuees reached Maymyo, their criticisms of the government evacuation operation intensified. Journalists listened to these complaints and reported them in their published books. Alfred Wagg, an American reporter, was determined to make a story of this and, whilst in India after the retreat, he planned a book which would focus on these criticisms. Wagg changed his mind when he was able to interview a number of Burma government figures, including Dorman-Smith, and he was also directed to talk to de Graaff-Hunter. Wagg shared the jibes common among journalists that civil defence had been a shambles and that de Graaff-Hunter, described as an 'ex-chorus boy', was to a large extent responsible.[24] Wagg's book appeared in 1943 and the relevant chapter was provocatively entitled 'Why No Civil Defence?' Considering that de Graaff-Hunter had previously been threatening to sue Wagg for libel, their interview appeared to go well and de Graaff-Hunter was able to put his case across convincingly. In effect this was that reorganising civil defence for Burma needed two years, whereas only six months at most were available.[25] He argued that despite the shortage of labour and building material, shelter accommodation had been provided 'for a very large proportion of the population'. However, de Graaff-Hunter went on to express his frustration that government plans to keep people in Rangoon fell apart as a result of the scale of the Japanese bombing raids which was unprecedented.[26] People ignored the shelters and also bypassed the government camps which had been provided outside the city, preferring to walk long distances northwards from Rangoon.[27]

De Graaff-Hunter explained that the very limited heavy fire-fighting equipment and personnel that were available had to be moved to other parts of the country as soon as it looked possible that Rangoon might fall and the equipment be lost, and that they played a valuable role there. However persuasive de Graaff-Hunter's responses to Wagg's questions were, he did not convince the Burma Office officials in London, and he returned home to Britain under a cloud of disapproval. One of the main reasons for this was that he did not appear to be very good at managing other officials involved in civil defence in Rangoon. He particularly alienated J.S. Vorley, a senior forest officer who replaced Marsh on 4 December 1941. It was Vorley who, in the middle of the retreat, was promoted to the rank of commissioner of civilian evacuation, and who effectively took charge of evacuation arrangements on the ground. He produced the first official *Report on the Evacuation* in June 1942, which convinced the Burma Office that it was de Graaff-Hunter's appointment and his administrative incompetence which was most to blame for the breakdown in evacuation arrangements in Burma.[28] But this unprecedented personal criticism of de Graaff-Hunter was by implication also a reproach directed at Dorman-Smith.

Fearing that the camps prepared for them outside Rangoon would be targets for Japanese attacks, the Indian evacuees bypassed them and walked over 150 miles towards Prome. There they hoped to cross the River Irrawaddy and travel by land through the Taungup Pass to eventually reach boats at Akyab on the Arakan Peninsula which would take them across to safety in Calcutta (see Map 2, p. 124). From the government point of view, it was vital to persuade workers to return to Rangoon, otherwise there was a danger that the infrastructure of the city and the vital docks would collapse. Special district commissioners using pamphlets, canteens and loudspeaker lorries were employed to coax the evacuees to return, and it seems they had some success, using the argument that there were no food supplies on routes further than Prome.[29] At this stage, journalists still had not been provided with transport so that they were unable to see the evacuee convoys for themselves. They concentrated on AVG stories in Rangoon instead. This meant that they were reliant on the government information on the evacuation. Newsreel cameramen filmed Dorman-Smith with the Burmese premier, Sir Paw Tun, meeting refugees returning to Rangoon and talking with one of them, an Indian whose wife had been killed.[30]

In some of the journalists' later books, however, they were critical of the government's handling of the evacuation from Rangoon of Indian, European and other refugees. Wilfred Burchett did not see the evacuation at first hand but reported what his Australian friend David Maurice, who worked for Imperial Chemical Industries in Burma, told him. Maurice was ashamed because he told Indians initially that they should stay put as the government would give them plenty of time to evacuate the city. He felt a special guilt because he told his own workers who were moving explosives from the wharves to continue working. When he realised that he was mistaken and that the government had no proper plans for Indian evacuation, he tried to rectify his mistake by warning Indians to leave.[31]

The British newspapers were slow to pick up on this mammoth exodus of up to 500,000 people, of whom perhaps 80,000 died in the process. Dan De Luce, the Associated Press correspondent, wrote a moving report on 28 February of 4,000 Indian refugees leaving the Pegu area.[32] They still had a journey of some 650 miles to reach India by land, and they faced attacks by Burmans on the way. De Luce aided his American readers' identification with the refugees by describing how they drew up their wagons at night like the old pioneers. Perhaps the best reporting of the refugee convoys, however, was by the photo-journalist, George Rodger, whose story 'Flight from Burma' was not published in *Life* magazine until 8 June 1942.[33] Rodger found the refugees at Prome at the end of February. He told in *Red Moon Rising* how they had been exploited by the local Burman population and police who demanded high prices for food and tolls to travel on the road. Rodger intervened to let the Indians through, threatening the Burmans with his pistol. Further south he came across a stream of refugees, some 50,000 to 60,000 he estimated:

Some of the men pulled heavy carts in which their women and children perched on top of their household goods, but the majority had been unable to bring more than a small bundle of personal things with them. I was struck by the incongruity of the articles that some of them had chosen to salvage from their homes when nothing but the most indispensable things could be carried. One man had a cross-cut saw over his shoulder, another lugged along a large tom-tom, several had umbrellas, and one carried a bicycle with a back wheel missing.[34]

Rodger's photos are very sympathetic to the human plight of the Indian refugees and foreshadow pictorially a later and much larger refugee exodus in the Partition of India in 1947.[35] In his book and article, Rodger showed himself to be well aware of the economic and social origins of the tensions between ethnic Burmans and Indians.[36] Other correspondents were similarly aware, although it is possible that they may have exaggerated the extent of the attacks on the refugees. J.S. Vorley thought so, and played down the alleged attacks on Indians on the roads.[37] British newsreels had provided short clips of film of the Indian refugees in their editions of 21 and 28 May, thanks to the work of Maurice Ford of British Paramount News.[38] British Movietone News cameraman Alec Tozer, who was in Calcutta after the retreat, was requested by the Ministry of Information to provide film of refugee camps in India in order to show that they were well-organised and to 'refute Axis propaganda inferring Allies showing no interest in welfare refugees'.[39] However, there is no evidence that he was able to produce any such film.

The issue of discriminatory treatment of European evacuees as against Indians was raised by Jawaharlal Nehru in his talks with Stafford Cripps in April 1942. It was referred to by Philip Jordan in the *News Chronicle* of 9 April in which he wrote that he had seen evidence that Europeans were given priority in airplanes taking evacuees from Burma to India and that Indian complaints were justified.[40] Such was the sensitivity over the issue that the Ministry of Information, Near East Division, wanted to censor the media's use of stories which seemed to support any preference being given to European evacuees. The example given was that of George Rodger's otherwise innocuous photo which appeared in *The Times* on 14 April of European adults and children waiting under the wings of an aircraft to be evacuated from Burma by air.[41]

The treatment of Indian refugees became an issue of controversy in the British parliament on 7 May 1942 when Labour members raised the government censorship of the Indian National Congress working committee's resolutions of 28 April 1942, which made strongly worded criticisms of the Burma government's lack of planning for civil defence and evacuation of residents of Rangoon. Additionally, one resolution claimed that 'racial discrimination was shown at the base camps in Burma and there was particular scandal of safer and more convenient route being practically reserved for non-Indians while Indians were forced to travel by longer, more difficult and more dangerous route.'[42] The government searched for evidence to refute the allegations but was not satisfied with the information being given by Dorman-Smith, who was in the process of leaving Burma by airplane to India on 4 May. Some help was provided by *The Times'* correspondent in Delhi whose dispatches on 4 and 8 May gave a very rosy view of conditions in the camps on the India side of the border and insisted that 'no distinction whatever is made between Indians and non-Indians in the refugee camps.'[43]

Correspondents Leave Burma

War correspondents had the opportunity to report the continuing mass exodus from Burma of civilians and soldiers at first hand, but most decided against it. Leland Stowe was typical in deciding against taking the overland route out of Burma because he did not believe that he could make a successful story out of it: 'Even though this was the world's most formidable mass flight, by the time it could be written it would make stale reading for daily newspapers and might be lucky if it got printed on page seven.'[44]

Six war correspondents took a different view and decided to take their luck with dangerous journeys by land out of Burma. William Munday, Dan De Luce, and Darrell Berrigan claimed to be the last correspondents to leave Burma by jeep along a 1,200-mile 'impassable route'. 'We were,' wrote Munday for the *News Chronicle*, 'I believe, the first to drive all the way from Mandalay to Calcutta.'[45]

Wilfred Burchett and George Rodger could also sense a good story in their escape by jeep through the Hukawng Valley and Pangsao Pass, especially as Burchett had been in a party that tested part of this route back in February. Rodger, who was reporting for *Time* magazine, did

Map 2: Evacuation Routes of Civilians and Journalists

not have quite the same problems with deadlines as the newspaper correspondents, and the journey would provide good photos of jungle conditions and tribal peoples *en route*. The two correspondents kept their journey secret from other journalists, and it is clear that their main motive was in getting a good story.[46] It was secondary, although valuable, that they provided detailed information on what was to become one of the main exit routes from Burma, although they probably did not have any idea that over 40,000 refugees might eventually have come through on this route.[47] Rodger wrote of his experiences in *Red Moon Rising*, which included some excellent photos of the escape by jeep and by foot, accompanied by Naga tribesmen as porters. Burchett wrote two books based on his experience, *Bombs Over Burma* (1944), and *Trek Back from Burma* (1944), which covered much of the same material. The journey over the Pangsao Pass to Ledo in Assam proved much harder than had been anticipated. This was partly because the monsoon rains had begun earlier than expected and turned the jeep tracks into quagmires. In the end, the journalists had to abandon their jeep and continue for 130 miles over steep jungle-covered mountain tracks on foot. The prospect seemed daunting as neither journalist had done much walking for a long time. Burchett asked Rodger how good a walker he was and was not reassured by his reply: 'I don't know, I always take taxis.'[48] They managed, however, to hire Naga porters to help them on their way. On arrival in India they were told that they were the first white men ever to come via the route they had taken.[49] Burchett originally wanted to return to Burma after his exit but, of course, circumstances had changed by the time he reached India and learnt that the Japanese had taken Lashio, the Allied armies were in full retreat and no return journey was possible.

The third correspondent who made a story of the overland exodus was Jack Belden, who wrote up his experiences in a detailed book, *Retreat with Stilwell*.[50] Belden found it good policy to stay near General Stilwell and his press officer, Fred Eldridge, and to transmit his messages to *Life* magazine through the Chinese nationalist headquarters in Chungking. The problem, according to Belden, was that Chungking still censored messages and even stopped some of Stilwell's communiqués which did not accord with their view of how the war was going.[51] Belden very much shared Stilwell's highly critical views of British imperialism and conduct of the war. Stilwell had to leave Burma in May by a little-used and difficult route along jungle-sided streams, across the Chindwin river at Homalin, and over the mountains towards Imphal: he felt he needed to avoid the large groups of refugees and the escaping Chinese troops as he realised that food would be a major requirement on the journey.[52] As Barbara Tuchman says: 'Through careful planning and relentless leadership Stilwell ... brought his party [115 people in all] out without a single person missing—the only group, military or civilian, to reach India without loss of life.'[53] This story made up a good part of Belden's book, while there was a good army photo report for *Life* magazine on 10 August 1942, entitled 'Flight From Burma', provided by Fred Eldridge.[54] Belden knew that he had a really good story and was even dismayed that the party was 'rescued' by British efforts as it crossed the final mountains into Assam.[55] A sense of camaraderie had grown up amongst the strange, ragged, international group that followed the fifty-nine-year-old US general out of Burma. Belden had come to admire, and even to fall in love with, the simple, unspoilt, affectionate and caring young Kachin, Karen and Burmese nurses who accompanied Dr Seagrave's medical unit. He contrasted this with his more critical view of many Americans, who

> revealed a profound insularity of thought, an egotistic self-centredness, and not only an ignorance of agrarian Asia ... but also a startling and somewhat arrogant desire to remain ignorant of those conditions, as if America, like the old Chinese empires, was sufficient unto itself... We Americans have no humility about other people. We have too much arrogance and pride.[56]

Conclusion

Journalistic practices and the inevitable preference for stories of European evacuees coloured and distorted the coverage of the large-scale civilian evacuation from Burma. In comparison with the evacuation of civilians from Malaya and Singapore, this was a much larger and more complex operation. There were over one million Indians in Burma and they were a vital part of the workforce, especially in the port of Rangoon. The Burmese ministers proved reluctant to provide money for shelters and evacuation facilities for the Indians, and there was a history of resentment by Burmans against what were regarded as temporary or exploitative outsiders. There undoubtedly was racial discrimination in the evacuation, but the type of blatant discrimination that had happened in Penang in Malaya was minimised in Burma, partly through direct instructions from the Government of Burma, and partly through awareness of the damage to Britain's international reputation that such discrimination would cause. The late call for non-essential civilians to leave Rangoon applied to both the European and Indian populations. Some of the discrimination in favour of Europeans, Anglo-Indians and Anglo-Burmese, which undoubtedly occurred, resulted from calculations that at least in Upper Burma, Indians would be safer at the hands of the Japanese than other groups would be. The government had in mind revelations of Japanese atrocities committed against European civilians when Hong Kong was occupied. It was, however, the escalating military failures that ultimately undermined planned schedules and modes of evacuation.

9

MAKING THE GOVERNMENT OF BURMA'S CASE

The British defeat in Burma was humiliating and, just as in the loss of Singapore, there was an inevitable search for scapegoats to blame for the catastrophe. Like Singapore, where Governor Sir Shenton Thomas took much of the blame for the demoralising nature of the surrender, so in Burma, Dorman-Smith was in the firing line for critics. Journalists who had largely held back during the military campaign now came forward with their damning indictments of the failures on the British side. Although correspondents recognised that this was primarily a military defeat, they had no wish to single out the military command-ers and even less the soldiers themselves. The army public relations set-up in Delhi, under Colonel Jehu, seems to have been keen to deflect any criticisms of the military onto the civilian administration.[1] There is no doubt that Dorman-Smith felt the lack of support he received when he returned to England to try to explain what had hap-pened. However, unlike Shenton Thomas, who remained a prisoner of war of the Japanese, Dorman-Smith had the time and the resources to make a case for the way he, his ministers and his civil servants had performed during the retreat. It is obvious that much of his defence was in direct response to some of the criticisms that were made by the war correspondents, either in their newspaper articles or in their books which appeared after the retreat. The governor's public case was set out in a variety of ways: journal articles, memoirs, supportive writings by his public relations team, threatened libel cases, a biography based on his unpublished memoirs, a propaganda film and, most extraordinarily, in financial and other material support for one of the journalists to alter his account of the retreat in ways sympathetic to the Government of Burma.[2]

The first opportunities for the Government of Burma to put its case to a wider audience in Britain came with two addresses given by leading officials, which were later published in respected journals. Thomas Lewis Hughes gave his talk to the Royal Central Asian Society on 3 November 1943 in London. Hughes was secretary to the Government of Burma between 1942 and 1946, and was very much reflecting the views of Dorman-Smith. Significantly, his talk started with an attack on Gallagher's recently published memoir, *Retreat in the East*, although the author was not actually named. Hughes cautioned his audience against 'accepting much that has already been written and published by alleged eye-witnesses or first-hand observers'.[3] Hughes scorned Gallagher's claims in his book to have been in Rangoon on the day that the final scorched earth policy was carried out and to have included photographs taken by himself. Hughes knew that Gallagher was in Maymyo at this time and could not possibly count this as a first-hand account. He went on to ridicule Gallagher's other stories of the last days of Rangoon, specifically of Burman attacks on those involved in demolition works and of the ramming of boats headed for Rangoon that contained armed Burmese and Japanese. The gentleman who was supposed, according to Gallagher, to be a leading figure in these last-minute demolitions, a Mr Mclean-Brown, had actually left Rangoon fifteen days before the demolitions.[4] Hughes concluded that 'the author of this particular book had collected much of his information in the bar of Calcutta's leading hotel...'

Hughes' address went on to provide a much wider riposte to the main criticisms that had been made of the civil government. It was published in the *Journal of the Royal Central Asian Society*, in pamphlet form and in the regular India Office Summary of Press Messages which was quite widely circulated.[5] So the Government of Burma was able to publish its version of the Burma campaign and, in effect, to highlight that the basic reason for the defeat was a military, not a civil one.

Dorman-Smith also criticised Gallagher's book when he spoke to the United Service Institution of India at Simla, but he was annoyed about a different failing of the correspondent.[6] He took exception to Gallagher's criticism of the so-called *burra sahibs* (British businessmen in Burma) whom he regarded as complacent and arrogant.[7] The governor had included a representative of these business leaders in his regular 'soviets' which he set up to coordinate civil response during the crisis in Rangoon. He knew that they had played an important part in the auxiliary defence forces, in evacuation arrangements and, most dangerously of all, in the final demolition work in Rangoon and elsewhere.

Dorman-Smith named another correspondent, the American Jack Belden, who in his book *Retreat with Stilwell*, published early in 1943, gave one of the main reasons for the Burma defeat as 'the emasculation of military authority owing to the original unwillingness to declare martial law'.[8] Dorman-Smith spent the largest part of his speech answering this criticism in quite convincing fashion. He emphasised the need to take into account the likely reaction of his ministers and the Burmese people to any declaration of martial law but, mostly, he did not feel that it was either necessary or practical in view of the limited number of military personnel available for key roles.

The Government of Burma public relations team also contributed to undermining the credibility of some of the journalists' accounts. George Appleton, who was both Archdeacon of Rangoon and director of public relations in the years 1943 to 1946, wrote: 'A highly inaccurate picture of Burma during the invasion months has been presented by war correspondents, most of whom had little real knowledge of the people or the country, and were quickly in and quickly out of Burma.' Appleton cited George Rodger's *Red Moon Rising* as a notable exception.[9] Powerful outside support came from an American, Major John Leroy Christian, who was chief of the Southern Asia Branch of the Military Intelligence Service during the Second World War. He wrote a negative review of Gallagher's *Action in the East* but, more importantly, a book entitled *Burma and the Japanese Invader*, which he completed in September 1944.[10] Christian thanked the public relations officers of the Government of Burma for information provided, and the book had a foreword by Dorman-Smith. Christian wrote that:

> The civil government of Burma has been the target for much criticism, usually by journalists with no experience in Burma before the war. The critics seldom remained long in Burma, and probably have no intention of returning to the country with their ready solutions. The fact is that no

country is ever ready for a sudden invasion such as the Japanese achieved with equal success in all countries of South East Asia and the adjacent islands. Nor is the sudden overthrow of representative government by martial law the key to successful defence of a country like Burma, as some journalists would have us believe.[11]

J.S. Vorley, who was a forest officer in Burma prior to the war, but who came to be in charge of the evacuation of civilians from Mandalay and Upper Burma, was not part of the public relations organisation and, indeed, could be critical of the governor and the way that the evacuation of Rangoon had been organised. However, in his memoir, written originally in 1950, Vorley takes swipes at a couple of unnamed journalists. One of them is probably Alfred Wagg, as he is described as an American who is writing a book on the campaign whilst in Delhi.

> I first heard of the author at about this time in Mandalay, when one of his dispatches passed through the Censor's office with a detailed description of how our troops at the front were being sniped at by traitor Burmans hiding in the tops of palm trees. This dispatch had been prepared in Maymyo, the hill station, at least a hundred miles away from the scene of the fighting, which this war correspondent had never visited.[12]

The issue of traitor Burmans or fifth columnists was one which often divided the correspondents from official opinion. Vorley, however, took exception to the way that the journalist described the situation in Mandalay as anarchic due to the collapse in morale of the civil administrators.[13]

Vorley had even clearer evidence of journalistic fabrication in the newspapers when some years later he read the story of an event which apparently took place in the last days before Rangoon fell. It told of a riot being put down at Government House by a Sikh bodyguard with a tommy gun. Vorley had been escorting the author, who made a very short reporting visit to Rangoon just before it fell, and knew that the story was completely fabricated. The correspondent is likely to have been the British journalist Richard Busvine, who wrote for the *Chicago Daily Times*. Vorley wrote that 'I have yet to meet again that war correspondent, but would like to, if only to tell him that my faith in newsprint has never been the same since.'

The most extraordinary example of the Government of Burma's attempts to put its case to a wider audience came not in conflict with the journalists but rather in cooperation with one of them, Alfred Wagg. Wagg, a roly-poly figure, was a latecomer to the Burma campaign, arriving from India about the end of February 1942. He was an American journalist who came strongly recommended by the British Information Services in Washington. He wrote for the *Daily Sketch* in London, the *Washington Evening Post* and *Liberty* magazine in the US.[14] Marsland Gander of the *Daily Telegraph* described Wagg as 'easily the most energetic and effervescent reporter I have ever met' and observed that he was beloved by the British brigadiers because he seemed to them typical of the go-getting American.[15] Wagg did not prove quite so popular with Lieutenant-Colonel Richmond who found out that Wagg was preparing a chapter which would be devoted to a long list of criticisms of Dorman-Smith. Wagg was persuaded to meet with the governor in Simla. He opened their conversation with the winning line that he had come to meet 'the most unpopular man in India' and that he was preparing a book to be published in England which would list seven accusations levelled at Dorman-Smith.[16]

The governor refuted the charges and apparently convinced Wagg that he had been misled by the head of the Inter-Services Public Relation Directorate, Brigadier Jehu, with the intention of diverting the blame for the army's humiliating defeat.[17] Wagg persuaded Dorman-Smith to provide him with background materials, introductions to key figures in governing and defending Burma and even financial support for his book. The Burma Office vetted each chapter as Wagg hurriedly wrote them for his publisher's deadline in March 1943. Officials even drafted a whole chapter which dealt with the Governor of Burma, and although Wagg re-worked this, he followed much of the India Office draft for this section.[18] In the end, the book was only published in a hardback format at the end of June 1943. Officials were not displeased with the result which they described as 'thin' but 'balanced' and giving 'a very much fairer picture of the events in Burma than anything that has yet appeared in print...'[19] The help given to Wagg indicates just how much the British were concerned about negative images of their rule in Burma and the military campaign there circulating in the US just at the turn of 1943, when American military support for the recapture of Burma was most needed.

Wagg's book proved to be more reflective about the Burma retreat than most other contemporary publications and attempted to depict something of the wider context of Burmese history and western relations with Asia. The book was reviewed by the *Statesman* in India, and the reviewer, quite possibly M.J. Pritchard, who had been a correspondent during the retreat, entitling his piece, 'Two-Sided Report', picked up on the dichotomy in the book:

> For about 160 pages it is deeply critical of authority. It is bluff, racy and rather daring. Then, for the last 30 pages Mr Wagg's virile manner changes. He meets the Governor of Burma, Sir Reginald Dorman-Smith, and sees the Light. Unfortunately, he fails to pass it on to his readers. These are left to reconcile the landscape of a shockingly administered country with the portrait of its efficient administrator.[20]

Finally, when Dorman-Smith returned to Burma as governor after the Japanese defeat, he began writing his memoirs. These were never to be published, but they were used to provide most of the information for the history written by Maurice Collis. Collis was a highly respected author and authority on Burma, having been a civil servant there since before the First World War. Collis admitted that this volume of history covering the 1940s would, in effect, be a biography of Dorman-Smith.[21] The book allows some glimpses into the pressures that Dorman-Smith was under during February and March 1942. It shows his sensitivity to press comments in this extract from his journal:

> 17 February. The war correspondents of the London newspapers ... seemed intolerably irritating in their frantic search for sensation. A scoop seemed their sole ambition, and anything that interfered with it, even public convenience or common prudence, was regarded as a deliberate attempt against the sacred freedom of the Press. The criticism in the London newspapers was also hard to bear when one knew so much more than a reporter ever could.[22]

One can see that it was not for lack of effort in defending himself that Dorman-Smith's reputation as Governor of Burma during the retreat has tended to have been a negative one on the part of historians. It was as if there was a battle for the verdict of history involving the army, the war correspondents and the governor, and none really comes out well from that particular conflict. Dorman-Smith had shown himself too sensitive to criticism and had picked on only the more hasty and extreme of the journalists' books. If the public relations organisation in Burma had been better prepared and established, and the journalists had been taken more into the confidence of the government and the armed forces, one cannot help but feel that the outcome would have been more understanding of the extreme problems that were faced in the Burma campaign.

EPILOGUE AND CONCLUSION

WHAT HAPPENED TO THE CORRESPONDENTS AFTER THE BURMA RETREAT?

Jack Belden was unusual among the reporters in returning to China almost immediately after the retreat to report on the American Volunteer Group (AVG) operating there.[1] He flew on bombing missions over Burma and China before taking a well-deserved rest in Srinagar, Kashmir, and this is where in October 1942 he wrote up his Burma experiences in *Retreat with Stilwell*. Most of the other correspondents stayed in India for a time. Calcutta was their first stop. Some needed time to recuperate from the illnesses and exhaustion they had suffered in the retreat. The correspondents met up in the Great Eastern Hotel where there were, according to Marsland Gander of the *Daily Telegraph*, 'good stories to be picked up as the hotels were full of women who had evacuated from Burma' and AVG pilots, now annoyed that they were soon to be taken over by the air force and would lose their bounty for planes shot down'.[2] Obviously there was potential for bias in the accounts of aggrieved British refugees, but Gander was against blaming the usual journalistic scapegoats—the civil administration and the pleasure-loving habits of the European population. 'Surely,' he argued, 'the blame can be traced back through the years to the highest levels of State, and at the other extreme back to the humble, ill-informed voter [who took no interest in our Far Eastern possessions].'[3] Gander joined up with Victor Thompson (*Daily Herald*), Gordon Young (*Daily Express*) and Alfred Wagg to report on the flow of refugees and armed forces coming through the mountains into north-east India. This provided opportunities to interview the commander-in-chief, General Wavell, and the returning generals, Alexander and Stilwell.

Some of the correspondents took the opportunity to stay in India to report on the all-important Cripps Mission in late March 1942. The Mission was a last-ditch attempt by the British wartime coalition to secure India's cooperation in the war in return for concessions which would allow India's political leaders to be involved in the government, and made promises of post-war dominion status. The talks failed ultimately, largely due to Churchill's unwillingness to make the necessary constitutional concessions in wartime. This left reporters like Leland Stowe very frustrated as they had argued the case all along that the only way for Britain to engage its colonial possessions in the fight against Japan was to offer immediate concessions leading to future independence. Stowe was dismayed, to say the least, that British attitudes in Calcutta and New Delhi seemed to be as complacent and bureaucratically minded as they had been in Malaya and Burma.[4] As far as he was concerned, if the Japanese had taken the opportunity to launch a naval and air assault on the Bengal coast at this time, it was likely that there would be just the same sort of panic and retreat that he had witnessed in Burma. Fortunately for the Allies, the Japanese became bogged down in New Guinea and the Solomon Islands, and their chance was gone.[5] Stowe was hoping that the US government would put pressure on its British ally to make concessions to nationalist demands for the sake of the larger war effort but he found that the American media misrepresented the failure of the Cripps Mission as the fault of the Indian politicians rather than that of Churchill and the colonial administration. He typified the American press 'lecture' to the Indian people as

'You've been offered dominion status and independence. Why don't you take it? Don't you Indians realize that we Allies are at war and we haven't got time to discuss details? ... The Japs may hit you at any moment. Don't you understand there's no time now to waste discussing mere details and ways and means?'[6]

From India, the bulk of correspondents went on to the Middle East and North Africa. Gander believed that most of them were pleased to be leaving the Eastern theatre because it could not compete for public attention with what was going on in Russia and North Africa.[7] Munday,

Belden, Busvine, MacDonald, Jordan, and De Luce all reported from North Africa at some time until the end of the campaign in May 1943. Certainly, conditions in the Desert War were very different from those of the jungles of Burma. For one thing it seemed even more difficult to accommodate women journalists in the desert, but regulations were subverted, much to the annoyance of Colonel Philip Astley, director of Army Press Relations in Cairo. Eve Curie had been escorted to the front in November 1941 by the prime minister's son Randolph Churchill, and had managed to obtain interviews with senior officers, which irritated the other correspondents who had been unable to do so. In March 1942, Clare Boothe Luce also broke the embargo and was taken to the front by the RAF as a distinguished visitor.[8] Alan Moorehead, the Australian war correspondent, had met both women and astutely compared them:

> Clare Boothe was blonde, lively, witty, gregarious, full of highly coloured opinions and completely American. Eve Curie was dark, quiet, aloof, full of shrewd abstract deductions and completely cosmopolitan. Both were very attractive... One could not help talking to Clare Boothe but agreeing with Eve Curie.[9]

The next campaign to cover would be the invasions of Sicily and the Italian peninsula. Roderick MacDonald was the only reporter to take part in the glider-borne landing in Sicily and was taken prisoner for a time before being released by British troops. A number of the Burma correspondents were involved in Italy, including Daniel De Luce, Ian Monroe, Alfred Wagg, Jack Belden and Bill Munday. Belden's story is interesting. On 9 September 1943, he landed with the US 5th Army near Paestum as part of the Salerno operation. He was accompanied by George Rodger who was taking photographs for *Life*. Belden was coming down with recurring malaria and feared that the Germans would be well prepared for the landing, and he was proved correct. The assault was vigorously resisted and Belden was shot in the leg, breaking his femur in two places. He commented that now he really knew the vulnerability that soldiers felt when they lay wounded, waiting for help to reach them before the enemy did.[10] His reports to *Life* have coincidental parallels with Ernest Hemingway's experiences in the Austro-Italian campaign in the First World War which was the basis for his novel *A Farewell to Arms*. Both men described lying helpless in the battlefield when wounded in the leg, and then falling in love with a nurse who was caring for them in hospital.[11] Belden was taken back to the US to recuperate, and did not return to the war until after the D-Day landings of June 1944.

Bill Munday was killed, along with two other correspondents in the aftermath of the Salerno landings.[12] Another Burma reporter who died in Italy was Roderick Macdonald of the *Sydney Morning Herald* and the *News Chronicle* who was killed by a land mine near Cassino in May 1944. War reporting was a dangerous business: it was estimated that forty-nine US and eighteen British war correspondents were killed from 1939 to 1945.[13] It was still statistically less dangerous than being a serving soldier. A casualty rate of 4% to 5% among Allied correspondents covering the European campaign from Normandy to the defeat of Germany in 1944–45 compared with a figure of 19% among the Allied forces.[14]

It is interesting to speculate whether the correspondents felt any guilt about not actually fighting in the war themselves. O'Dowd Gallagher, perhaps finally finding an outlet for his spleen, volunteered for the Royal Armoured Corps when he returned to Britain, and Eve Curie served in Italy as a volunteer in the women's medical corps of the Free French Army, being given the Croix de Guerre.[15] However, most of the journalists rightly seemed to feel that their war reporting was their war service.

Other than physical danger, there is also an issue of the psychological pressures placed on war correspondents. Today, we acknowledge post-traumatic stress disorder, for instance amongst soldiers who have served in Iraq or Afghanistan. In the Second World War, there was far less understanding of the condition among soldiers, and virtually none among war correspondents. Yet the correspondents often had to endure longer tours of duty than the soldiers and were often faced with horrific situations, with the added difficulty that they were not trained for dealing with them. Indeed, there had developed a glamorous image of the war reporter which Fay Anderson describes very well: 'Essentially reporters were imagined as an archetypal cliché—resilient, hard-drinking, hedonistic, churlish, and cynical. Let us call it the Hemingway syndrome—the celebrated machismo.'[16]

Under the stress of illness and of exhaustion, many of the reporters in Burma contracted malaria or dysentery, and it is not surprising that some might have suffered some form of mental breakdown. This could have been what happened to Jack Belden at Yenangyaung. Leland Stowe admitted in his notebooks to suffering from loneliness and exhaustion. For him, the stress may well have been due to reconciling his highly negative private views on the campaign with his role as a war correspondent reporting the Allied war effort in a way that was palatable to censors and editors. Some correspondents found that the way to cope with the stress was to take breaks away from the fighting. George Rodger and Wilfred Burchett went to recover to Lake Inle and the Shan States, where they met Alec Tozer doing the same.[17] Rodger had been covering the war for fifteen months, and was showing signs of exhaustion. His letter to his wife Cicely on 17 February 1942 indicates this pressure:

> Our ranks [of correspondents] are getting pretty well thinned out now after the ones we lost in Libya. Tozer is about the oldest on the job now and I come pretty well near the next. I am getting stale on the job too, and I don't feel I can do my best any more. That is a bad frame of mind to get into, so, when I've cleared up here, I think I'll suggest I pack up. Of course it has cost *Life* a lot to send me out here, so I must justify the expense first.[18]

George Rodger's most traumatic experience was not to be on the battlefields but at the end of the war in Europe when the Allies reached the Nazi concentration camps. He was one of a number of photographers who entered the Bergen-Belsen concentration camp in 1945. The experience was a horrific one, and forced him to reconsider his role as a photojournalist: 'When I could look at the horror of Belsen—and think only of a nice photographic composition I knew something had happened to me, and it had to stop.'[19] He did not work as a war correspondent again. He left *Life* and was a founding member of Magnum Photos, set up in 1947 as a photographic cooperative which allowed its members to keep copyright in their own work. The original members agreed to focus on particular geographic areas and Rodger was assigned the Middle East and North Africa. This allowed him to pursue his interest in photographing indigenous peoples, their cultures and environments. He had been one of the hardest-working war correspondents, but now this was finally behind him.

It is interesting that so many of the correspondents seemed to become radicalised by their wartime experiences. The polarisation of politics in the 1930s and 1940s was one aspect of this, particularly the perceived heroism of the communists in the fight against fascism in Spain, China and the Soviet Union. Leland Stowe was very moved by the sacrifices made by the American and RAF pilots in Burma and contrasted it with the way that life went on in America, apparently oblivious to the realities of the war in the Far East: 'mankind is busy raking in big wartime profits. Mankind is feeling cheerful because the stock markets are going up again.'[20] Later, he made a strong case in his book for America to recognise 'that the Soviet experiment has come of age' and that it must come to terms with the fact that 'the majority of European countries are going to be more socialistic, more radical, and more left-wing after the war...'[21] But there was also a revulsion against European imperialism and a sense that its days were numbered. Belden wrote in *Still Time to Die*:

> The Burma War was a sham and a farce. Imperialism and colonialism, no matter how paternalistic and civilized, is an oppressive and a rotten system. And the representatives of it, in this historic epoch, are but caricatures of what in another time and age were Kipling heroes.[22]

Anti-imperialism was not, however, the sole prerogative of the left. Clare Boothe, who seemed to move increasingly to the right during the war, was a strong critic of British imperialism. There is no doubt that some American reporters identified the nationalist struggle against British rule as paralleling the United States' own history of revolution.

Just as many soldiers returning after the war found it difficult to come to terms with civilian life, so some correspondents felt distanced by their wartime experiences from their home country. Jack Belden was a case in point. When he returned to the US to regain mobility after his injuries, he was highly critical of its society and politics. He wrote:

> America, because she was a wealthy country, is getting her Fascism late. I believe this country is pregnant with reaction. I hope the birth of Fascism here will be abortive. I see no guarantee that it will be. I believe it must be fought. I think there are men in this country in business, in government and in the army who are just like men in other countries in business, in government and in the army. And I think they do not give two cents for the people.[23]

Belden found himself the subject of Federal Bureau of Investigation surveillance. It was almost inevitable that he would fall out of favour with his employers at *Time-Life*. He was always seen as something of an outsider at the company and his criticisms of Henry Luce's promotion of the 'American Century' in his book *Still Time to Die* certainly did not endear him to his boss. He missed out on covering the D-Day landings but did report on the Normandy campaign that followed and led to the recapture of Paris and the drive into Germany. His last story for *Life* was published on 1 January 1945 and then he was fired.

Whether it was war reporting or China that acted as the stronger magnet, Belden returned there in late 1946. His reports on the civil war between nationalists and communists would not have won him back his job at *Time-Life*. He reported from the communist-held areas, and although he was critical of communist dictatorial tendencies he argued against the owner Henry Luce's line that the US should give full backing to Chiang Kai-Shek and the nationalists. Having had articles rejected by a couple of magazines, he wrote *China Shakes the World* (1949). The book was well regarded by many critics but sold poorly in the aftermath of the communist victory on the mainland in October 1949 and the growing McCarthyite witch-hunt of suspected communist sympathisers. Belden found himself increasingly out of tune with America and seemed happier in Paris, where he eventually died in 1989.

Another of the Burma correspondents who fell foul of the changing Cold War climate was Wilfred Burchett. His fall from grace with the western governments was altogether more spectacular, however. There were already signs in Burchett's background, and in his writing at the end of the Burma War, of a growing critique of western capitalist society.[24] He returned to China in June 1942 at the request of the *Daily Express*, hoping to get an interview with Generalissimo Chiang Kai-Shek. He spent weeks travelling through China while waiting for his interview opportunity, and was increasingly angry at the Kuomintang regime expending so much of its energies against the rival communists rather than against the Japanese. Eventually he did manage to interview the generalissimo and had a carefully prepared set of questions to put to him. However, the interview was a failure as Chiang Kai-Shek was too busy to give proper replies. Significantly, Burchett did not blame the generalissimo for the corrupt police state that Kuomintang China had become, but rather those officials and army officers who kept him ignorant of their actions. Burchett had a little more success in interviewing Madame Chiang, a connection that he was to find useful in the future. He went to India in October 1942 and at the very end of the year participated in a botched British offensive in the Arakan Peninsula, in which he was badly wounded when Japanese aircraft strafed his boat. While spending three months recovering in hospital he heard of Major Orde Wingate, who seemed very different, more radical and less stuffy than many of the high-ranking British officers he had come across. He spent several weeks in Delhi interviewing Wingate who was recuperating from his first and very arduous, long-range mission behind enemy lines in Burma. In 1944 Burchett published *Wingate Adventure*, based on his dozen interviews. The book was published in Australia in June 1944 and was the first to be based on interviews with Wingate and other participants in Operation Longcloth, as the first mission was called. It appeared after the death of Wingate, who was killed in an aeroplane crash during the second long-range operation on 24 March 1944, along with two correspondents, Stuart Emeny of the *News Chronicle* and Stanley Wills of the *Daily Herald*. *Wingate Adventure* was a largely uncritical account of the first mission, seen from the perspective of Wingate and his admirers. Since then there has been a never-ending and voluminous debate on the military value of that mission. The general consensus seems to be that it contributed little to the overall military campaign and was a costly diversion of men and resources. However, there is also a recognition that it provided a valuable boost to army morale after the failure of the Arakan campaign and that it paved the way for much larger and more successful long-range operations in 1944. Burchett was therefore contributing to an important propaganda exercise when the reputation of the army in Burma was at a very low ebb. Was this, however, the proper role of a war correspondent, especially one with increasingly radical views? Phillip Knightley is not impressed with Burchett's 'over-glamorizing a comparatively minor and costly operation', and explains the distortion in terms of Burchett's identification with and admiration for Wingate as an outsider, his 'distaste for British Army blimps [Indian Army GHQ, in particular] and his attraction to guerrilla warfare'.[25] In truth, Burchett was not yet the engaged journalist that Knightley would have liked him to be. He was, after all, working for the strongly pro-Empire *Daily Express* newspaper, was the subject of strong wartime censorship and needed the money that a bestselling book would provide.[26]

EPILOGUE AND CONCLUSION

In 1944 Burchett was sent to cover the Pacific War with the US Navy, but censorship restrictions, and the fact that the British public now had their attention focused on the culmination of the European campaigns, meant that he still did not manage to achieve wider recognition for his journalism. His greatest scoop—and he was a journalist who thrived on beating the opposition to a story—came at the end of the war with Japan when he was the first reporter to reach Hiroshima, not long after the atomic bomb had been dropped on the city. His report was a stark warning to the world of the danger of future use of these weapons, not just from the immediate deaths they caused but also from the impact of radiation sickness.[27] The US government dismissed Burchett's claims, and this marked a turning-point in his attitude to American foreign policy. He became increasingly sympathetic to communist regimes in China, the Soviet Union, Korea, Cambodia and Vietnam, with the result that he and his family were denied Australian passports for seventeen years. Burchett divided opinion in Australia, some accusing him of being a Soviet spy, while others considering him a 'rebel journalist', a martyr for the cause of free expression. He was a prolific writer but his Burma journalism and his book on the Burma retreat, *Bombs Over Burma*, had none of the later ideological colour of his Cold War writings.[28] His best book was probably *Democracy with a Tommygun*, published in 1946, in which he showed his deeply felt commitment to freedom and democracy, his genuine sympathy for the downtrodden masses and his antagonism to imperialism.[29] He wrote thirty-five books in all, many translated into several languages, and he is almost certainly the most written-about of all the Burma retreat correspondents. He died in Bulgaria in 1983.

Conclusion

A veteran reporter from the First World War reviewing O'Dowd Gallagher's book wrote that 'Never in any war before this have newspaper men taken exactly the same risks as the fighting men.'[30] Reporters in Burma had flown with RAF bomber crews, been with the tanks as they broke through enemy road blocks, escaped from sinking battleships off the Malayan coast, and driven their jeeps through thousands of miles of uncertain roads whilst being strafed by Japanese fighters. One cannot but admire their courage and resilience. They saw their job as keeping the public informed of how the war was going, whilst not in any way undermining the war effort. Wartime censorship severely circumscribed what they could publish at the time, but they used their notes to write much more thoughtful and critical accounts after the campaign had finished. They wanted to contribute to improving the war effort by explaining where things had gone wrong, and their assessments are not very different from those of later historians. They were well in advance of politicians in seeing that the days of empire in Southeast Asia were numbered, and that the only way to win the support of local populations for the war effort was to recognise this and promise future self-government. The correspondents were not just onlookers but participants in the war in Burma. They carried guns and knew that they would receive no concessions if they fell into the hands of the Japanese. Time and again they put down their cameras and notebooks to do what they could to help wounded civilians or engendered refugees. Some might have behaved like 'prima donnas' in the demands they made, and perhaps in the stories they embellished, but they were a minority. Many of them did believe that they were writing the first draft of history, providing the eye-witness accounts of the soldiers' experiences, analysing what was happening and recording the testimony of those who witnessed what they had not been able to. In some cases, they made an immediate difference: Stowe to the improved running of the Burma Road, Burchett in persuading the British to provide a better welcome and support to incoming Chinese troops, and Rodger and Burchett in pioneering one of the routes over the Naga Hills that was to be used by many refugees later. A number of their books deserve to be treated as classics of war reporting, Jack Belden's *Retreat with Stilwell* and *Still Time to Die* can stand comparison with the best. The books, newsreels and photographs are a valuable source for historians, though like any other source they must be treated with caution. Censorship set firm limits on what they could report and the pressures of the media market meant that positive, exciting and timely tales of military actions were the stories that editors, the military, politicians and the general public wanted from them, and the temptation was always there to take shortcuts to provide them.

APPENDIX 1

WAR CORRESPONDENTS IN BURMA, DECEMBER 1941 TO JUNE 1942

Superscript numbers after names indicate that the correspondents travelled or worked together in Burma.

	Correspondent	Enters Burma	Leaves Burma-all 1942	Nationality	Affiliation	Book(s)
1	Jack BELDEN (1910–89)	11 Mar. 42 with Stilwell from China	end Apr. with Stilwell to India	USA	Independent & *Time/Life; Daily Mail; Daily Herald*	*Retreat with Stilwell* (by Mar. 1943)
2	Darrell BERRIGAN[5] (1916–1965)	From Thailand 11 Dec. 41	end April with De Luce & Munday	USA	United Press Agency	
3	Claire BOOTHE Luce (1903–1987)	5 Apr. 42 from Calcutta	10 Apr. by air to Chungking	USA	*Time/Life*	
4	Wilfred (sometimes called Peter) BURCHETT[1] (1911–83)	22 Jan. 42 from Chungking	early Apr. via Hukawng Valley	Australian	*Daily Express & Sydney Daily Telegraph*	*Bombs Over Burma* (1944); *Trek Back from Burma* (1944)
5	Richard BUSVINE (1904–1987)	Mar. 42	Mar. evacuated by boat from Rangoon to Madras	British	*Chicago Daily Times*	*Gullible Travels* (1945)
6	Eve CURIE (1904–2007)	12 Feb. 42	Mid-Feb. flew to Chungking	French	*New York Herald Tribune and Allied Newspapers (Daily Sketch)*	*Journey Among Warriors* (1943)

147

Correspondent	Enters Burma	Leaves Burma-all 1942	Nationality	Affiliation	Book(s)
7 Dan DE LUCE[5] (1911–2002)	Jan. 42	end Apr. by jeep with Munday & Berrigan	USA	Associated Press Agency	
8 Maurice FORD (1910–1974)	c. 25 Jan. 42	c. 6 Apr. by air	British	British Paramount News Cameraman	
9 E. O'Dowd ('O.D.') GALLAGHER (1911–)[3]	22 Dec. 41 from Singapore	12 Mar. by air to Calcutta	South African	*Daily Express*	*Retreat in the East / Action in the East (1942)*
10 Leonard Marsland GANDER (1902–1986)	May 42 in Assam-Burma Border	May 42 from Naga Hills-last correspondent to leave Burma?	British	*Daily Telegraph*	*Long Road to Leros* (1945)
11 Thomas HEALY[2] b. 1901?	12 Feb. 42	6 May 42 flew to India from Loiwing	Australian	*Daily Mirror*	*Tourist Under Fire* (1945)
12 James L HODSON (1891–1956)	25 Feb. 42	8 Mar. 42	British	*Daily Sketch* & Allied Newspapers	*War in the Sun* (1942)
13 Philip JORDAN (1902–1951)	25 Feb. 42	8 Mar. 42	British	*News Chronicle*	
14 Roderick MACDONALD (1912–1944)[4]	27 Dec. 41 from Chungking	c. 17 Feb. via Burma Road to Chungking	Australian	*Sydney Morning Herald* &*London News Chronicle*	*Dawn Like Thunder* (1944)
15 Ronald MATTHEWS	11 Dec. 41 with Berrigan from Thailand	24 Jan. 42 for Singapore and Batavia	British	*Daily Herald*	
Correspondent	Enters Burma	Leaves Burma-all 1942	Nationality	Affiliation	Book(s)
16 William MUNDAY[2] (1910–43)	mid. Feb. 42	end Apr. by jeep to India with De Luce & Berrigan	Australian	*Sydney Morning Herald* / *News Chronicle*	
17 Ian MUNRO	c. 1 Jan. 42	c. 15 Apr. by jeep & car with Tozer	British	Reuters, London & A.P. of India, Madras	
18 M.J. PRITCHARD	c. 25 Jan. 42		British?	*Statesman* of India & London *Times*	
19 George RODGER[1] (1908–1995)	26 Jan. 42	early Apr. via Hukawng Valley	British	*Life* magazine Photographer	*Red Moon Rising* (1943) *Far on the Ringing Plains: 75,000 Miles With a Photo Reporter* (New York: 1944)

20	Cedric SALTER (1907–)	7 Jan. 42 from Turkey	29 Mar. by air to Calcutta	British	*Daily Mail*	Wrote a chapter in Young's *Outposts of Victory* (1943)
21	Henry A. 'Harry' STANDISH	11 Dec. 41 from Thailand with Berrigan	25 Jan. to Singapore	Australian	*Sydney Morning Herald / Daily Telegraph* (London)	
22	Leland STOWE[3] (1899–1994)	16 Dec. 1941 from Chungking	12 Mar. from Magwe flew to Calcutta	USA	*Chicago Daily News; Daily Telegraph* (London)	*They Shall Not Sleep* (1944)
23	Victor THOMPSON[4]	c. 8 Mar. 42	21 Apr. by air to Calcutta	British	*Daily Herald*	
24	ALEC TOZER (1913–1974)	c. 25 Jan. 42	c. 15 Apr. by Jeep over Naga Hills	British	Movietone News Cameraman	
25	Norman TRESHAM	c. 7 Feb. 42	c. 4 May	British	*Daily Mail*	
26	Alfred WAGG[4]	late Feb. / early March 42 from India	21 Apr. by air to Calcutta	USA	*Daily Sketch; Liberty magazine; Washington Evening Post*	*A Million Died* (1943)

APPENDIX 2

GEORGE RODGER STORIES FOR LIFE MAGAZINE
(AS RECORDED IN RODGER'S DIARIES) ALL DATES 1942

Story	Date sent	where sent from	Appears in _Life_	In _Illustrated_
AVG	1 Feb.	Rangoon	30 Mar. 'Flying Tigers in Burma'	23 May
Rangoon	4 Feb.	Rangoon	8 June	
Y-B Railway	27 Feb.	Maymyo	not used	16 May?
Burma Rd	1 Mar.	Maymyo	1 photo 10 Aug.	16 May?
Evacuated Rangoon	7 Mar.	Maymyo	8 June	
Recapture of Shwegyin	15 Mar.	Maymyo	2 photos in 22 June Burma Mission 2	20 June
Chinese Army	1 Apr.		not used	
Stilwell Toungoo	3 Apr.		not used	
Bombing Thazi	3 Apr.		not used	27 June Indian refugees
Stilwell & Generalissimo	9 Apr.		18 May	
Escape From Burma			12 photos 10 Aug.	

NOTES

PREFACE: 'THE FIRST DRAFT OF HISTORY'?

1. See http://www.readex.com/blog/newspapers-rough-draft-history, last accessed 5 August 2015.
2. John Simpson, *Unreliable Sources: How the 20th Century Was Reported*, London: Macmillan, 2010, p. x.
3. Michael Nicholson, *A State of War Exists: Reporters in the Line of Fire*, London: Biteback Publishing, 2012, p. xxiv.

INTRODUCTION: WAR CORRESPONDENTS

1. Among the books which focus on the 1942 campaign are James Lunt, *A Hell of a Licking: The Retreat from Burma 1941–2*, London: Collins, 1986; Alfred Draper, *Dawns Like Thunder: Retreat from Burma, 1942*. Barnsley: Pen & Sword, 1987; Ian Lyall Grant & Kazuo Tamayama, *Burma 1942: The Japanese Invasion; Both Sides Tell the Story of a Savage Jungle War*, Chichester: Zampi Press, 1999; Alan Warren, *The Road from Rangoon to Mandalay*, London: Continuum, 2011; Jon Latimer, *Burma: The Forgotten War*, London: John Murray: 2005; Robert Lyman, *Slim, Master of War: Burma and the Birth of Modern Warfare*, London: Constable & Robinson, 2004.
2. By far the best example is Christopher Bayly and Tim Harper, *Forgotten Armies: Britain's Asian Empire & the War with Japan*, London: Penguin Books, 2005.
3. See e.g. Michael D. Leigh, *The Evacuation of Civilians from Burma: Analysing the 1942 Colonial Disaster*, London: Bloomsbury Academic, 2014; Felicity Goodall, *Exodus Burma: The British Escape Through the Jungles of Death 1942*, Stroud: History Press, 2011.

4. An exception is Alfred Draper's book, *op. cit.* Draper was himself a journalist, which may explain his greater interest in using the war correspondents as sources.

5. A recent example of a relevant cultural studies approach to studying the work of war correspondents is Gareth Bentley, 'Journalistic Agency and the Subjective Turn in British Foreign Correspondent Discourse', PhD thesis, SOAS, University of London, 2013.

6. Some examples are Richard Collier, *The Warcos: The War Correspondents of World War Two*, London: Weidenfeld & Nicholson, London 1989; Trevor Royle, *War Report: The War Correspondent's View of Battle from the Crimea to the Falklands*, London: Grafton Books, 1987.

7. Phillip Knightley, *The First Casualty: The War Correspondent as Hero, Propagandist and Myth-Maker from Crimea to Iraq*, Baltimore, MA: Johns Hopkins University Press, 3rd ed., 2004.

8. Max Hastings, *Going to the Wars*, London: Pan Macmillan, 2001, p. 140.

9. See Appendix 1. The numbers cannot be established entirely accurately as the system of accreditation of correspondents in Burma seemed to break down as the retreat took place, and many of the Burma records were destroyed in two phases of the retreat. The official *Report on the Working of the Services Public Relations Office, Burma, during the Year 1941– 1942* [SPRO Report], lists twenty-eight correspondents but this covers the period from June 1941 and therefore includes correspondents who may have spent only a little time in Burma before the war started. See Kenneth Wallace-Crabbe MSS, University of Melbourne Archives, 2011, 0094, Box 1. The figure of twenty-six correspondents in Burma compares with ninety-two accredited war correspondents in North Africa covering the Desert War in North Africa in 1942, and 558 for the D-Day landings in 1944. See Knightley, *The First Casualty*, p. 332.

10. An exception was Lubeck of the *Rangoon Gazette* who returned his pass after a very short time. No Burmese language journalists applied for accreditation. SPRO Report, p. 4.

11. For a good discussion of the issue of war correspondents' self-censorship see Brian P.D. Hannon, 'British and Dominion War Correspondents in the Western Theatres of the Second World War, PhD thesis, University of Edinburgh, 2015, pp. 153–70. https://www.era.lib. ed.ac.uk/bitstream/handle/1842/10651/Hannon2015.pdf?sequence= 2&isAllowed=y, last accessed 2 April 2016.

12. J.L. Hodson (*Daily Sketch*) wrote in favour of correspondents being allowed to carry weapons and to have official officer status within the army in an article written after he returned to England. He used his experiences of the dangers in the last days at Rangoon to back his argument. *Newspaper World*, 2 May 1942, p. 1.

13. Fred Eldridge, General Stilwell's public relations Officer, claimed that General Alexander established a censorship rule prohibiting the use of the word 'withdrawal' in newspaper copy, arbitrarily substituting the word 'battle' wherever it appeared. See *Wrath in Burma: The Uncensored Story of General Stilwell and International Maneuvers in the Far East*, New York: Doubleday, 1946, p. 83. However, Eldridge's book has a very strong anti-British bias, and cannot always be relied on.

14. *Daily Sketch*, 23 February 1942, p. 3.

15. Eve Curie, *Journey Among Warriors*, London: Heinemann, 1943, p. 322.

16. *Ibid*, p. 323.

1. BURMA 1942: THE WAR CORRESPONDENTS' PERSPECTIVE

1. *Sunday Express*, 12 April 1942, p. 6.

2. O.D. Gallagher, *Retreat in the East*, London: Harrap, 1942, pp. 136–40. Gallagher had plenty of time to observe the activities at the Mingaladon Golf Club as he stayed there with two other colleagues, Leland Stowe and Daniel Berrigan, for several weeks. The governor, Dorman-Smith, responded directly to Gallagher's criticisms of the business community in his talk to the United Service Institution of India which was published in their journal, vol. lxiii, 1943, pp. 240–52. He made the points that businessmen had volunteered for military duty and played a vital part in the final, dangerous demolition work in Rangoon in March 1942.

3. Leland Stowe, *They Shall Not Sleep*, New York: Alfred A. Knopf, 1944, p. 89.

4. T.E. Healy, *Tourist Under Fire: The Journal of a War-Time Traveler*, New York: H. Holt & Co, 1945, p. 91.

5. See 'Attitude of the Burmese People in the Recent Campaign in Burma', F.S. Arnold MSS, Eur F145/6a, OIOC.

6. Stowe, *They Shall Not Sleep*, p. 137. These views were supported by the survey of Burmese attitudes. See for instance the 'Critical Analysis' by W.R. Bickford, deputy secretary, Reconstruction Dept., Arnold MSS, Eur F145/6a, pp. 136–41, OIOC.

7. These are estimates as the 1941 Census records were destroyed in the process of the war. See Dorman-Smith MSS, Eur E215/32a, f. 58, OIOC.

8. Stowe, *They Shall Not Sleep*, pp. 96–7.

9. For further discussion of this issue see Chapter Seven.

10. F.S.V. Donnison, *British Military Administration in the Far East 1943–46*, London: HMSO, 1956, p. 9.

11. See Robert Lyman, *The Generals: From Defeat to Victory, Leadership in Asia,*

1941–45, London: Constable, 2008, pp. 100–103, for an excellent picture of the paucity of Burma's defences in December 1941. See also Jon Latimer, *Burma: The Forgotten War*, London: John Murray, 2005, pp 20–1; Monteath, Draft Paper, 3 May 1942, WO106/3760, TNA. Sir David Monteath, under-secretary of state for Burma, used the low number of troops kept in peacetime Burma as an argument in defence of British rule in Burma from American criticisms, arguing that it indicated the lack of need for civil repression, which in turn showed Burmese acceptance of British rule.

12. Frank McLynn says that in 1939 the armed forces in Burma contained only 472 Burmans as against 3,197 Karens, Chins and Kachins: *The Burma Campaign: Disaster into Triumph, 1942–45*, New Haven, CT: Yale University Press, 2011, p. 7.

13. Fergal Keane, *Road of Bones: The Siege of Kohima 1944: The Epic Story of the Last Great Stand of Empire*, London: Harper Press, 2010, p. 4.

14. J. Belden, *Retreat with Stilwell*, New York: Alfred A. Knopf, 1943, p. 3. Belden wrote his book by March 1943, but another journalist, Darrell Berrigan of the United Press agency, later said that the first three chapters of the book were written by 'a friend'. Toby Wiant, also an agency war correspondent, believed that this was Berrigan himself. See Susan E. Wiant and Walter Cronkite, *Between the Bylines: A Father's Legacy*, New York: Fordham University Press, 2010, p. 114. In any case, the views seem typical of American war correspondents.

15. Belden, *Retreat with Stilwell*, p. 5.

16. *Ibid.*

17. Wavell to War Office (WO) 15 Dec. 1941, W106/2662, War Office: Directorate of Military Operations and Military Intelligence, f.8a, TNA.

18. Wavell to WO for Chiefs of Staff, 1 January 1942, W106/2662, f.63a, TNA. Wavell's fullest defence of his decision only to take two divisions of the Chinese 5th Army and not the 6th Army is set out in his reply to Churchill, 26 January 1942, WO106/2689. What Wavell failed to acknowledge was the blow he had dealt to Chiang Kai-Shek's amour-propre.

19. British Paramount News dope sheet, shipment 110, 'The Troops Arrive', 5 February 1942, IWM.

20. Hutton Report, WO106/2666, p. 4, TNA.

21. The British expected the main Japanese attack to be through the Shan States, which proved mistaken.

22. See FO371/31621 (file F4285), TNA, for details. Pearl Buck had written an article in the *The New York Times* on 31 May 1942 repeating this allegation, which triggered a concerted British government response,

but concerns went back much earlier. See Field Marshal Sir John Dill to CIGS, 22 January 1942, WO106/2662, f.81, TNA. For the correspondents' assertions of British delays in bringing in Chinese troops see Belden, *Retreat with Stilwell*, p. 15; W.G. Burchett, *Bombs Over Burma*, Melbourne: F.W. Cheshire, 1944, pp. 27–31.

23. Wavell dispatch, 1 July 1942, WO106/2666, p. 7, TNA.

24. General Hutton thought so. See his Report, W106/2666, p. 34, TNA: 'It is easy to see that even one more [Infantry] Brigade received early in January would have sufficed to turn the scale in practically every battle from Kawkareik to Rangoon.'

25. Wavell Dispatch, WO106/2666, p. 9, TNA.

2. THE GOVERNOR OF BURMA AND HIS CRITICS

1. Of course, there are exceptions to this rule but they usually only occur in extreme situations such as in the Dardanelles campaign of 1915 where the reporting of Ellis Ashmead-Bartlett is supposed to have contributed to stopping the disastrous campaign.

2. For press criticism of Shenton Thomas in Singapore see Alan Warren, *Britain's Greatest Defeat: Singapore 1942*. London: Hambledon Continuum, 2006, p. 212.

3. T.E. Healy, *Tourist Under Fire: The Journal of a War-Time Traveler*. New York: H. Holt & Co., 1945, p. 140. Healy was very critical of Dorman-Smith and his handling of the evacuation of Rangoon.

4. Jon Latimer, *Burma: The Forgotten War*, London: John Murray, 2005, p. 65. General Stilwell called him 'Doormat Smith' according to Fred Eldridge, *Wrath in Burma; The Uncensored Story of General Stilwell and International Maneuvers in the Far East*, New York: Doubleday, 1946, p. 53.

5. See for example Max Hastings, *All Hell Let Loose: The World at War 1939–1945*, London: Harper Press, 2011, p. 219; Kwasi Kwarteng, *Ghosts of Empire: Britain's Legacies in the Modern World*, London: Bloomsbury, 2010, p. 196.

6. The most balanced and up-to-date treatment of Dorman-Smith, Burma and the war with Japan is C. Bayly and T. Harper, *Forgotten Armies: Britain's Asian Empire and the War with Japan*, London: Penguin, 2005.

7. Brian Short, *The Battle of the Fields: Rural Community and Authority in Britain during the Second World War*, Woodbridge: Boydell Press, 2014, p. 30.

8. R.H. Taylor, 'Constitutional Developments in Burma', entry in Oii Keat Gin (ed.), *Southeast Asia: A Historical Encyclopedia from Angkor Wat to East Timor*, Santa Barbara, CA: ABC-CLIO, 2004, p. 385.

9. Aron Shai, *Origins of the War in the East: Britain, China and Japan, 1937–1939*, Routledge: 2011, e-edn., pp. 114–15.

10. Maurice Collis, *Last and First in Burma (1941–1948)*, London: Faber & Faber, 1956, p. 23. Collis' book is very much based on Dorman-Smith's draft and unpublished memoirs and is favourably disposed to its subject. See Collis MSS Eur D. 1034/2, 'Dorman-Smith Notes', OIOC.

11. R.H. Taylor, 'Constitutional Developments'.

12. Collis, *Last and First*, pp. 25–6.

13. Colonel Blimp was initially the invention of the *Evening Standard* cartoonist David Low, and depicted a retired, upper-class, British army officer of the 1930s who held on to ridiculously reactionary, outdated and prejudiced viewpoints. The personality was taken up in Powell and Pressburger's wartime film, *The Life and Death of Colonel Blimp* (Rank, 1943).

14. Collis MSS Eur D1034/2, f.9, Dorman-Smith Notes [comments on Collis' draft for his book *Last and First in Burma*, written c. August 1954], OIOC.

15. Bayly and Harper, *Forgotten Armies*, p. 86.

16. I have relied on Michael D. Leigh, *The Evacuation of Civilians from Burma: Analysing the 1942 Colonial Disaster*, London: Bloomsbury, 2014, for much of the following sections on evacuation policy.

17. Dorman-Smith later wrote that the Burma civil service and others were not pleased with this appointment. Collis MSS Eur D1034/2, ff. 13–17. The initial request was Dorman-Smith to Amery, 19 June 1941, B60/41; 'Civil Defence in Burma: appointment of R. de Graaff-Hunter as Director of Civil Defence, M/3/1090, OIOC. Incidentally, this short file shows just how aware at this date Dorman-Smith and Leo Amery, the Secretary of State for Burma, were of the possibility of Japanese air-raids and the consequences of such attacks. Dorman-Smith had also requested that a transport expert be sent out but this was turned down as Burma was not seen as a priority. E. Foucar, 'Draft Narrative of the First Burma Campaign December 1941–May 1942', p. 232, CAB44/324, TNA. Foucar was a Rangoon lawyer who became Services Public Relations Officer. His report was designed to improve military training: it supported the de Graaff-Hunter line on civil defence. See pp. 46–7.

18. The information for this section on civil defence is taken from the interview which de Graaff-Hunter gave to the journalist Alfred Wagg which was published soon after. See A. Wagg, *A Million Died! A Story of War in the Far East*, London: Nicholson & Watson, 1943, Chapter XXI, 'Why No Civil Defence?'

19. Belden, *Retreat with Stilwell*, p. 5. It is likely that Belden took this view from General Stilwell's entourage. In his memoir, Stilwell's PRO, Fred

Eldridge, repeated the same erroneous view that 'the British military commander in the field could not deploy his troops without the consent of the British civil governor, who insisted on retaining the normal disposition of garrison troops in lower Burma'. Eldridge, *Wrath in Burma*, p. 41. Eldridge's book has a strong anti-British bias, which reflected the views of Stilwell.

20. James Lunt to Maurice Collis, 11 November 1955, MSS Eur D1034, OIOC, cited in Latimer, *Burma: The Forgotten War*, p. 48, n. 33.
21. Latimer, *Burma*, p. 48.
22. Technically he had command of the Burma Rifles, but this had no practical effect in wartime.
23. See Belden, *Retreat with Stilwell*, p. 15; W.G. Burchett, *Bombs Over Burma*, Melbourne: F.W. Cheshire, 1944, pp. 28–31.
24. Dorman-Smith to Collis, 13 June 1954, Collis MSS, Eur D1034/2, ff. 148–9, 'Wavell and the Chinese troops', OIOC. Wavell added to his arguments for restricting the numbers of Chinese troops admitted immediately, saying that 'the Governor particularly asked me not to accept more Chinese for Burma than was absolutely necessary'. Wavell to Churchill, 23 January 1942, WO106/2689, TNA.
25. Latimer, *Burma*, p. 53.
26. See Bayly and Harper, *Forgotten Armies*, p. 164.
27. *The Times*, 20 March 1942, p. 3.
28. *Daily Mirror*, 14 March 1942, p. 2.
29. See Stowe, *They Shall Not Sleep*, p. 90; O.D. Gallagher, *Retreat in the East*, London: Harrap, 1942, pp. 78–82, for instance. This issue is discussed more fully in Chapter Nine.
30. This issue is very well dealt with in Leigh, *The Evacuation of Civilians*, pp. 46–7.
31. This he did in 'Report on the Burma Campaign 1941–1942' by H.E. the Rt. Hon. Sir Reginald Dorman-Smith GBE, Governor of Burma, Simla, November 1943, Simla: Government of India Press, 1943, pp. 7–8, M/8/15, OIOC.
32. *Ibid*, p. 8.
33. W. Slim, *Defeat into Victory*, London: Pan Macmillan, 2009, p. 117.
34. Hutton to War Office, 21 February 1942, WO106/2681, 'Operations Burma: telegrams 151–250', f. 171c, TNA.
35. Wavell to Hutton, 21 February 1942, WO106/2681, ff. 174–5, TNA.
36. Slim, *Defeat into Victory*, pp. 115–21.
37. Gallagher, *Retreat in the East*, p. 78.
38. British Movietone News, issue 662, 9 February 1942, 'Rangoon Resolute', http://bufvc.ac.uk/newsonscreen/search/index.php/story/12138, last accessed 18 January 2016. Lady Dorman-Smith's diary also

records two of her husband's visits to the docks on 30 December and 15 January, MSS Eur E215/41, OIOC.

39. Cutting from *Daily Telegraph*, 9 December 1941, MSS Eur E215/41, OIOC.

40. Lady Dorman-Smith's diary for 1942, entries for 8 and 9 February 1942, MSS Eur E215/41, OIOC.

41. For Gallagher's criticisms see his *Retreat in the East*, p. 76.

42. J.L. Hodson, *War in the Sun*, London: Victor Gollancz, 1942, p. 332. For Dorman-Smith's generally negative views on the war correspondents see Collis MSS Eur D1034/2, f.107, OIOC. It is interesting to see how well some of the correspondents got on with Dorman-Smith when they were able to meet him in person. Wilfred Burchett, who was a pretty critical commentator, wrote: 'On behalf of that much-maligned Governor of Burma, I must say that I always found him readily accessible and quick to act when he was convinced of the necessity of action.' W.G. Burchett, *Bombs Over Burma*, p. 75. This was based on an interview following Burchett's complaints about the poor welcome given to Chinese troops entering Burma.

43. Hodson's report featured in the *Daily Sketch*, 7 March 1942, p. 8, 'Big Moves Coming in Burma Within Next Few Days.'; Jordan's reports appeared in the *News Chronicle*, 7 March 1942, p. 1; 11 March, p. 1. Both correspondents now told of the involvement of Burmese fifth columnists armed by the Japanese in their advance on Rangoon.

44. See Wagg, *A Million Died!*, Chapter XX, 'I Talk to Burma's Governor'. See Chapter Nine for more details.

45. Dorman-Smith to Amery, 8 March 1942, WO106/2681, f. 221, TNA.

46. See 'Drafts of Dorman-Smith's unfinished memoirs', MSS Eur 215/32b, f. 170, OIOC.

47. See Dorman-Smith to Amery, 19 June 1941; Amery to Morrison, 4 July 1941, B60/41 'Civil Defence in Burma: appointment of R. de Graaff-Hunter as Director of Civil Defence', M/3/1090, OIOC.

3. EARLY BIRDS OR 'VULTURES'?

1. Dorman-Smith MSS Eur 215/32b, 'Drafts of Dorman-Smith's unfinished memoirs and of his articles on the invasion of Burma etc.' ff. 159–159b, OIOC.

2. For his views on Chungking see *Chicago Daily News* (CDN), 24 December 1941, p. 2; for his attitudes to China see Leland Stowe, *They Shall Not Sleep*, New York: Alfred A. Knopf, 1944, Chapter III, 'China Inches Towards Democracy'.

3. Stowe, *They Shall Not Sleep*, pp. 60–1.

4. *Ibid*, pp. 76–7; copies of telegrams, Carroll Binder, CDN Foreign Editor, to Stowe, 1, 2,10, 26 January 1942, kindly provided from Stowe MSS by Newberry Library, Chicago. It was the last three articles that were published, as they arrived first.

5. CDN, 30 December 1941, p. 1, contd. p. 6.

6. CDN, 31 December 1941, p. 1.

7. Stowe, *They Shall Not Sleep*, p. 78.

8. *Ibid*, p. 83.

9. Stowe recorded statements in his notebooks from members of the American military mission saying that his articles had brought about an improvement on the Burma Road and a more cooperative attitude from the Chinese See Col. St John, cited in Stowe notebook ii, f.58, 15 January 1942; Major Russell, cited in Stowe notebook iv, f.36, 8 March 1942, Stowe MSS, Wisconsin Historical Society [WHS].

10. *Ibid*, p. xvi.

11. Eve Curie, *Journey Among Warriors*. London: Heinemann, 1943, pp. 330–1.

12. Paul Preston, *We Saw Spain Die: Foreign Correspondents in the Spanish Civil War*, London: Constable & Robinson, 2008, p. 60.

13. *Daily Express*, 17 December 1941, p. 1.

14. Amery to Dorman-Smith, 29 January 1942, 5 February 1942, M3/857, B153/40(i), War: propaganda: publicity organisation in Burma and liaison with UK, 27 July 1938–27 July 1943, OIOC.

15. Dorman-Smith to Amery, 10 February 1942, *ibid*.

16. CDN, 3 January 1942, p. 2.

17. Stowe, *They Shall Not Sleep*, p. 90.

18. *Ibid*, p. 88.

19. *Ibid*, p. 92. Stowe's notebooks confirm that this was not just a matter of hindsight. Almost from his arrival in Rangoon he had been predicting the fall of Burma. See, for example entry for 26 December 1941, 'Very little reason to expect Burma to hold', notebook, 'Battles in Burma & British "Colonial Rot"', vol. 1, 17 to 30 December 1941, p. 55, Stowe MSS, WHS.

20. See for instance his notebook, *op. cit.*, entry f. 34, 22 December 1941.

21. CDN, 16 January 1942, p. 2. Gallagher made the same positive arguments in the *Daily Express*, 15 January 1942, p. 1. Often, it was left to the newspaper's military correspondent based in London to add some realism to the war correspondents' offerings.

22. CDN, 5 January 1942, p. 1, contd. back page.

23. See, for instance, Stowe, *They Shall Not Sleep*, p. 90.

24. *Daily Express*, 14 January 1942, p. 1, contd. p. 4.

25. Gallagher still took up an argument on behalf of his fellow journal-

ists that they should not have been required to leave Rangoon under the rule governing war correspondents, which allowed them free movement provided they did not interfere with military operations. He cited the Chief of Imperial General Staff order of 31 January 1942 2(a) and (d), *Action in the East*, pp. 259–60.

26. *Sunday Times*, 1 March 1942, p. 1, contd. p. 5. Philip Jordan's report, dated 3 March, was published in the *News Chronicle*, 8 March 1942, p. 2. It said that it was 'a party that made Dunkirk look like a picnic'. These Dunkirk analogies may have come from interviewing General Alexander who had been a key figure in the evacuation of British troops there.

27. James Lunt, *A Hell of a Licking: The Retreat from Burma 1941–2*, London: Collins, 1986, p. 127.

28. Stowe first heard of the British brigades cut off on the wrong side of the Sittang on 26 February, five days after it happened, Stowe notebook iv, f. 1, 26 February 1942, Stowe MSS, WHS, but seems originally to have seen it more as a story of heroic rescue by a newly arrived tank regiment. It was not until 2 March that the American Major Merrill confirmed the story, *ibid*, f. 10, 2 March 1942, and six days later a British officer who had been in the battle spoke of the loss of a thousand men and much equipment there, *ibid*, f. 37, 8 March 1942. By this time the story was probably too old to be regarded as a scoop.

29. See Stowe, *They Shall Not Sleep*, pp. 120–2.

30. For the bombing raid see Gallagher, *Retreat in the East*, Chapter XI.

31. This was the very problem that E.B. White complained of in an influential article in *Harper's Magazine* of April 1942 entitled 'The Newspaper Reader Finds It Very Hard to Get at the Truth'. White argued that negative news stories were hidden away at the bottom of much more positive articles and, therefore, the American public found it very difficult to discern accurately how the war was going. Reprinted in Samuel Hynes *et al* (eds), *Reporting World War II: Part 1: American Journalism, 1938–1944*, New York: Library of America, 1995, pp. 300–2.

32. Gallagher, *Action in the East*, p. 183.

33. Stowe commented in his notebook on the effect of the monotony of life in Rangoon and the lack of a sexual life in wartime, notebook ii, f. 52, 14 January 1942.

34. Stowe notebook ii, f. 53, 14 January 1942, 'Battles in Burma'; notebook iv, f. 58, 12 March 1942, Stowe MSS, WHS.

35. Stowe notebook i, f.78, 29 December 1941.

36. Stowe notebook iii, f.53, 9 February 1942.

37. Stowe notebook ii, f.76, 22 January 1942.

38. Stowe notebook iii, f. 49, 8 February 1942.

39. Stowe notebook iv, f. 39, 9 March 1942.

40. It would not have been difficult to obtain an interview with Dorman-Smith, for instance. Roderick Macdonald wrote that he asked for an interview on 31 December and received one the next day, New Year's Day at 9.30 am. See Roderick Macdonald, *Dawn Like Thunder*, London: Hodder & Stoughton, 1944, p. 68. Wilfred Burchett also said that he found the governor 'readily accessible and quick to act when he was convinced of the necessity of action'. See W.G. Burchett, *Bombs Over Burma*, Melbourne: F.W. Cheshire, 1944, p. 75.

41. Stowe notebook iv, f. 55, 12 March 1942. Stowe MSS, WHS.

42. *Ibid*, ff. 59–62, 12 March 1942.

43. CDN, 23 March 1942, p. 2.

44. Gallagher later boasted that he had written the book in thirteen days, HS 9/555/2, Special Operations Executive, personnel file, Edward O'Dowd Gallagher, TNA. It was republished in the US under the more positive title *Action in the East*, New York: Doubleday-Doran, 1943.

45. Vol. 3, 1, November 1943, pp. 88–9.

46. George Orwell, *Keeping Our Little Corner Clean, 1942–1943 (Collected Works of George Orwell, vol. XIV)*. rev. ed. London: Secker & Warburg, 2001, pp. 8–9.

4. ORGANISING THE WAR CORRESPONDENTS IN BURMA

1. 18 July 1941, J.C.R. Proud's Report on the Visit to Burma of the Services Publicity Officer M3/857, B153/40(i) 'War: propaganda: publicity organisation in Burma and liaison with UK, 27 July 1938 to 27 July 1943', ff. 146–52, OIOC.

2. Newham was the editor of the *Civil and Military Gazette*, Lahore, and later was the editor of *The Pioneer* in Allahabad.

3. Newham was replaced on 18 April by a Mr Pollock, but it was too late by then to achieve much as the rapid Japanese advance forced the publicity machine to retreat further and further northwards. See E. Foucar, 'Draft Narrative of the First Burma Campaign December 1941–May 1942', CAB44/324, p. 14, OIOC.

4. See Lord Hood's 'Report on Propaganda and Political Warfare in the Far East, Appendix F: Burma', L/I/1/1081, August 1942, OIOC.

5. Dorman-Smith to Amery, 18 September 1941, M/3/859, B153/40(v) 'War: propaganda: publicity organisation in Burma: appointment of officers on special duty in Defence Department', 12 August 1941– 2 September 1946, TNA.

6. On the journalists' resentment see Leland Stowe, *They Shall Not Sleep*, New York: Alfred A. Knopf, 1944, pp. 103–4. Stowe's views recorded in his contemporary notebooks are much stronger, describing Cook as a 'pompous, conceited, pipsqueak—looks down on press—Full of own importance', Stowe notebook, 8 February 1942, 'Battles in Burma', vol. III, p. 53, Stowe MSS, WHS. For Cook's attitude to the press see Cook to A.H. Joyce [Chief Press Officer, India & Burma Office] 3 May 1941, MSS Eur 215/37, OIOC.
7. All information on the setting up of the SPRO is from E. Foucar, 'Report on the Workings of the Services Public Relations Office, (SPRO Report), Kenneth Wallace-Crabbe Papers, University of Melbourne Archives, pp. 1–2.
8. For biographical information see http://www.daao.org.au/bio/kenneth-eyre-inverell-wallace-crabbe/biography/, last accessed 18 January 2016. His papers are held at the University of Melbourne library.
9. SPRO Report, p. 4. It is not known who the errant journalist was.
10. The frustration of this process is described by Leland Stowe in his Burma notebook I, 'Battles in Burma & British "Colonial Rot"' Dec. 17 to 30, 1941', f. 76, 29 December 1941, Stowe MSS, WHS. It seems that at this stage the governor's office was also involved in censoring correspondents' dispatches. Two days later, Stowe learnt that India was also censoring everything leaving Burma and Malaya, causing further delays in transmission. Notebook II, 'Battles in Burma', f. 1, 1 January 1942.
11. T.E. Healy, *Tourist Under Fire: The Journal of a War-Time Traveler*. New York: H. Holt & Co., 1945, p. 112.
12. SPRO Report, p. 6.
13. Burma: Censorship Regulations, 1938, Chapter VI, 'Press Censorship', p. 88, WO33/1567, TNA.
14. E.C.V. Foucar, *I Lived in Burma*, London: Dennis Dobson, 1956, p. 123.
15. Leland Stowe, notebook IV, f. 46, 10 March 1942, Stowe MSS, WHS.
16. See 'Note dictated by Colonel Jehu', DPR, Defence Department, Government of India, 14 March 1942, L/I/1/732, 'Censorship Indian [Cases] 1939–43', file 462/18b, OIOC.
17. See the case of Roderick Macdonald, as reported in his book *Dawn Like Thunder*, London: Hodder & Stoughton, 1944, pp. 81–2. Interestingly, Macdonald was trying to have certain military lessons learnt from the early defeats in southern Burma, but, although his articles were passed by Burma censors, they were stopped in India and excisions required. Leland Stowe also believed that India was censoring everything coming out of Malaya and Burma and that this was causing a delay in journalists' dispatches, sometimes of days. Stowe, notebook II, f. 1, 1 January 1942, Stowe MSS, WHS.

18. Alfred Draper, *Dawns Like Thunder: Retreat from Burma, 1942*, Barnsley: Pen & Sword, 1987, pp. 40–1.
19. These issues are well dealt with in Anne Sebba, *Battling for News: The Rise of the Woman Reporter*, London: Hodder & Stoughton, 1994, Chapters 10–12.
20. Curie wrote of her experiences in *Journey Among Warriors*, London: Heinemann, 1943.
21. *Ibid*, p. 316.
22. *Ibid*, p. 320.
23. *Ibid*, p. 323.
24. *Daily Sketch*, 23 February 1942, p. 3.
25. For more information on Clare Boothe in Burma see Chapter Five.

5. GEORGE RODGER AND *LIFE* MAGAZINE PHOTO-JOURNALISM

1. Theodore Peterson, *Magazines in the Twentieth Century*, Urbana, IL: University of Illinois Press, 1956, p. 56. *Life*, 26 October 1942, p. 127, claimed more than 23 million civilian readers and that nearly two out of every three Americans in the military read the magazine. For a more cautious estimate of the readership of *Life* and its possible influence see James L. Baughman, 'Who Read *Life*? The Circulation of America's Favorite Magazine', in Erika Doss (ed.), *Looking at Life Magazine*, Washington DC: Smithsonian Institution Press, 2001, pp. 41–51.
2. Biographical information is from Carole Naggar, *George Rodger: An Adventure in Photography, 1908–1995*, Syracuse, NY: Syracuse University Press, 2003, and Martin Caiger-Smith's preface to Colin Osman (ed.), *George Rodger Magnum Opus: Fifty Years in Photojournalism*, London: Nishen, 1987. As was stated in *Life*, 30 March 1942, 'George Rodger has gone to more sweat and pain to get a few pictures in LIFE than any other LIFE photographer. He has photographed the Free French in Africa, the sandy war of Libya, the grimy war of Ethiopia, the travail of Syria, Iran and Iraq, the Northwest Frontier, India.'
3. Naggar, *George Rodger*, p. 4.
4. *Life*, 10 August 1942, '75,000 miles', pp. 61–7. Copies of *Life* magazine can be found online at https://books.google.co.uk/books?id=N0EEAAAAMBAJ&redir_esc=y#all_issues_anchor, last accessed 11 January 2016, and the relevant Burma editions have been conveniently adapted by the excellent China-Burma-India website http://cbi-theater.home.comcast.net/~cbi-theater/menu/cbi_home.html, last accessed 18 January 2016.
5. George Rodger, *Red Moon Rising*, London: Cresset Press, 1943, pp. 15–16.

6. The British consul-general in New York had asked for Rodger to be supported by the government, particularly to meet American interest in photographs of American materiel going up the Burma Road and of troops sent to Burma from China. Amery to Dorman-Smith, 8 February 1942, M/3/857, B153/40(i) 'War: propaganda: publicity organisation in Burma and liaison with UK', 27 July 1938–27 July 1943', f.80, OIOC.

7. Naggar, *George Rodger*, p. 89, n.3.

8. After this, his photos and captions would usually go unseen by him and it might take two months or more before he saw how his photos had turned out.

9. George Rodger, *Far on the Ringing Plains: 75,000 Miles with a Photo Reporter*, New York: Macmillan, 1944, pp. 293–4.

10. This personalisation of stories was popular with American editors, but could also be seen as a distraction from reporting some of the harsher realities of war and the wider issues of significance. See John Maxwell Hamilton, *Journalism's Roving Eye: A History of American Foreign Reporting*, Baton Rouge, LA: Louisiana State University Press, 2009, p. 313.

11. His death on 30 January 1942 is confirmed in Daniel Ford's 'Warbirds' website: http://www.warbirdforum.com/casuals.htm, last accessed 18 January 2016.

12. *Daily Express*, 24 December 1941, p. 4.

13. *Chicago Daily News* (CDN), 26 December 1941, p. 1.

14. CDN, 1 January 1942, p. 1. Correspondents often compared events in the places they were reporting to other significant wartime places or events, for instance Dunkirk if a positive spin on a retreat was required, or Tobruk for a gallant defence. Although journalists complained of Dorman-Smith's over-optimistic use of Tobruk as a parallel with the defence of southern Burma, they were as likely to use such analogies in their own writing.

15. Leland Stowe, *They Shall Not Sleep*, New York: Alfred A. Knopf, 1944, p. 146. AVG pilots received $600 (£150) per month and $500 (£125) for each plane shot down, *Daily Telegraph*, 4 May 1942, p. 4. Bill Munday calculated that AVG pilots who survived their full Burma tour each would make about $10,000, *Sydney Morning Herald*, 16 June 1942, p. 6, http://trove.nla.gov.au/newspaper/article/17803939?searchTerm=William%20Munday&searchLimits=#, last accessed 25 March 2016.

16. Stowe, *They Shall Not Sleep*, p. 154.

17. Jerome Klinkowitz, *With the Tigers Over China, 1941–1942*, Lexington, KY: University of Kentucky Press, 1999), pp. 50–2.

18. *Ibid*, p. 52.

19. *Ibid*, p. 50.
20. Gallagher remarks that 'the American news agencies drove their reporters frantic with demands for more A.V.G. stories'. O.D. Gallagher, *Retreat in the East*, London: Harrap, 1942, p. 96.
21. Rodger, *Red Moon Rising*, p. 15.
22. *Ibid*, p. 101.
23. *Ibid*, pp. 35–6.
24. *Ibid*, p. 63.
25. *Ibid*, p. 70.
26. Information about his cameras is taken from Naggar, *George Rodger*, p. 57. She points out that the Rolleiflex was medium-format and produced photos of a finer grain which would be suitable for *Life*'s requirements for cover photos. He seemed to use film rolls with twelve exposures. He could use the faster Leica camera for European magazines such as *Illustrated*.
27. Rodger, *Red Moon Rising*, p. 73. Naggar, *George Rodger*, p. 95, confirms the lack of suitable images. What is surprising is that although Rodger admits to the almost impossible conditions for taking photographs on the day of the battle, he makes no reference to the reconstruction which took place for photographers the next day. See *Red Moon Rising*, pp. 71–6. He even describes the soldiers advancing over the fence, but his supporting photograph (Plate XXX, facing p. 67) shows a soldier climbing over an entirely different fence from that shown in the newsreel. The clarity of the photos in his book and in the *Life* magazine article (see Figure 5.3) would seem to indicate that they were taken in the re-enactment.
28. Rodger, *Red Moon Rising*, p. 74.
29. *Ibid*.
30. Rodger, Burma Diary entries for 12, 13 March 1942, Smarden Archive.
31. Burchett, *Bombs Over Burma*, p. 135. Burchett also gave the impression that he witnessed the battle when he wrote his report for the *Sunday Express*, 22 March 1942, p. 8.
32. E.C.V. Foucar, *I Lived in Burma*, London: Dennis Dobson, 1956, pp. 133–4. The newsreel must have been taken by Alec Tozer. See Chapter Six for more details.
33. *Illustrated*, 'Soldiers of the Propaganda Army', 20 June 1942, p. 13.
34. Rodger quoted in Colin Naylor (ed.), *Contemporary Photographers*, London: Macmillan, 1982, p. 867, cited in Naggar, *George Rodger*, p. 74.
35. Rodger, *Red Moon Rising*, pp. 95–6.
36. *Ibid*, pp. 97–8.

37. Clare Boothe Luce described it thus in her report, 'U.S. General Stilwell Commands Chinese on Burma Front' in *Life*, 27 April 1942: 'American headquarters, in cool, fragrant Maymyo, is in the mission house, with the eight or ten cottages in the compound for officers. These are surrounded by a lovely spring garden, rose arbors and a great hedge of poinsettias. The sweet smell of eucalyptus is always in the air. The 30-odd officers at the mess, with a scattering of Chinese liaison officers, were served delicious strawberries and lousy coffee by Burmese Indian servants.'

38. Rodger, *Red Moon Rising*, p. 99.

39. Frank Dorn, *Walkout:With Stilwell in Burma*, New York: T.Y. Crowell, 1971, p. 62.

40. See Rodger, *Red Moon Rising*, plates XLVIII a & b.

41. *Life*, 22 June 1942, 'Burma Mission, Part II', report dated 9 April 1942, p. 83.

42. *Ibid*, p. 80.

43. *Life*, 'Burma Mission', Part I, 15 June 1942, p. 100.

44. Collis MSS Eur D. 1034/2, Dorman-Smith notes for book *Last and First in Burma*, f.107, OIOC.

45. Published in *Life*, 27 April 1942. It is probable that she had the freedom to publish these views because she sent them via the Chinese capital, Chungking.

46. *Life*, 27 April 1942.

47. Rodger, *Far on the Ringing Plains*, pp. 283–4.

48. *Ibid*.

49. For Burchett's first exploratory journey through the Hukawng Valley see his *Bombs Over Burma*, Chapter XI, 'The New Route to India', which describes the detailed survey of the route which he contributed to.

50. See Rodger, *Far on the Ringing Plains*, pp. 293–4.

51. George Rodger letter to Cicely Hussey-Freke, Khyukok [China-Burma border], Burma, 17 February 1942, cited in Naggar, *George Rodger*, p. 93.

52. Rodger, *Red Moon Rising*, 'Acknowledgements'.

53. Rodger, *Far on the Ringing Plains*, p. 284.

6. NEWSREEL CAMERAMEN: ALEC TOZER AND MAURICE FORD

1. A notable exception is the recent Colonial Film project, http://www.colonialfilm.org.uk/home, which catalogues and gives detailed commentaries on newsreel and documentary films on colonial history topics. The online database covers film material held by archives such as the

Imperial War Museum as well as selected newsreels. It is important, however, to recognise that only a fraction of the film shot by the cameramen actually reached cinema screens, after censoring and editing.

2. For more information on newsreel cameramen see the British Universities Film & Video Council's (BUFVC) website, which holds an invaluable database on newsreels, contains links to streamed newsreel footage, and has archived manuscript material such as dope sheets (cameraman's record of shots taken) and background, shot lists and commentary drafts where available. BUFVC sources and web links have been referred to in this article wherever possible. See http://bufvc. ac.uk/newsonscreen/search/index.php/person/301, last accessed 18 January 2016, for Ford's career details.

3. See http://www.historicfilms.com/tapes/20495 [start 1:15;05; stop 1:18:20], last accessed 18 January 2016, for good film of Ford's filming of the Blitz in January 1941, with shots of a moustachioed Ford.

4. For details of Alec Tozer's career (1913–74) see http://bufvc.ac.uk/ newsonscreen/search/index.php/person/932, last accessed 18 January 2016. It was calculated that Tozer served overseas for four years and three months, including further spells in Burma in 1943 and 1945, *The Cine-Technician*, November–December 1945, available in http://archive. org/stream/cinetech911asso/cinetech911asso_djvu.txt, last accessed 18 January 2016.

5. http://terencegallacher.wordpress.com/2012/02/28/cameraman-tales- alec-tozer-italian-prisoner-of-war/, last accessed 18 January 2016.

6. The other newsreels were Gaumont British News, Universal News and Pathé News.

7. Dope sheets are invaluable as evidence. The best description of them is given in Jonathan Stuart Setliff, 'The March of Time and the American Century', PhD., University of Maryland, 2007, pp. 136–7: 'Dope sheets indicated the exact order, location, date and subject of each shot exposed on a roll of film, together with the name[s] of the cameraman … the production number, the amount of footage exposed, the kind of film stock used, processing instructions for the laboratory, information about the presence or absence of competing newsreel cameramen, and information about the way in which the film was being shipped. The names of all individuals shown in each shot were indicated, as were their positions within a shot.' In addition, during wartime indication was given of when the films and scripts were censored. Cameraman differed in how much supporting information they provided.

8. George Rodger Burma diary, entries for 31 January, 2 February 1942, Smarden archive.

9. 'Movietone's War Time News—Reported by Leslie Mitchell: On the Burma Front', British Movietone News (BMN) Issue No. 669, 30 March

1942. http://bufvc.ac.uk/newsonscreen/search/index.php/story/ 12196, last accessed 18 January 2016.

10. 'Street Scenes, Rangoon, Burma, 25 January 1942', Imperial War Museum (IWM) BAY 226, The IWM holds the original dope sheets and some of the Paramount films: references to film clips are to their catalogue numbers; 'Scenes in Bomb Damaged Rangoon, 28 January 1942' and 'Air Force and Japs Downed, Burma, 30 Jan. 1942', IWM BAY 232–1: http://www.colonialfilm.org.uk/node/5584 & http:// www.colonialfilm.org.uk/node/5585, last accessed 18 January 2016.

11. O'Dowd Gallagher published his criticisms in *Retreat in the East*, London: Harrap, 1942, pp. 76–7.

12. See Nicholas Reeves, *The Power of Film Propaganda: Myth or Reality?* London: Cassell, 1999, pp. 156–7.

13. *Ibid.*

14. For some details of the debates about the working of the rota arrangement in this period see Minute Book 2 of the Newsreel Association of Great Britain, especially the minutes of 5 February, 26 March and 7 May 1942, British Film Institute Library (BFI), London.

15. Ford was lucky in this respect in that Paramount was allowed to present an exclusive newsreel displaying Ford's Burma footage, which was credited at thirteen minutes as the 'longest newsreel ever issued by British Paramount'; 'Burma: A War Correspondent's Dispatch', NPA 1173, 28 May 1942, IWM. For the response to Paramount's request, see Minute Book 2 of the Newsreel Association, entries for 21 May 1942 (item 1056) and 4 June 1942 (item 1074), BFI.

16. A good example is Alec Tozer's film of British troops defending the Salween river front which must have been taken at the very end of January 1942 but did not appear in British cinemas until 30 March, with an apology for the delay by the commentator, Leslie Mitchell 'Movietone's War Time News—Reported by Leslie Mitchell: On the Burma Front', BMN Issue No. 669, 30 March 1942. http://bufvc. ac.uk/newsonscreen/search/index.php/story/12196, last accessed 18 January 2016. The film of what is admitted to be a British setback, the loss of Moulmein, is balanced with more positive, and more recent, footage of the arrival of Chinese troops in Burma.

17. BPN dispatch 108, 2 February 1942, 'Night Fighters of Burma'; 'AA Bofors Manned by Indian Troops', 15 February 1942, dispatch 121, dope sheets, IWM.

18. http://www.colonialfilm.org.uk/node/5585, last accessed 18 January 2016.

19. British Paramount News (BPN) dope sheet, shipment 115, 'AVG Personalities', 7 February 1942, Shipment 116, IWM.

20. BPN, cameraman's dope sheet 22 Feb. 1942, shipments 122, 124, 126, 128; shipment 130, 23 February 1942, IWM.

21. BPN Issue 1173, 28 May 1942, NPA1173, IWM. Further details from 113 Squadron website http://113squadron.com/id117.htm, last accessed 18 January 2016. Although the film was passed by censors in Burma, it is interesting that the filming dates and identification of individual aircrew were not mentioned in the final newsreel. Although there was no regulation against naming RAF personnel in the press and media during the war, it does seem that there was a greater reluctance to name them in the Burma campaign, certainly greater than for the AVG pilots.

22. Some cameramen wrote brief summaries, but Maurice Ford was an example of someone who wrote very full and colourful dope sheets, which amounted to suggested commentaries for the future newsreel.

23. BPN dope sheet, shipment 106, 'Scenes in Bomb Damaged Rangoon', 28 January 1942, IWM.

24. BPN dope sheet, shipment 110, 'The Troops Arrive', 5 February 1942, IWM.

25. *Ibid*.

26. Nicholas Pronay, 'British Newsreels in the 1930s: 1. Audience and Producers', *History*, 56, 188, October 1971, p. 416.

27. BPN dope sheet, shipment 113, 'Burma Road Racket' 1–2 February 1942, IWM.

28. See Chapter Three for more details.

29. BPN dope sheet, shipment 113, 'Burma Road Racket', filmed 1–2 February 1942, IWM.

30. BPN Issue no. 1156, 'Burma Crisis', 30 March 1942, http://www.itnsource.com/en/shotlist/BHC_RTV/1942/03/30/BGX408200149/?s=Burma%20Road. See also BMN Issue 671, 12 April 1942,'Battle of Burma Communications', http://bufvc.ac.uk/newsonscreen/search/index.php/story/12217, last accessed 18 January 2016; Pathé Gazette, 'Aid for China-Burma Road', 13 April 1942; GBN, 13 April 1942, 'The Far East Front-India-Burma-China—the Battle of the Roads and railways'. The British Library of Information in New York monitored the showing of British material in American newsreels. It noted that the Burma Road film which was shown by all the newsreel companies was 'one of the finest and most stimulating newsreels for some time past.' Gullan to Darvall, 13 April 1942, INF1/568, ff.191–2, The National Archives, London (TNA).

31. BMN, Issue 671, 'Battle of Burma Communications', 12 April 1942, http://bufvc.ac.uk/newsonscreen/search/index.php/story/12217, last accessed 18 January 2016.

32. George Rodger, *Red Moon Rising*, London: Cresset Press, 1943, Chapter 3, 'Burma Railway'.
33. *Ibid*, p. 71. It seems likely that all film and photographs of the Kumaoni soldiers (in bush hats) are also reconstructions. Kumaon is part of present-day Uttarakhand state in India's North-East Himalayan frontier area.
34. Gerald Sanger, 'A News Reel Man's Conscience', *Sight and Sound*, 22 (summer 1941), cited in Nicholas Hiley and Luke McKernan, 'Reconstructing the News: British Newsreel Documentation and the British Universities Newsreel Project', *Film History*, 13 (2001), pp. 185–99. It is difficult to be absolutely certain about this issue and I am grateful for correspondence with the late Terry Gallacher who worked for British Movietone after the war and who remained unconvinced that this film is faked. Further written evidence of newsreel faking later in the Burma campaign is provided in an article by Alan Lawson, of S.E.A.C. British Film Unit in *The Cine-Technician* (May–June 1945), but this may be influenced by the rivalry between official film units and newsreel cameramen at a later stage of the war.
35. Tozer's film of this reconstruction of Indian troops advancing through Shwegyin was shown as 'Movietone's War Time News—Reported by Leslie Mitchell: Battle of Burma', BMN, issue 673A, 30 April 1942: http://bufvc.ac.uk/newsonscreen/search/index.php/story/12237, last accessed 18 January 2016. The alternative Pathé newsreel, 'Burma—Latest Pictures', Pathé Gazette, Issue 42/35, 30 April 1942, can be seen at http://bufvc.ac.uk/newsonscreen/search/index.php/story/99397, last accessed 18 January 2016. Gaumont British News, 'Allied Armies in Burma', 30 April 1942, BGU408210039, also listed the shot of the falling soldier although it is not included in the film clip on ITN Source.
36. 'British Troops Fight Rearguard Action Against Japanese Forces', ITN Source ref: BGX408220153
37. For a fuller version of the film of the Gloucester Regiment see the clip provided by courtesy of the IWM: BAY 253–6, 'The Front Line of Burma. Gloucesters in Action', http://www.youtube.com/watch?v=iJSYvx79krQ. This indicates that the film was taken much earlier in late March 1942. For full details see the Colonial Film synopsis http://www.colonialfilm.org.uk/node/5600, last accessed 18 January 2016.
38. BMN Issue 673A, 30 April 1942, 'Burma Fighting and Chiang Kai Sheks', http://bufvc.ac.uk/newsonscreen/search/index.php/story/12237, last accessed 18 January 2016.
39. BPN dope sheet, shipment 133, 28 February 1942, IWM.

40. http://bufvc.ac.uk/newsonscreen/search/index.php/story/12138, last accessed 18 January 2016.

41. BPN, shipment 114, 3 February 1942, 'Special, First Pictures of Burma's New Prime Minister', IWM.

42. 'BURMA/DEFENCE: Oilfields of Yenangyaung before capture', 4 May 1942, ITN Source ref: GX408220138, BPN, Issue 1166, http://bufvc. ac.uk/newsonscreen/search/index.php/story/38232, last accessed 18 January 2016.

43. R. Clarke, *With Alex at War: From the Irrawaddy to the Po 1941–1945*, Barnsley: Pen & Sword, 2000, p. 15, cited in J. Latimer, *Burma: The Forgotten War*, London: John Murray, 2004 p. 67, n. 57.

44. Commentary, 'The Far East Front', GBN, Issue 859, 30 March 1942. http://bufvc.ac.uk/newsonscreen/search/index.php/document/62623_commentary, last accessed 18 January 2016. Alec Tozer's film.

45. *Ibid.*

46. This is certainly the view put forward in the GBN, issue 874, 21 May 1942, 'Far East Front. Burma. Action in Tharrawaddy', http://bufvc. ac.uk/newsonscreen/search/index.php/document/62762_commentary, last accessed 18 January 2016.

47. 'Scorched Earth in Burma', GBN, Issue 879, 8 June 1942; http://bufvc.ac.uk/newsonscreen/search/index.php/document/62807_commentary, last accessed 18 January 2016. Tozer was to return to film the war in Burma in 1943 and in 1945. He was also one of the cameramen chosen to film the D-Day operations. He continued working for Movietone after the war and helped film the Coronation in 1953, http://bufvc.ac.uk/newsonscreen/search/index.php/person/932, last accessed 18 January 2016.

48. Alec Tozer, 'War Filming in the Far East', *The Journal of British Kinematograph Society*, 9, 1 (January–March 1946), pp. 19–21.

49. www.colonialfilm.org.uk/node/5591, last accessed 18 January 2016.

50. *Ibid.*

7. REPORTING THE BATTLES

1. W.G. Burchett, *Bombs Over Burma*, Melbourne: F.W. Cheshire, 1944, p. 18.

2. Roderick Macdonald, *Dawn Like Thunder*, London: Hodder & Stoughton, 1944, pp. 76–7.

3. *Ibid*, pp. 80–2.

4. *News Chronicle*, 3 February 1942, p. 1, contd. p. 4; 'JAPANESE TACTICS IN JUNGLE', *Sydney Morning Herald*, 4 February 1942, p. 9, http://nla.gov.au/nla.news-article17786459, last accessed 17 May 2016.

5. T.E. Healy, *Tourist Under Fire: The Journal of a War-Time Traveler*, New York: H. Holt & Co., 1945, p. 98.

6. See Fay Anderson and Richard Trembath (eds), *Witnesses to War: The History of Australian War Reporting*, Melbourne: Melbourne University Publishing, 2011, Chapter 4.

7. *News Chronicle*, 12 March 1942, p. 2.

8. *Ibid*, 13 March 1942, p. 1.

9. *Daily Mirror*, 13 March 1942, p. 1.

10. *Ibid*, p. 2.

11. Healy, *Tourist Under Fire*, p. 121. It is a pity that very few of the correspondents' wartime photos seem to have been made available to a wider audience.

12. *Daily Mirror*, 14 March 1942, p. 5.

13. *News Chronicle*, 25 March 1942, p. 2.

14. See Fay Anderson, 'Collective Silence: The Australian Press Reporting of Suffering during the World Wars', *Journalism History*, 440 (2014), pp. 148–57.

15. Healy, *Tourist Under Fire*, p. 137.

16. WO to GOC Burma, 13 March 1942, WO 106/3760, 'War Office: Directorate of Military Operations and Military Intelligence, and predecessors: Correspondence and Papers. War of 1939–1945. India. Burma: publicity and propaganda', TNA.

17. Churchill had earlier told the Middle East commander of his desire to see British units named wherever possible in reports. PM to Auchinleck, 12 December 1941, W0106/2662, f. 4a, TNA.

18. Healy, *Tourist Under Fire*, p. 139.

19. See Chapter Eight for more details. *Daily Mirror*, 14 March 1942, p. 2, 'Poor Leadership Betrayed Rangoon'.

20. Healy, *Tourist Under Fire*, p. 137; 'WHY RANGOON WAS ABANDONED', *The Sydney Morning Herald* (NSW: 1842–1954) 21 March 1942, p. 9, http://nla.gov.au/nla.news-article17793431, last accessed 11 November 2015.

21. *News Chronicle*, 14 March 1942, p. 1, 'Why the Japs Won in Burma'.

22. These pressures were common. See the telegram sent by the foreign editor of the *Daily Express* to their reporter Gordon Young in Delhi at this time, 'Opposition off wiping us exface earth Burma messages columns long crammed personal adventure blood sweat tears...' Gordon Young, *Outposts of Victory*, London: Hodder & Stoughton, 1943, pp. 28–9.

23. *News Chronicle*, 4 April 1942, p. 1, contd. pp. 4–5.

24. Healy, *Tourist Under Fire*, p. 146.

25. *News Chronicle*, 23 March 1942, p. 1. This claim would have been dis-

puted by the *Daily Express* correspondent, Wilfred Burchett, who had a meeting at Pyu, near Toungoo, with the Chinese commander of the 200ᵗʰ Division of the 5ᵗʰ Army, General Thai en Lai, on 19 March. Burchett, *Bombs Over Burma* pp. 140–1; *Daily Express*, 25 March 1942, p. 1.

26. See Alan K. Lathrop, 'The Employment of Chinese Nationalist Troops in the First Burma Campaign', *Journal of Southeast Asian Studies*, 12, 2 (September 1981), pp. 412–14.

27. 'EARLY CHECK TO ENEMY EXPECTED', *The Sydney Morning Herald* (NSW: 1842–1954) 25 March 1942, p. 9, http://nla.gov.au/nla.news-article17794000, last accessed 13 November 2015.

28. Field Marshal Sir John Dill believed that the complaints originated from Mr Currie, an American who administered Lend-Lease for China. Dill to General Sir Alan Brooke, Chief of Imperial General Staff, 22 January 1942, WO106/2662, f.81, TNA.

29. Churchill to Wavell, 23 January 1942, WO106/2689, TNA.

30. Due to an early error, the *Daily Express* continued to name him as Peter Burchett.

31. Burchett, *Bombs Over Burma*, pp. 27–9.

32. *Ibid*, pp. 64–5. Burchett talked in his autobiography of his frustration 'that 70,000 battle-hardened Chinese troops were kept out of Burma while the British had less than 12,000 men at the front, most of whom had never heard a shot fired'. W. Burchett *et al* (eds), *Memoirs of a Rebel Journalist: The Autobiography of Wilfred Burchett*, Sydney: UNSW Press, 2005, p. 170.

33. Burchett, *Bombs Over Burma*, pp. 75–6. The McDougall report on his visit to Chungking at the end of January 1941 cited Burchett's tele-gram as contributing to negative views of Britain in the Chinese cap-ital and showed the methods by which Burchett had tried to send his dispatch to the US: M/3/860, B153/40(Vi) 'War: propaganda: pub-licity in Chungking, China in view of anti-British feeling, 10 Feb.-12 May 1942', OIOC.

34. Burchett, *Bombs Over Burma*, p. 76.

35. *Ibid*, p. 77.

36. J. Belden, *Retreat with Stilwell*, New York: Alfred A. Knopf, 1943. p. 228.

37. *News Chronicle*, 13 April 1942, p. 4.

38. Also present was an Australian photographer provided by the Ministry of Information and then working for the SPRO in Burma, Reggie Edwards.

39. Belden, *Retreat with Stilwell*, p. 171.

40. C.L. Chennault, *Way of a Fighter, The Memoirs of C.L. Chennault*, R.B. Hotz (ed.) New York: Putnam's Sons, 1949, pp. 148–9, cited in

Jon Latimer, *Burma: The Forgotten War*, London: John Murray, 2005, p. 98.

41. *Daily Mail*, 30 April 1942, p. 4.

42. A. Wagg, *A Million Died! A Story of War in the Far East*, London: Nicholson & Watson, 1943, Chapter XI, 'The Battle of Yenangyaung' by Darrell Berrigan, p. 84.

43. Barbara Tuchman, *Sand Against the Wind: Stilwell and the American Experience in China 1941–45*, London: Futura, 1981, p. 230.

44. Burchett, *Bombs Over Burma*, p. 12.

45. Carol Dagg, 'Jack Belden', in Jeffery B. Cook (ed.), *Dictionary of Literary Biography*, vol. 364, *American World War Two Correspondents*, Detroit, MI: Bruccoli Layman, 2012, pp. 3–7; Gary G. Yerkey, *Still Time to Live: A Biography of Jack Belden*, Washington DC: GK Press, 2011.

46. Belden, *Retreat with Stilwell*, p. 157.

47. *Daily Mail*, 1 May 1942, p. 1, contd. p. 4; 4 May 1942, p. 1; *Life*, 12, 20, 18 May 1942.

48. J. Belden, *Still Time to Die*, New York: Harper, 1944.

49. *Daily Mail*, 5 May 1942, p. 1, 'Burma: Final Summing Up'.

50. Belden, *Retreat with Stilwell*, p. 165.

51. *Ibid*, p. 166.

52. *Ibid*, p. 58, Chapter VII, 'The People's War', is a superb analysis of the British failure to successfully engage with their Burmese subjects.

53. Belden, *Still Time to Die*, pp. 311–12.

54. Interestingly, Belden's style did not deter rival newspaper editors. Charles Foley, foreign editor of the *Daily Express*, tried his hardest to recruit Belden to report on India/Burma after the retreat was over and even asked Burma Office officials to help him. However, Belden declined and went to North Africa. Foley to A.H. Joyce, 4 November 1942, L/I/1/274, 'British Press: Daily Express', OIOC.

55. Belden, *Retreat with Stilwell*, p. 225.

56. George Rodger, *Red Moon Rising*, London: Cresset Press, 1943, p. 94.

57. Belden, *Retreat with Stilwell*, p. 227.

58. *Daily Mirror*, 31 March 1942, p. 1; *The Times* 31 March 1942, p. 4c.

59. *Daily Mirror*, 1 April 1942, p. 1.

60. *Ibid*, 10 April 1942, p. 2. Such stories were given more substance by the detailed report from an Indian soldier, Ranjit Singh of 7th Burma Rifles, of Japanese bayoneting of prisoners FO371/31811/F6408, TNA.

61. Cedric Salter, 'Nightmare in Paradise', in Gordon Young, *Outposts of Victory*, London: Hodder & Stoughton, 1943, pp. 69–70.

62. See, 'Drafts of Dorman-Smith's unfinished memoirs', MSS Eur 215/32b, f.170, OIOC. The War Office was also concerned about the

impression such stories were making in America and wanted more stories publicised of the activities of loyal Burmans, both troops and civilians. War Office to Wavell, repeated to General Alexander, 15 April 1942, WO 106/3760, TNA.

63. C. Bayly and T. Harper, *Forgotten Armies: Britain's Asian Empire & the War with Japan*, London: Penguin Books, 2005, p. 164.
64. Certainly the evidence listed in army intelligence of individual acts suspected of being perpetrated by fifth columnists compiled at the end of March 1942 looks pretty flimsy. Advance Burma HQ Army to C-in-C India, 28 February 1942, WO106/2662, f.184, TNA.
65. Bayly and Harper, *Forgotten Armies*, p. 171.
66. *Ibid*, p. 172.
67. Salter, 'Nightmare in Paradise', pp. 69–70.
68. Rodger, *Red Moon Rising*, p. 75.
69. Wavell Dispatch, WO106/2666, p. 12, TNA.

8. JOURNALISTS AND THE EVACUATION OF CIVILIANS FROM BURMA, 1942

1. The best estimate for the number of Indians who died in the evacuation is the government figure of 80,000.
2. For Gallagher's description of his contact with the refugees and the dangers they faced from attacks by Burmese, see O.D. Gallagher, *Retreat in the East*, London: Harrap, 1942, pp. 175–7.
3. Michael D. Leigh, *The Evacuation of Civilians from Burma: Analysing the 1942 Colonial Disaster*, London, Bloomsbury, London, 2014, p. 130.
4. *Ibid*, p. 123.
5. See Appendix 1 for details of how and when individual reporters left Burma.
6. A recent popular account, but one based on good research is Felicity Goodall, *Exodus Burma: The British Escape Through the Jungles of Death 1942*, Stroud: History Press, 2011. A good deal of original material on the evacuation of Britons from India has been collected by the Anglo-Burmese Library: http://www.angloburmeselibrary.com/, last accessed 18 January 2016. Leigh, *The Evacuation of Civilians*, makes a more conservative estimate of the number of civilian evacuees than some contemporary estimates but he believes that the death toll might well be higher than the government was willing to allow. He admits that we may never have an accurate number of evacuees and lives lost.
8. *Ibid*, p. 50; Hugh Tinker, 'A Forgotten Long March: The Indian Exodus from Burma', *Journal of Southeast Asian Studies*, 6, 1 (1975), pp. 1–15.
9. Tinker, 'A Forgotten Long March', p. 4.
10. Leigh, *The Evacuation of Civilians*, p. 37.

11. Dorman-Smith set out his defence of de Graaff-Hunter's critique of the Marsh Plan in his report of November 1943, 'Report on the Burma Campaign 1941–1942', Simla: Government of India Press, Part VI, Chapter 4, MSS Eur E215/28 OIOC.

12. *Ibid*, p. 8.

13. Leigh, *The Evacuation of Civilians*, p. 50.

14. 'Movietone's War Time News—Reported by Leslie Mitchell: On the Burma Front', British Movietone News (BMN), issue No. 669, 30 March 1942, http://bufvc.ac.uk/newsonscreen/search/index.php/story/12196, last accessed 18 January 2016.

15. *Daily Express*, 24 December 1941, p. 4.

16. O.D. Gallagher, *Retreat in the East*, London: Harrap, 1942, pp. 76–7.

17. *Daily Mirror*, 14 March 1942, p. 2.

18. T.E. Healy, *Tourist Under Fire: The Journal of a War-Time Traveler*, New York: H. Holt & Co, 1945, p. 137.

19. *Ibid*, Chapter 12.

20. *Chicago Daily News*, 3 March 1942, p. 6.

21. Leigh is also critical of the tendency of reporters to treat the Indian refugees as an undifferentiated mass. See *The Evacuation of Civilians*, p. 54.

22. 'HALF A MILLION FLEEING INDIANS', *The Sydney Morning Herald* (NSW: 1842–1954) 18 March 1942: 9. Web. 16 July 2015, http://nla.gov.au/nla.news-article17792850, last accessed 16 January 2016.

23. Healy, *Tourist Under Fire*, p. 116.

24. Alfred and Valerie Wagg, *A Million Died*, Bombay: Thacker & Co., Ltd., 1945. '"A Million Died!" by A. Wagg, General File re. Publication in UK', M/3/1353, OIOC. The chorus boy epithet perhaps derived from the time de Graaff-Hunter had previously spent in Hollywood.

25. Wagg, *A Million Died!*, p. 182.

26. Some 800 high-explosive bombs had been dropped on Rangoon in the Japanese attacks on 23 and 25 December. See Leigh, *The Evacuation of Civilians*, p. 45.

27. Wagg, *A Million Died!*, p. 185.

28. Leigh, *The Evacuation of Civilians*, p. 43.

29. O.D. Gallagher's report, *Daily Express*, 5 January 1942, p. 1, contd. back page.

30. British Movietone News, issue 662, 9 February 1942, 'Rangoon Resolute'.

31. W.G. Burchett, *Bombs Over Burma*, Melbourne: F.W. Cheshire, 1944. pp. 127–8.

32. *Chicago Tribune*, 3 March 1942, p. 5.

33. Available online: http://cbi-theater.home.comcast.net/~cbi-theater/life060842/life060842.html, last accessed 3 December 2015.

34. George Rodger, *Red Moon Rising*. London: Cresset Press, 1943, pp. 62–4.

35. See the photos in *Ibid*, pp. 46, 55, 58.

36. *Ibid*, p. 64.

37. 'Report on the Work of Civil Evacuation and Welfare in Burma from 1 December 1941 to 31 May 1942' by J.S. Vorley Esq., CBE, IFS, 'Evacuation of Indians and Europeans from Burma', p. 48, f.120, M/3/955, OIOC.

38. 'British Troops Fight Rearguard Action Against Japanese Forces', British Paramount News, ITN Source ref: BGX408220153, 28 May 1942 'Burma'; British Paramount News, issue no. 1173, 28 May 1942, http://bufvc.ac.uk/newsonscreen/search/index.php/story/38266, last accessed 18 January 2016.

39. Ministry of Information, Minutes of War News Film Sub-Committee held on Monday June 15, 1942, minute 390. 'Refugees in India' (386) M/3/955, f. 299, OIOC.

40. *News Chronicle*, p. 1, contd. p. 4.

41. *The Times*, 14 April 1942, p. 8; also shown in the *News Chronicle* of the same date.

42. Government of India, Home Department, to Secretary of State for India, 1 May 1942, M/3/955, f.396, OIOC.

43. *The Times*, 8 May 1942, p. 3, 'Refugees from Burma', 'Overseas Publicity Telegram from Ministry of Information to its representatives abroad, 5 May 1942, M/3/955, f. 380, OIOC. Alfred Wagg also endorsed this view in his censored dispatch to the *Daily Express*, Wagg dispatch to Allied Newspapers, 2 July 1942, M/3/955, ff. 287–8, OIOC.

44. Leland Stowe, *They Shall Not Sleep*, New York: Alfred A. Knopf, 1944, pp. 131–2.

45. *News Chronicle*, 13 May 1942, p. 1, contd. p. 4. Interestingly, the *Spectator* magazine, 14 May 1942, pointed out that whereas Dan De Luce's report emphasised his own heroic role in the exit (*Daily Mail*, 13 May, p. 4), Munday more modestly told of the joint exploits of all three reporters. 'I had mud-sores, Berrigan malaria and De Luce alone was sound when arriving in India.' This was an heroic story of jour- nalistic endeavour that could be published quite quickly and was fol- lowed by analysis from India of the causes of the defeat. William Munday, 'Why We Were Beaten in Burma', *News Chronicle*, 14 May, p. 2.

46. Evidence of this can be seen from the fact that Rodger considered at one point picking up one or two European female evacuees as he thought this would make a better story. See Burchett, *Bombs over Burma*, p. 193.

47. According to Cornelius North, the forest officer who was mostly responsible for organising it. Vorley estimated 20–30,000. See J.S. and H.M. Vorley, *The Road from Mandalay*, Windsor: Wilton 65, 2002, p. 123.
48. Burchett, *Bombs over Burma*, p. 203.
49. Rodger, *Red Moon Rising*, p. 126.
50. J. Belden, *Retreat with Stilwell*, New York: Alfred A. Knopf, 1943.
51. *Ibid*, pp. 275–6.
52. Barbara W. Tuchman, *Sand Against the Wind: Stilwell and the American Experience in China, 1911–45*, London: Futura, 1981, p. 376.
53. *Ibid*, p. 382.
54. https://books.google.co.uk/books?id=sk4EAAAAMBAJ&pg=PA26&source=gbs_toc_r&cad=2#v=onepage&q&f=false, last accessed 15 January 2016.
55. Belden, *Retreat with Stilwell*, pp. 365–6. It is an interesting indication of standard war correspondent equipment that, despite all those on the walkout being commanded to only carry minimal personal belongings, Belden kept hold of his beloved typewriter for half of the journey, and his camera for all of it.
56. *Ibid*, p. 319.

9. MAKING THE GOVERNMENT OF BURMA'S CASE

1. F.S.V. Donnison MSS, Eur B357, f.374, OIOC.
2. This was a filmed interview with Dorman-Smith made by the South East Asia Command (SEAC) Photo Unit on 28 October 1944 and obviously aimed at an American audience, MWY206, IWM.
3. 'Mr T.L. Hughes' address on the Burma campaign to the Central Asian Society', WO106/2693, f.14, TNA.
4. The relevant parts of Gallagher's book *Retreat in the East*, London: Harrap, 1942, are pp. 174–5 and the photographs facing pp. 144–5.
5. T.L. Hughes, 'The Campaign in and Evacuation of Burma', *JRCAS*, 1, 1, 1944, pp. 80–93. It was also published in an altered form to take account of War Office objections. See T.L. Hughes, *What Happened in Burma*, London: Brittain Publishing, 1944. For the War Office comments see 'Article on Burma by Mr Hughes, Private Secretary to the Governor of Burma, Dec. 1941 to May 1942', WO106/2693, TNA.
6. Sir Reginald Dorman-Smith, 'Civil Government under Invasion Conditions', *Journal of the United Service Institution of India*, lxxiii, 1943, pp. 240–52.
7. *Ibid*, p. 251.
8. J. Belden, *Retreat with Stilwell*, New York: Alfred. A. Knopf, 1943, pp. 246–9.

9. George Appleton, Project Canterbury, *The War and After Burma*, http://anglicanhistory.org/asia/burma/appleton1946/, last accessed 4 November 2015.

10. J.L. Christian review of O.D Gallagher, *Action in the East*, New York: Doubleday-Doran, 1942 in *Journal of Asian Studies*, 3, 1 (November 1943) XVII, xiii, pp. 87–8.

11. John Leroy Christian, *Burma and the Japanese Invader*, Bombay: Thacker & Co, 1945, p. 349.

12. J.S. and H.M. Vorley, *The Road from Mandalay*, Windsor: Wilton 65, 2002, pp. 53–65.

13. *Ibid*, p. 24. It has not been possible to verify this story. His reflections on his short time in Rangoon can be found in Richard Busvine, *Gullible Travels*, Constable: London, 1945, Chapter 18.

14. Amery to Linlithgow, 16 January 1942, M/3/857, OIOC.

15. L.M. Gander, *Long Road to Leros*, London: Macdonald & Co., 1945, pp. 114–5.

16. This was to be *A Million Died! A Story of War in the Far East*, London: Nicholson & Watson, 1943.

17. Jehu later admitted to F.S.V. Donnison that he had been told to conduct a campaign to put the blame on the civil authorities. See F.S.V. Donnison MSS, Eur B358/f. 374, OIOC.

18. See the enclosure to Walton to Wagg, 24 February 1943, M/3/1353, OIOC. The under-secretary commented that two Burma Office officials, '…Walton and Clague have become part, if not primary, authors of the book. I don't know what the title will be, but I am sure it ought to be "by Walton-Wagg".' Sir David Monteath to Dorman-Smith, 12 March 1943, Dorman-Smith MSS, Eur E215/3, OIOC.

19. See Walton to Hughes, 2 July 1943, M/3/1354, OIOC; '"A Million Died" by A. Wagg: Question of title, publication arrangements etc.', Amery to Dorman-Smith, 14 May 1943, *Ibid*; T.L. Hughes to Walton, 14 June 1943, *Ibid*.

20. Wallace MSS, Eur 338/4, OIOC, 'Notes and correspondence kept by Wallace when Secretary to the Defence Dept., Government of Burma, Simla, mainly relating to conditions in Burma 1939–42, and dealing with war damage claims. 1942–7'. Review of Wagg's *A Million Died!* in *Statesman* (Delhi edition) 14 November 1943, f.69, enclosure to 'Extract from Mr Wallace's twelfth fortnightly letter dated 15 Nov. 1943 to Mr Johnston of Burma Office', *Ibid*, OIOC.

21. Maurice Collis, *Last and First in Burma (1941–1948)*, London: Faber & Faber, 1956.

22. *Ibid*, p. 88.

EPILOGUE AND CONCLUSION

1. Though Alec Tozer also went to China to film Chinese aircrew being trained. He then filmed part of the first Arakan campaign in Burma in the spring of 1943. His newsreel was typically upbeat for a campaign that ended disastrously. Tozer did at least have the satisfaction of being in Burma in 1945 for the recapture of Mandalay and the successful advance of the 14th Army towards Rangoon.

2. L.M. Gander, *Long Road to Leros*, London: Macdonald & Co., 1945, p. 93. Gander mentions meeting up with Gallagher, Hodson, Thompson, Wagg and Salter of the ex-Burma correspondents.

3. *Ibid*, pp. 123–4. Actually, Gander's dispatch to the *Daily Telegraph* on 22 May was, by implication, critical of the civil administration and may have been influenced by his interview with General Alexander. However, the article is intended as advice to the Government of India on how to avoid the civilian panic caused by Japanese bombing in Rangoon, which had led to the collapse of vital services. *Daily Telegraph*, 22 May, p. 3, 'Nehru's Film Appeal to Indians to "Stay Put"—Lessons of Burma Invasion'.

4. Leland Stowe, *They Shall Not Sleep*, New York: Alfred A. Knopf, 1944, pp. 169–75.

5. *Ibid*, pp. 182–3.

6. *Ibid*, p. 203.

7. Gander, *Long Road*, p. 153.

8. Anne Sebba, *Battling for News: The Rise of the Woman Reporter*, London: Hodder & Stoughton, 1994, p. 153.

9. Alan Moorehead, *Desert War Trilogy*, London: Aurum Press, 2009 (first published London: Hamish Hamilton, 1944), p. 285.

10. 'Hey, Soldier, I'm wounded', *Life*, 27 September 1943, pp. 25–35.

11. See *Life*, 20 March 1944, 'Sequel to Salerno', pp. 100–6 about his feelings for an American nurse in an army hospital in North Africa.

12. The others were Stewart Sale of Reuters and Alexander Austin of the *Daily Herald*.

13. Robert W. Desmond, *Tides of War: World News Reporting 1940–1945*, Iowa City, IA: University of Iowa Press, 1984, p. 453.

14. *Ibid*.

15. However, Gallagher did not see active service as he was recruited to the Special Operations Executive working in the Middle East. Ironically, he fell out with his superiors there too. See his SOE personnel file, HS 9/555/2, TNA.

16. Fay Anderson, 'Collective Silence: The Australian Press Reporting of Suffering during the World Wars', *Journalism History*, 440, 3 (Fall 2014), p. 153.

17. George Rodger, *Red Moon Rising*, London: Cresset Press, 1943, pp. 92–3.
18. Carole Naggar, *George Rodger: An Adventure in Photography, 1908–1995*, Syracuse, NY: Syracuse University Press, 2003, p. 93.
19. http://www.georgerodgerphotographs.com/biography/, last accessed 4 June 2015.
20. Stowe, *They Shall Not Sleep*, pp. 158–9.
21. *Ibid*, pp. 331 & 351.
22. J. Belden, *Still Time to Die*, New York: Harper, 1944, p. 319.
23. *Ibid*, p. 322.
24. For a good summary of Burchett's career see Tom Heenan, 'Burchett, Wilfred Graham (1911–1983)', *Australian Dictionary of Biography*, National Centre of Biography, Australian National University, http://adb.anu.edu.au/biography/burchett-wilfred-graham-12265/text22015, published first in hardcopy 2007, last accessed 5 June 2015. The ideological battle over Burchett's post-war communist allegiances is well analysed in Miller, Jamie, 'Once Were Warriors: Wilfred Burchett, Robert Manne and the Forgotten History War', *The New Critic*, IAS, University of Western Australia, 8 (September 2008): http://www.ias.uwa.edu.au/new-critic/eight/Miller, last accessed 10 February 2016.
25. Phillip Knightley, 'Cracking the Jap: Burchett on World War Two', in Ben Kiernan (ed.), *Burchett: Reporting the Other Side of the World 1939–1983*, London: Quartet Books, 1986, pp. 3–12.
26. Apparently *Wingate Adventure* had a circulation of over 20,000 copies, according to Burchett's pamphlet, *War-Mongers Unmasked, no. 1: History of Cold War in Germany*, Melbourne: World Unity Publications, 1950, in KV 2/3960, Wilfred G. Burchett, Security Services File, 16 May 1938–20 August 1951, TNA. Burchett was supporting a wife and young son from his first marriage and was known to be short of money.
27. 'The Atomic Plague', *Daily Express*, 5 September 1945, reprinted in George Burchett & Nick Shimmin (eds) *Rebel Journalism: The Writings of Wilfred Burchett*. Cambridge: Cambridge University Press, 2007, pp. 2–5.
28. For Burchett's views in the Korean War see Steven Casey, 'Wilfred Burchett and the UN Command's Media Relations during the Korean War, 1951–52', *Journal of Military History*, 74,3 (2010), pp. 821–45.
29. Wilfred Burchett, *Democracy with a Tommygun*, Melbourne: F.W. Cheshire, 1946.
30. Hamilton Fyfe, *The War Illustrated*, 2 October 1942, vol. 6, p. 243.

BIBLIOGRAPHY

MANUSCRIPT SOURCES

Oriental and India Office Collection, British Library

Arnold MSS Eur F145/6
Donnison MSS Eur B357
Dorman-Smith MSS Eur E215: including Diaries of Lady Dorman-Smith and
    papers of Major E.T. Cook
Maybury MSS Eur D1080
Potter MSS Eur C414
Collis MSS Eur D1034
Clague MSS Eur E252
Wallace MSS Eur E338

OFFICIAL PAPERS

Oriental and India Office Collection, British Library

L/P&J/12 Political intelligence files

Burma Office Papers

M/3: Burma Office Records
M/8: Burma Office Miscellaneous Records
Information Department: L/I/1

The National Archives, Kew, London

CAB44 Committee of Imperial Defence, Historical Branch and Cabinet
    Office, Historical Section: War Histories: Draft Chapters and Narratives,
    Military
FO371 Foreign Office: Political Departments: General Correspondence from
    1906–1966

BIBLIOGRAPHY

FO643/4 Burma Office, Burma Secretariat, and Foreign Office, Embassy, Rangoon, Burma: General Correspondence

FO930 Ministry of Information and Foreign Office: Foreign Publicity Files

HS1 Special Operations Executive: Far East: Registered Files

INF 1 Ministry of Information: Files of Correspondence

WO33 War Office: Reports, Memoranda and Papers (O and A Series)

WO106 War Office: Directorate of Military Operations and Military Intelligence

WO172 War Office: British and Allied Land Forces, South East Asia: War Diaries, Second World War

WO203 War Office: South East Asia Command: Military Headquarters Papers, Second World War

W0208 War Office: Directorate of Military Operations and Intelligence, and Directorate of Military Intelligence; Ministry of Defence, Defence Intelligence Staff: Files

Imperial War Museum, London

Photographic Department

George Rodger Photos provided for Ministry of Information. Catalogued under James Jarché collection

Film Department

MW 206: Interview with Sir Reginald Dorman-Smith, 28 October 1944, by an American officer of South East Asia Command.

British Paramount News: Newsreels and Dope Sheets

Interview, recorded with live sound, given by Sir Reginald Dorman-Smith, Governor-in-Exile of Burma

British Film Institute, London

Minute Books of the Newsreel Association of Great Britain

British Universities Film and Video

News on Screen Newsreel Database and Associated film clips and supporting documents; biographical information on cameramen

Wisconsin Historical Society, Madison, WI, US

Leland Stowe MSS, notebooks December 1941 to March 1942

RECORDINGS

Recording of Interview with George Rodger, 1992, OIOC, British Library

BIBLIOGRAPHY

NEWSREELS

British Universities Film and Video Council database, News on Screen, gives information including documentation, dope sheets and links to Movietone and Pathé newsreels online
British Movietone News, online at www.movietone.com
British Paramount News: film and dope sheets at Imperial War Museum
Pathé Gazette: online at www.britishpathe.com

NEWSPAPERS AND MAGAZINES (via Newsroom at British Library unless otherwise stated)

Chicago Daily News
Daily Express
Daily Herald
Daily Mail
Daily Mirror
Daily Sketch
Daily Telegraph
Illustrated (magazine)
Illustrated Weekly of India
Life (magazine)
Manchester Guardian
News Chronicle
Newspaper World
New York Herald Tribune
Observer
Picture Post (magazine)
Sydney Morning Herald (via http://trove.nla.gov.au/, National Library of Australia, for this and other Australian newspapers)
Statesman (Calcutta)
Sunday Express
The Sunday Times
The Times
War Illustrated (magazine)

INTERVIEWS

Mrs Jinx Rodger; Ms Sarah de Graaff Hunter; Mr Anthony Foucar

BOOKS AND ARTICLES

Allen, L., *Burma: The Longest War 1941–1945*, London: Phoenix Press, 2000.
Anderson, Fay, 'Collective Silence: The Australian Press Reporting of Suffering during the World Wars', *Journalism History* 440, 3 (Fall 2014), pp. 148–57.

BIBLIOGRAPHY

Anderson, Fay and Richard Trembath (eds), *Witnesses to War: The History of Australian War Reporting*, Melbourne: Melbourne University Publishing, 2011.

Appleton, George, Project Canterbury, *The War and After Burma*, http://anglicanhistory.org/asia/burma/appleton1946/, accessed 4 November 2015.

Baughman, James L., *Henry R, Luce and the Rise of the American News Media*, Baltimore, MD: Johns Hopkins Press, 2001.

Bayly, Christopher and Tim Harper, *Forgotten Armies: Britain's Asian Empire & the War with Japan*, London: Penguin Books, 2005.

Belden, Jack, *Retreat with Stilwell*, New York: Alfred A. Knopf, 1943.

——, *Still Time to Die*, New York: Harper, 1944.

Brinkley, Alan, *The Publisher: Henry Luce and His American Century*, New York: Alfred A. Knopf, 2010.

Brown, Cecil, *Suez to Singapore*, New York: Random House, 1942.

Burchett, George and Nick Shimmin (eds), *Rebel Journalism: The Writings of Wilfred Burchett*, Cambridge: Cambridge University Press, 2007.

——, *Memoirs of a Rebel Journalist: The Autobiography of Wilfred Burchett*, New South Publishing, 2006.

Burchett, W.G., *Bombs Over Burma*, Melbourne: F. W. Cheshire, 1944.

——, *Wingate Adventure*, Melbourne: F. W. Cheshire, 1944.

——, *Democracy with a Tommygun*, Melbourne: F. W. Cheshire, 1946.

Burgess, Pat, *Warco: Australian Reporters at War*, Richmond, Victoria: William Heinemann Australia, 1986.

Cady, John F.A., *History of Modern Burma*, Ithaca, NY: Cornell University Press, 1958.

Callahan, Raymond, *Burma, 1942–1945*, London: Davis-Poynter, 1978.

Carruthers, Susan L., *The Media at War: Communication and Conflict in the Twentieth Century*, London: Macmillan, 2000.

Casey, Steven, 'Reporting from the Battlefield: Censorship and Journalism', in Bosworth, Richard and Maiolo, Joseph (eds), *The Cambridge History of the Second World War*, vol. 2, Cambridge: Cambridge University Press, 2015, pp. 117–38.

——, 'Wilfred Burchett and the UN Command's Media Relations during the Korean War, 1951–52', *Journal of Military History*, 74, 3 (2010), pp. 821–45.

Charney, Michael W., *History of Modern Burma*, Cambridge: Cambridge University Press, 2009.

Chennault, C.L. and R. B. Hotz (eds), *Way of a Fighter: The Memoirs of C. L. Chennault*, New York: Putnam's Sons, 1949.

Choi, Suhi. 'The Repertoire, Not the Archive: The 1950 *Life* and *Time*'s Coverage of the Korean War', *Media, War and Conflict*, 8, 2 (August 2015): pp. 264–80.

BIBLIOGRAPHY

Christian, J.L., review of O.D Gallagher, *Action in the East*, *Journal of Asian Studies*, 3, 1 (November 1943) XVII, xiii, pp 87–8.

Clarke, Rupert, *With Alex at War: From the Irrawaddy to the Po, 1941–1945*, Barnsley: Pen & Sword, 2000.

Coatney, Caryn, 'From Burma Battles to "The Bright Lights of Brisbane". How an Australian Wartime Prime Minister Won, Lost and Recaptured American Journalists' Support, 1941 to 1945', *Journalism History*, 40, 4 (winter 2015), pp. 229–39.

Collier, Richard, *The Warcos: The War Correspondents of World War Two*, London: Weidenfeld & Nicholson, 1989.

Collis, Maurice, *Last and First in Burma (1941–1948)*, London: Faber & Faber, 1956.

Conboy, Martin (ed.), *How Journalism Uses History*, London: Routledge, 2012.

Curie, Eve, *Journey Among Warriors*, London: Heinemann, 1943.

Desmond, Robert W., *Tides of War: World News Reporting 1940–1945*, Iowa City, IA: University of Iowa Press, 1984.

Donnison, David, *Last of the Guardians: A Story of Burma, Britain and a Family*, Newtown: Superscript, 2005.

Donnison, F.S.V., *British Military Administration in the Far East, 1943–46*, London: HMSO, 1956.

———, *Burma*, London: Ernest Benn, 1970.

Dorman-Smith, Sir Reginald, 'Civil Government under Invasion Conditions', *Journal of the United Service Institution of India*, lxxiii (1943), pp. 240–52.

Dorn, Frank, *Walkout: With Stilwell in Burma*, New York: T.Y. Crowell, 1971.

Doss, Erica (ed.), *Looking at Life Magazine*, Washington DC: Smithsonian Institution Press, 2001.

Draper, Alfred, *Dawns Like Thunder: Retreat from Burma, 1942*, Barnsley: Pen & Sword, 1987.

Dunlop, Graham, *Military Economics, Culture and Logistics in the Burma Campaign, 1942–1945*, London: Pickering & Chatto, 2009.

Eldridge, Fred, *Wrath in Burma: The Uncensored Story of General Stilwell and International Maneuvers in the Far East*, New York: Doubleday, 1946.

Evans, Geoffrey and Anthony Brett James, *Imphal: A Flower on Lofty Height*, London: Macmillan, 1962.

Fitzpatrick, Captain Gerald, *Chinese Save Brits—in Burma (Battle of Yenangyaung)*, Fitzpatrick Publishing, 2013.

Ford, Daniel, *Flying Tigers: Claire Chennault and His American Volunteers, 1941–1942*, New York: Harper Collins/Smithsonian Books, 2007.

Foucar, E.C.V., *I Lived in Burma*, London: Dennis Dobson, 1956.

Fowler, William, *We Gave Our Today: Burma 1941–1945*, London: Weidenfeld & Nicholson, 2009.

Furnivall, J.S., *Colonial Policy and Practice: A Comparative Study of Burma and the Netherlands India*, Cambridge: Cambridge University Press, 1948.

BIBLIOGRAPHY

Gallagher, O'Dowd, *Action in the East*, New York: Doubleday-Doran, 1943.
———, *Retreat in the East*, London: Harrap, 1942.
Gander, Leonard Marsland, *Long Road to Leros*, London: Macdonald & Co., 1945.
Gladstone, Kay, 'The AFPU: The Origins of British Army Combat Filming during the Second World War', *Film History*, 14 (2002): pp. 316–31.
Goodall, Felicity, *Exodus Burma: The British Escape Through the Jungles of Death 1942*, Stroud: History Press, 2011.
Grant, Ian Lyall and Kazuo Tamayama, *Burma 1942: The Japanese Invasion; Both Sides Tell the Story of a Savage Jungle War*, Chichester: Zampi Press, 1999.
Griffiths, Dennis (ed.), *The Encyclopedia of the British Press 1422–1992*, London: Macmillan, 1992.
Gunnison, Royal Arch, *So Sorry, No Peace*, New York: Viking Press, 1944.
Hack, Karl and Kevin Blackburn, *Did Singapore Have to Fall? Churchill and the Impregnable Fortress*, London: Routledge Curzon, 2004.
Hamilton, John Maxwell, *Journalism's Roving Eye: A History of American Foreign Reporting*, Baton Rouge, LA: Louisiana State University Press, 2009.
Hamilton, John Maxwell and Regina G. Lawrence, *Foreign Correspondence*, London: Routledge, 2012.
Hastings, Max, *All Hell Let Loose: The World at War 1939–1945*, London: Harper Press, 2011.
Healy, Thomas Edward, *Tourist Under Fire: The Journal of a War-Time Traveler*, New York: H. Holt & Co., 1945.
Heenan, Tom, *From Traveller to Traitor: The Life of Wilfred Burchett*, Melbourne: Academic Monographs, 2006.
Hemingway, Kenneth, *Wings Over Burma*, London: Quality Press, 1944.
Hendershot, Clarence, 'Role of the Shan States in the Japanese Conquest of Burma', *The Far Eastern Quarterly*, 2, 3 (May 1943), pp. 253–8.
Herzstein, Robert E., *Henry R. Luce, Time, and the American Crusade in Asia*, Cambridge: Cambridge University Press, 2005.
Higashi, Sumiko, 'Melodrama, Realism and Race: World War Two Newsreels and Propaganda Film'. *Cinema Journal*, 37, 3 (spring 1998), pp. 38–61.
Hillenbrand, Martin J., *Fragments of Our Time: Memoirs of a Diplomat*, Athens, GA: University of Georgia Press, 1998.
Holmes, Richard, *The World at War: The Landmark Oral History from the Previously Unpublished Archives*, London: Ebury Press, 2007.
Hood, Jean, *War Correspondent: Reporting Under Fire Since 1850*, London: Conway/IWM, 2011.
Horne, Gerald, *Race War: White Supremacy and the Japanese attack on the British Empire*, New York: NYU Press, 2003.
Hughes, T.L., 'The Campaign in and Evacuation of Burma', *Journal of Royal Central Asian Society* 1, 1, (1944), pp. 80–93.

BIBLIOGRAPHY

————, *What Happened in Burma*, London: Brittain Publishing, 1944.

Hynes, Samuel *et al* (eds), *Reporting World War II: Part 1: American Journalism, 1938–1944*, New York: Library of America, 1995.

Jackson, Ashley, *The British Empire and the Second World War*, London: Hambledon Continuum, 2006.

Jeffreys, Alan, *The British Army in the Far East 1941–1945*, Oxford: Osprey, 2005.

Keane, Fergal, *Road of Bones: The Siege of Kohima 1944*, London: Harper Press, 2010.

Khan, Yasmin, *The Raj at War: A People's History of India's Second World War*, London: Bodley Head, 2015.

Kiernan, Ben (ed.), *Burchett: Reporting the Other Side of the World 1939–1983*, London: Quartet Books, 1986.

Kirby, Major-General S. Woodburn, *The War Against Japan: Vol. II, India's Most Dangerous Hour*, Uckfield: Naval & Military Press, 2004.

Knightley, Phillip, *The First Casualty: The War Correspondent as Hero, Propagandist and Myth-Maker from Crimea to Iraq*, Baltimore, MA: Johns Hopkins University Press, 3rd ed., 2004.

————, 'Cracking the Jap: Burchett on World War Two', in Kiernan, Ben (ed.), *Burchett: Reporting the Other Side of the World 1939–1983*, London: Quartet Books, 1986, pp. 3–12.

Knott, Richard, *The Trio: Three War Correspondents of World War Two*, Stroud: History Press, 2015.

Korte, Barbara, *Represented Reporters: Images of War Correspondents in Memoirs and Fiction*, New Brunswick, NJ: Transaction Publications, 2009.

Kupfer, Charles, *Indomitable Will: Turning Defeat into Victory from Pearl Harbor to Midway*, London: Continuum, 2012.

Kwarteng, Kwasi, *Ghosts of Empire: Britain's Legacies in the Modern World*, London: Bloomsbury, 2010.

Lathrop, Alan K., 'The Employment of Chinese Nationalist Troops in the First Burma Campaign', *Journal of South-East Asian Studies* 12, 2 (September 1981), pp. 403–42.

Latimer, J., *Burma: The Forgotten War*, London: John Murray, 2004.

Leigh, Michael D., *The Evacuation of Civilians from Burma: Analysing the 1942 Colonial Disaster*, London: Bloomsbury Academic, 2014.

Lunt, James, '"A Hell of a Licking": Some Reflections on the Retreat from Burma, December 1941–May 1942'. *RUSI Journal* 130, 5 (1985), pp. 55–8.

————, *A Hell of a Licking: The Retreat from Burma 1941–2*, London: Collins, 1986.

Lyman, Robert, *Slim, Master of War: Burma and the Birth of Modern Warfare*, London: Constable & Robinson, 2004.

————, *The Generals: From Defeat to Victory, Leadership in Asia, 1941–45*, London: Constable, 2008.

Macdonald, Roderick, *Dawn Like Thunder*, London: Hodder & Stoughton, 1944.

MacKinnon, Stephen R. and Oris Friesen, *China Reporting: An Oral History of American Journalism in the 1930s and 1940s*, Los Angeles, CA: UCLA, 1990.

Mains, Tony, *The Retreat from Burma: An Intelligence Officer's Personal Story*, London: Foulsham, 1973.

Mander, Mary S., *Pen and Sword: American War Correspondents, 1898–1975*, Urbana, IL: University of Illinois Press, 2010.

Mankekar, D.R., *Leaves from a War Reporter's Diary*, New Delhi: Vikas, 1977.

Marshall, Andrew, *The Trouser People: Burma in the Shadows of Empire*, Bangkok: River Books, 2012.

Marston, Daniel P., *The Indian Army and the End of the Raj*, Cambridge: Cambridge University Press, 2014.

————, *Phoenix from the Ashes*, Westport, CT: Praeger, 2003.

Marston, Daniel P. and Chandar Sundaram, *A Military History of India and South Asia: From the East India Company to the Nuclear Era*, Bloomington, IN: Indiana University Press, 2008.

Maslowski, Peter, *The American Military Photographers of World War II*, New York: The Free Press, 1993.

Matthews, Herbert L., *A World in Revolution: A Newspaperman's Memoir*, New York: Charles Scribner's Sons, 1971.

Maw, Ba, *Breakthrough in Burma: Memoirs of a Revolution, 1939–1946*, New Haven, CT: Yale University Press, 1968.

Maybury, Maurice, *Heaven-Born in Burma Vol. 2: Flight of the Heaven-Born*. Castle Cary: Folio Hadspen, 1985.

McEwen, Yvonne and Fiona A. Fisken (eds), *War, Journalism and History: War Correspondents in the Two World Wars*, Oxford: Peter Lang, 2012.

McKernan, Luke, 'Newsreels: Form and Function', in Howells, R. and Matson, W., *Using Visual Evidence*, Maidenhead: Open University Press, 2009, pp. 95–106.

McKerns, Joseph P. (ed.), *Biographical Dictionary of American Journalism*, New York: Greenwoods Press, 1989.

Mclynn, F., *The Burma Campaign: Disaster into Triumph, 1942–45*, New Haven, CT: Yale University Press, 2011.

Messinger, Gary S., *The Battle for the Mind: War and Peace in the Era of Mass Communication*, Amherst, MA: University of Massachusetts Press, 2011.

Millem, Fred, 'Rangoon Battalion' [letters from India about his role in the Rangoon Battalion, in eleven parts] *BBC People's War—WW2*, Archive of World War Two memories. http://www.bbc.co.uk/history/ww2peopleswar/categories/c55521/, accessed 2 January 2016.

Mitter, Rana, *China's War with Japan, 1937–1945: The Struggle for Survival*, London: Penguin Books, 2013.

BIBLIOGRAPHY

Moeller, Susan, *Shooting War: Photography and the American Experience of Combat*, New York: Basic Books, 1990.

Mole, Robert, *The Temple Bells Are Calling: Memories of Burma*, Susan Mole, 2001.

Moorcraft, Paul L. and Philip M. Taylor, *Shooting the Messenger: The Political Impact of War Reporting*, London: Biteback Publishing, 2011.

Moorehead, Alan, *A Late Education: Episodes in a Life*, London: Hamish Hamilton, 1970.

———, *Desert War Trilogy*, London: Aurum Press 2009 (first published London: Hamish Hamilton, 1944).

Moreira, Peter, *Hemingway on the China Front: His WWII Mission with Martha Gellhorn*, Washington DC: Potomac Books, 2006.

Moreman, Tim, *The Jungle, Japanese and the British Commonwealth Armies at War, 1941–45: Fighting Methods, Doctrine and Training for Jungle Warfare*, London: Routledge, 2014.

Morrison, Ian, *Malayan Postscript*, London: Faber & Faber, 1942.

———, *This War against Japan; Thoughts on the Present Conflict in the Far East*, London: Faber & Faber, 1944.

Morris, Sylvia Jukes, *Rage for Fame: The Ascent of Clare Boothe Luce*, New York: Random House USA, 1997.

Murray, Jacqui, *Watching the Sun Rise: Australian Reporting of Japan 1931 to the Fall of Singapore*, Lanham, MD: Lexington Books, 2004.

Naggar, Carole, *George Rodger: An Adventure in Photography, 1908–1995*, Syracuse, NY: Syracuse University Press, 2003.

Nicholson, Michael, *A State of War Exists: Reporters in the Line of Fire*, London: Biteback Publishing, 2012.

Noble, Ronnie, *Shoot First! Assignments of a Newsreel Camera-Man*, London: Pan Books, 1957.

Orwell, George, *Keeping Our Little Corner Clean, 1942–1943 (Collected Works of George Orwell)*, rev. ed., London: Secker & Warburg, 2001.

Pearn, B.R., *The Burman: 1939–1944*, London: India-Burma Association, 1945.

Pedelty, Mark, *War Stories: The Culture of Foreign Correspondents*, New York: Routledge, 1995.

Pe, M. Thein, *What Happened in Burma: The Frank Revelations of a Young Burmese Revolutionary Leader Who Has Recently Escaped from Burma to India*, Allahabad: Kitabistan, 1943.

Perlmutter, David D., *Picturing China in the American Press: The Visual Portrayal of Sino-American Relations in Time Magazine*, Lanham, MD: Lexington Books, 2007.

Prasad, B., *The Retreat from Burma, 1941–42*, Delhi: Combined Inter-Services Historical Section (India & Pakistan), 1959.

BIBLIOGRAPHY

Preston, Paul, *We Saw Spain Die: Foreign Correspondents in the Spanish Civil War*, London: Constable & Robinson, 2008.

Raghavan, Srinath, *India's War: The Making of Modern South Asia 1939–1945*, London: Allen Lane, 2016.

Rankin, Nicholas, *Telegram from Guernica: The Extraordinary Life of George Steer, War Correspondent*, London: Faber & Faber, 2003.

Rasor, Eugene L., *The China-Burma-India Campaign, 1931–1945: Historiography and Annotated Bibliography*, Westport, CT: Greenwood Press, 1998.

Read, Donald, *The Power of News: The History of Reuters*, Oxford: Oxford University Press, 1999.

Reeves, Nicholas, *The Power of Film Propaganda: Myth or Reality?* London: Cassell, 1999.

Rodger, George, *Far on the Ringing Plains: 75,000 Miles with a Photo Reporter*, New York: Macmillan, 1944.

———, *Red Moon Rising*, London: Cresset Press, 1943.

Roeder, George H., *The Censored War: American Visual Experience During World War Two*, New Haven, CT: Yale University Press, 1993.

Rooney, David, *Stilwell the Patriot: Vinegar Joe, the Brits and Chiang Kai-Shek*, London: Chatham Publishing, 2005

Roth, Mitchel P. (ed.), *Encyclopedia of War Journalism*, Armenia, NY: Grey House, 2nd ed., 2010.

Royle, Trevor, *War Report: The War Correspondent's View of Battle from the Crimea to the Falklands*, London: Grafton Books, 1987.

Sadan, Mandy, *A Guide to Colonial Sources on Burma in the India Office Records, British Library*, Bangkok: Orchid Press, 2008.

Sanger, Gerald, 'A News Reel Man's Conscience', *Sight and Sound*, 22 (summer 1941) cited in Hiley, Nicholas and McKernan, Luke, 'Reconstructing the News: British Newsreel Documentation and the British Universities Newsreel Project', *Film History*, 13 (2001), 185–99.

Sebba, Anna, *Battling for News: The Rise of the Woman Reporter*, London: Hodder & Stoughton, 1994.

Shores, Christopher, Brian Cull and Yasuho Izawa, *Bloody Shambles, Vol. 1: The Drift to War to the Fall of Singapore*, London: Grub Street, 1992.

———, *Bloody Shambles: The Complete Account of the Air War in the Far East, from the Defence of Sumatra to the Fall of Burma, 1942, Vol. 2*, London: Grub Street, 2005.

Short, Brian, *The Battle of the Fields: Rural Community and Authority in Britain during the Second World War*, Woodbridge: Boydell Press, 2014.

Silberstein-Loeb, Jonathan, *The International Distribution of News: The Associated Press, Press Association, and Reuters, 1848–1947*, Cambridge: Cambridge University Press, 2014.

BIBLIOGRAPHY

Simpson, John, *Unreliable Sources: How the 20th Century Was Reported*, London: Macmillan, 2010.

Slim, W., *Defeat into Victory*, London: Pan Macmillan, 2009.

Smith, Colin, *Singapore Burning: Heroism and Surrender in World War II*, London: Viking, 2005.

Smith, R.B. and A. J. Stockwell (eds), *British Policy and the Transfer of Power in Asia: Documentary Perspectives*, London: SOAS, 1988.

Stagg, John. 'Make-up of Newsreels', *Journal of the British Kinematograph Society*, 9, 1 (March 1946) p. 27.

Stockwell, Sarah (ed.), *The British Empire: Themes and Perspectives*, Oxford: Blackwell, 2008.

Stowe, Leland, *They Shall Not Sleep*, New York: Alfred A. Knopf, 1944.

Swanberg, William A., *Luce and His Empire*, New York: Scribner, 1972.

Sweeney, Michael S., *Secrets of Victory: The Office of Censorship and the American Press and Radio in World War II*, Chapel Hill, NC: University of North Carolina Press, 2001.

————, *The Military and the Press: An Uneasy Truce*, Evanston, IL: Northwestern University Press, 2006.

Tanner, R.E.S. and Tanner, D.A., *Burma 1942: Memories of a Retreat: The Diary of Ralph Tanner, KOYLI*, Stroud: History Press, 2009.

Tarling, Nicholas, *The Cambridge History of Southeast Asia: Volume Two, Part Two. From World War II to the Present*, Cambridge: Cambridge University Press, 1993.

Taylor, Philip M., *Munitions of the Mind: A History of Propaganda from the Ancient World to the Present Day*, Manchester: Manchester University Press, 3rd ed., 2003.

Taylor, Robert H., 'Politics in Late Colonial Burma: The Case of U Saw', *Modern Asian Studies* 1, 2 (1976), pp. 161–93.

————, 'Constitutional Developments in Burma', entry in Keat Gin Ooi (ed.), *South-East Asia: A Historical Encyclopedia from Angkor Wat to East Timor*, Santa Barbara, CA, ABC-CLIO, 2004, pp. 383–5.

Thant, Myint-U, *The River of Lost Footsteps: Histories of Burma*, London: Faber & Faber, 2006.

Theippan, Maung Wa, *Wartime in Burma: A Diary, January to June 1942*, Athens, OH: Ohio University Press, 2009.

Thompson, Peter, *The Battle for Singapore: The True Story of the Greatest Catastrophe of World War II*, London: Portrait, 2005.

Tinker, Hugh, 'A Forgotten Long March: The Indian Exodus from Burma, 1942'. *Journal of Southeast Asian Studies*, 6, 1 (March 1975), pp. 1–15.

Torney-Parlicki, Prue, *Somewhere in Asia: War, Journalism and Australia's Neighbours, 1941–1975*, Sydney: University of New South Wales Press, 2000.

BIBLIOGRAPHY

Torrance, A.R. and K. Morenweiser, *British Empire Civil Censorship Devices—World War II: British Asia, Section 3*, London: Civil Censorship Study Group, 1997.

Tozer, Alec, 'War Filming in the Far East'. *Journal of the British Kinematograph Society*, 9, 1 (January–March 1946) p. 19–21.

Trembath, Richard, '"Wherever There Was a Battle": Australian War Correspondents and the British Press', http://www.nla.gov.au/ojs/index.php/australian-studies/article/viewFile/1763/2138, accessed 2 January 2016.

Tuchman, Barbara, *Sand Against the Wind: Stilwell and the American Experience in China 1941–45*, London: Futura, 1981.

Van de Ven, Hans, 'Stilwell in the Stocks: The Chinese Nationalists and the Allied Powers in the Second World War', *Asian Affairs*, 34, 3 (November 2003), pp. 243–59.

———, *War and Nationalism in China, 1925–45*, London: Routledge, 2003.

Vorley, J.S. and Vorley, H.M., *The Road from Mandalay*, Windsor: Wilton 65, 2002.

Wagg, Alfred, *A Million Died!: A Story of War in the Far East*, London: Nicholson & Watson, 1943.

Warren, Alan, *Britain's Greatest Defeat: Singapore 1942*, London: Hambledon Continuum, 2006.

———, *The Road from Rangoon to Mandalay*, London: Continuum, 2011.

Webster, Donovan, *The Burma Road: The Epic Story of the China-Burma-India Theater in World War II*, New York: Farrar Straus & Giroux, 2003.

West, W.J. (ed.), *Orwell: The War Commentaries*, New York: Schocken Books, 1985.

Wiant, Susan E., and Walter Cronkite, *Between the Bylines: A Father's Legacy*, New York: Fordham University Press, 2010.

Williams, Kevin, 'War Correspondents as Sources for History: Problems and Possibilities in Journalism and Historiography', *Media History*, 18, 3–4 (2012), pp. 341–60.

Wilson, Cat, *Churchill on the Far East in the Second World War: Hiding the History of the 'Special Relationship'*, London: Palgrave Macmillan, 2014.

Woods, Philip, 'Filming the Retreat from Burma, 1942: British Newsreel Coverage of the Longest Retreat in British Army History'. *Historical Journal of Film, Radio and Television* 35, no. 3 (September 2015), pp. 438–53.

Yerkey, Gary G., *Still Time to Live: A Biography of Jack Belden*, Washington DC: GK Press, 2011.

Young, George Gordon, *Outposts of Victory*, London: Hodder & Stoughton, 1943.

Yurkevich, A., 'The Chinese Army in the Burma Campaigns of World War II (1942–1945)', *Far Eastern Affairs* 38, 3 (September 2010), pp. 95–109.

BIBLIOGRAPHY

Theses

Bentley, Gareth. 'Journalistic Agency and the Subjective Turn in British Foreign Correspondent Discourse', PhD, SOAS, University of London, 2013.

Ehrman, James M., 'Ways of War and the American Experience in the China-Burma-India Theatre, 1942–46', PhD, Kansas State University, 2006. https://books.google.co.uk/books?id=M5CSOPXpwrwC&printsec=frontcover#v=onepage&q&f=false, accessed 2 January 2016.

Hannon, Brian P.D., 'British and Dominion War Correspondents in the Western Theatres of the Second World War'. PhD, University of Edinburgh, 2015. https://www.era.lib.ed.ac.uk/bitstream/handle/1842/10651/Hannon2015.pdf?sequence=2&isAllowed=y, accessed 29 March 2016.

Setliff, Jonathan Stuart, 'The March of Time and the American Century', PhD, University of Maryland, 2007, https://books.google.co.uk/books?id=Mh_paMpNqw4C&pg=PP3&source=gbs_selected_pages&cad=2#v=onepage&q&f=false, last accessed 18 January 2016.

INDEX

Cameronians, 98, 104
Gurkha, 17, 18, 89, 104
Hussars, 98
18th Division, 18
1st Burma Division, 103
1st Burma Regiment, 46
1st Gloucestershire Regiment, 16, 104
200th Division, 104
2nd King's Own Yorkshire Light Infantry (KOYLI), 16, 104
46th Infantry Brigade, 18
48th Infantry Brigade, 18
West Yorkshire regiment, 98, 104
British Movietone News, 82, 89
British Paramount News, 18, 81, 84
Brown, Cecil, 42, 45
Burchett, Wilfred, xvii, xix, 12, 29, 69, 78, 88, 95, 97, 100, 104, 108, 141, 146
  admired Chinese army and Chiang Kai Shek, 102
  and Rodger help bombing casualties at Thazi, 74
  and Rodger leave Burma by jeep and foot through Hukawng Valley, 123–125
  career after Burma, 143–5
  reports criticisms of Indian evacuation, 121
  sends story of delays in Chinese troops being brought in to Burma direct to Chungking, 102
  tells of Shwegyin re-enactment, 71
Burma
  correspondents view of its colonial society, economics and politics, 12–4
  geography of, 11–2
  population of, 14–5
  state of armed forces in 1941, 16–7
Burma campaign, 16, 17
Burma Independence Army, 109
Burma Road, 12, 25, 36, 40, 69, 87
Burmese ministers, 125–6
Busvine, Richard, 132, 139

Calcutta, 21, 50, 114, 120, 130, 137
Censorship, 5–6, 56–60, 96, 99
Chennault, Colonel Claire, 67, 104
Chicago Daily News, 32, 38, 39, 44
China, American view of, 39
Chindwin, River, 12, 126
Chinese Army, 19, 37, 101
  38th Division, 104
  5th Army, 102
  6th Army, 74
  at Toungou, 21
  correspondents critical of treatment of slow Chinese entry into Burma, 101–3
  help rescue British troops at Yenanyaung, 97, 103
Chins, 17, 104
Chittagong, 114
Christian, Winslow L., 50, 131–2
Chungking, 29, 37, 38, 68, 77, 78, 95, 101, 102, 125
Churchill, Winston, 16, 18, 28, 33, 48, 97, 99, 101, 138
Churchill, Randolph, 60, 139
Cochrane, Sir Archibald, 24–5
Cole, Tom, 66
'Collateral Damage', 107–9
Collis, Maurice, 77, 134
Conducting officers, 95

INDEX

INDEX